New Frontiers in Regional Science: Asian Perspectives

Volume 67

This series is a constellation of works by scholars in the field of regional science and in related disciplines specifically focusing on dynamism in Asia.

Asia is the most dynamic part of the world. Japan, Korea, Taiwan, and Singapore experienced rapid and miracle economic growth in the 1970s. Malaysia, Indonesia, and Thailand followed in the 1980s. China, India, and Vietnam are now rising countries in Asia and are even leading the world economy. Due to their rapid economic development and growth, Asian countries continue to face a variety of urgent issues including regional and institutional unbalanced growth, environmental problems, poverty amidst prosperity, an ageing society, the collapse of the bubble economy, and deflation, among others.

Asian countries are diversified as they have their own cultural, historical, and geographical as well as political conditions. Due to this fact, scholars specializing in regional science as an inter- and multi-discipline have taken leading roles in providing mitigating policy proposals based on robust interdisciplinary analysis of multifaceted regional issues and subjects in Asia. This series not only will present unique research results from Asia that are unfamiliar in other parts of the world because of language barriers, but also will publish advanced research results from those regions that have focused on regional and urban issues in Asia from different perspectives.

The series aims to expand the frontiers of regional science through diffusion of intrinsically developed and advanced modern regional science methodologies in Asia and other areas of the world. Readers will be inspired to realize that regional and urban issues in the world are so vast that their established methodologies still have space for development and refinement, and to understand the importance of the interdisciplinary and multidisciplinary approach that is inherent in regional science for analyzing and resolving urgent regional and urban issues in Asia.

Topics under consideration in this series include the theory of social cost and benefit analysis and criteria of public investments, socio-economic vulnerability against disasters, food security and policy, agro-food systems in China, industrial clustering in Asia, comprehensive management of water environment and resources in a river basin, the international trade bloc and food security, migration and labor market in Asia, land policy and local property tax, Information and Communication Technology planning, consumer "shop-around" movements, and regeneration of downtowns, among others.

Researchers who are interested in publishing their books in this Series should obtain a proposal form from Yoshiro Higano (Editor in Chief, higano@jsrsai.jp) and return the completed form to him.

Shuetsu Takahashi • Mitsuyoshi Yanagihara •
Kei Hosoya • Tsuyoshi Shinozaki
Editors

Modern Macroeconomics with Historical Perspectives

Springer

Editors
Shuetsu Takahashi
Faculty of Economics
Tohoku Gakuin University
Sendai, Miyagi, Japan

Mitsuyoshi Yanagihara
Graduate School of Economics
Nagoya University
Nagoya, Aichi, Japan

Kei Hosoya
Faculty of Economics
Kokugakuin University
Shibuya, Tokyo, Japan

Tsuyoshi Shinozaki
Faculty of Economics
Tohoku Gakuin University
Sendai, Miyagi, Japan

ISSN 2199-5974 ISSN 2199-5982 (electronic)
New Frontiers in Regional Science: Asian Perspectives
ISBN 978-981-99-1066-3 ISBN 978-981-99-1067-0 (eBook)
https://doi.org/10.1007/978-981-99-1067-0

This Springer imprint is published by the registered company Springer Nature Singapore Pte Ltd.
The registered company address is: 152 Beach Road, #21-01/04 Gateway East, Singapore 189721, Singapore

Preface

Modern Macroeconomics with Historical Perspectives is a collection of papers by 12 researchers who have approached various *problems* in the core and peripheral areas of modern macroeconomics from their respective professional perspectives. Most researchers here have regional science as one of their main fields of analysis. Because the Japan Section of the Regional Science Association International (JSRSAI) is the place for their research activities, several studies have focused on economic activities in regional spaces. Editors have collected papers that not only analyze cutting-edge topics in modern macroeconomics but also reconsider the problems they encompass from a regional scientific perspective and a historical perspective and make an ambitious contribution to solving important issues facing the Japanese economy and other advanced countries.

Papers in these chapters are characterized by elaborate theoretical and empirical analyses based on all or some of the three analytical perspectives of theory, institutions, and history. While there are good reasons and background for the need for such multifaceted and multilayered analysis, let us consider, for example, the current situation of the Japanese economy. Unfortunately, Japan is considered a world leader in terms of declining birthrates and its aging population, and this has a serious impact on many areas of the economy and society. While the demographic trend of declining birthrates and its aging population has been predicted for decades, Japan, unfortunately, also experienced a "bubble economy" in the 1980s and the 1990s, when it had to extensively handle this situation. Generally, while Japanese society was unable to overcome the deep and extensive damage caused by the bubble economy, the economy has somehow managed to sustain itself throughout the chaos of negative events such as the Lehman Shock and the Great East Japan Earthquake and Tsunami.

Hence, the Japanese economy is now considered "a department store of economic and social problems." The declining birthrates and its aging population mentioned

The original version of this book has been revised: Preface and List of Contributors have been added.

above have directly introduced a crisis in the social security system and indirectly contributed to the long-term downward trend in labor productivity. The economic consequences of this situation are evident. Continuing accumulation of massive public debt, which is already considered to be in the danger zone, is a major problem in itself. However, this is also highly worrisome from a long-term perspective in that it may seriously impede the fiscal flexibility of the future Japanese economy. Considering such severe fiscal constraints, carefully examining the effects of fiscal and monetary policies from multiple perspectives is essential. However, little effort has been made to do so, and the reality is that we have only been left with symptomatic treatments for a series of problems that continue to emerge.

Given this reflection on current state of affairs, positioning the future as an extension of the past to engage in meaningful policy discussions based on an economic framework is useful. In summary, it is a reminder of the importance of "history," but the "institutions" that fundamentally define our economic activities can be a meaningful subject of consideration only if they are placed in a historical context. Throughout this book, the authors have attempted to "integrate" contemporary macroeconomic analysis with a historical analysis of the institutional environment. This approach is expected to lead to discoveries that are unattainable through conventional "narrow" analysis. Recently, a series of studies by Daron Acemoglu, a world-renowned theoretical economist, and James Robinson, a world-renowned historical economist, have widely recognized the usefulness of this type of research stance (Acemoglu and Robinson 2006, 2012). Going back a bit further, Masahiko Aoki's "Comparative Institutional Analysis" should be closer to the stream's source (Aoki 2001). These contributions demonstrate that meaningful economic analysis is possible through deep insight into institutions rooted in historical knowledge. The current economic policies surrounding us are largely characterized by historical path dependency. Even today's ruling party cannot easily ignore such historical paths. Through the organic combination of theory, institutions, and history that this book attempts overall, we hope to gain new insights that cannot be captured by theoretical analysis alone and formulate new policy theory supported by a historical perspective.

Before outlining the content of each chapter, we briefly describe the background of this book. Professor Emeritus Shuetsu Takahashi is at the center of the authors. Professor Takahashi has made outstanding achievements in the fields of macroeconomics and microeconomics and has also contributed to regional science, serving as the president of the Japan Section of the Regional Science Association International. In the latter half of their career as a researcher, Professor Takahashi has also been involved in elaborate economic analyses of topics in the field of history, especially in the closing years of the Tokugawa Shogunate (the late Edo period), under the influence of Professor Emeritus Shozaburo Fujino of Hitotsubashi University, his graduate school advisor. The authors of this book are researchers who have had a close relationship with Professor Takahashi as undergraduate students, graduate students, work colleagues, and academic colleagues during his life as a researcher. Accordingly, the authors' fields of expertise are diverse, which is a positive feature of this book; however, another feature is the loose solidarity in the analytical framework centered on the theoretical analysis rooted in history and institutions, which we have already mentioned.

As noted at the beginning of this preface, some chapters fall directly under the category of regional science and regional studies—one of the unique features of the present book—and research on modern macroeconomics considering historical perspectives. While we have already highlighted that in addition to employing the standard approaches of modern economics, efforts have been devoted to spatially capturing the structure of the local economy in terms of institutions and history. The research fields of the researchers contributing to this book can be broadly divided into several areas: Japanese economic history, including regional economic history; institutional economics focusing on social security systems; and economic dynamics using an overlapping generations model. Moreover, we also included researchers involved in applied microeconomics and econometrics. The following paragraphs provide an overview of each chapter (10 chapters in total).

Chapter 1, "Declining Population Growth and the Serendipity Theorem" by Shuetsu Takahashi, focuses on the Serendipity Theorem presented by American economist Paul A. Samuelson to investigate the optimum population growth rate for a society with a declining population. First, the relationship between the population growth rate and capital level is theoretically clarified when serendipity theorem holds. Next, we demonstrate that under certain preferences and production technologies, optimum population growth rate can be negative. This result is not only important from a historical demographic perspective but also serves as a benchmark for analyzing the situation that many advanced economies are expected to face in the future. The situation in question is an unfavorable case from conventional wisdom; however, the results of the analysis are quite interesting in that the situation can be expected to improve if information and communication technology and artificial intelligence are more utilized in the production sector. Although considerable progress has been made in recent years in research on the social impact of artificial intelligence, the novel analysis in this chapter, which considers population issues as its starting point, will be a valuable contribution.

In growth theory literature, including endogenous growth theory, several variations are known regarding the treatment of leisure in the utility function in addition to consumption. Moreover, leisure should be considered a composite of pure leisure time and leisure goods consumption. Chapter 2, "Consumption of Leisure Goods, Leisure Time, and Inheritance of Tastes for Leisure in an Overlapping Generations Model" by Mitsuyoshi Yanagihara and Weizhen Hu, approaches this leisure formulation problem by constructing an overlapping generations model implementing production externalities. Hence, despite the production function being a simple AK type, a uniquely determined and economically meaningful stationary equilibrium is always a periodic solution. Another interesting result is that levels of leisure consumption and capital stock in equilibrium decrease when the preference for combined leisure increases owing to certain factors. As seen in recent years, the use of artificial intelligence is expected to transform the working styles of many people; thus, their relationship with leisure may also change. This is a phase of substantial transformation based on historical perspectives. The analysis in this chapter will be of great help in deeply considering the implications of such transformations.

The overlapping generations model is often used as a framework for analyzing the impact of human capital formation, including public and private education. In Chap. 3, "Overlapping Generations Model with Relative Preference for Children's Human Capital" by Hideya Kato, the general tendency of parents to want to raise the education level of their children is considered a kind of habit formation. The analysis is developed using an overlapping generations model with educational investment. An important assumption in the analysis is that parents are concerned with the level of their children's human capital relative to their own human capital, which differentiates the analysis from previous studies and allows it to be conducted under more favorable dynamic conditions. From a policy perspective, the focus is on education subsidies and intergenerational transfer payments and how these instruments could be used to achieve a socially optimum solution in a decentralized (market) economy. The starting point of the analysis in this chapter, which is considered from parents' perspective, is essential when discussing the educational system. This is because, whether good or bad, parental involvement is usually quite large, for example, in school choice. We hope that the results of this analysis can be applied to the formulation of future policies.

In retrospect, the expenditure of the Japanese on private life insurance is not small, and examining its impact on people's economic lives and the macroeconomy would be interesting. Chapter 4, "The Impact of Life Insurance on Human Capital Investment During the Steady Growth Period in Japan: Simulation Analysis in an Overlapping Generations Model with Endogenous Growth" by Yuko Shindo, develops a three-period overlapping generations model that considers human capital as a source of endogenous growth and reveals the macroeconomic impact of life insurance in Japan during the period 1975–1994 based on numerical analysis. The results show that life insurance positively affects the number of years of schooling, which promotes the accumulation of human capital in turn, thereby increasing the rate of income growth. While this is an interesting result, it seems that the analytical framework presented can be meaningfully applied to other issues surrounding education in addition to life insurance. For people living with risk, there is no doubt that not only public but also private insurance is a very important "system." The fact that their significance has been quantitatively clarified is more important than expected.

In recent macroeconomic dynamic analyses, attention has been paid to how modes of preference formation of agents affect the patterns of economic development and the importance of deep parameters. Chapter 5, "The Effects of Patience in a Growth Model with Infrastructure and a Related Externality" by Kei Hosoya, implements a time preference function wherein the rate of time preference is determined by the ratio of total consumption to infrastructure level, and the equilibrium dynamics of the model are revealed in detail. We assumed two contrasting cases of people's patience, which are reflected in differences in specific functional form. Such differences in preferences may lead to significant changes in the model's long-term equilibrium dynamics. Moreover, the status of each equilibrium was also quantitatively evaluated through numerical analysis of tested parameters. Historically, factors directly affecting savings behavior (e.g., thrift and perseverance) have been considered fundamental requirements for determining economic growth trends. Along with the quality of the institutions surrounding an economy, the consumption and savings propensities of its inhabitants have been and continue being key factors in considering fundamental questions, such as "Why does this country experience growth while that country does not?"

In Japan, rapidly declining birthrates and its aging population under the social security system, which is essentially a pay-as-you-go system, have created a particularly serious intergenerational inequality problem. Chapter 6, "Intergenerational Inequalities and Policy Options for Achieving Generational Balance in Japan" by Yasuhito Sato, estimates the benefits and burdens in the year 2019 for each generation based on an intergenerational accounting method using the most recent data available for Japan at the time of writing this chapter. This chapter compares policy options to improve marked intergenerational imbalance. While intergenerational imbalance in Japan remains large, this has reduced over the past decade. Further reduction in the imbalance would also require a substantial additional tax burden. Moreover, a significant conflict of interest exists between younger and older generations over policy measures for restoring equilibrium. Throughout history, social security systems, including pensions, have been affected in various respects and have come to be what they are today. Although discussing social security systems based on profit and loss is not appropriate, the reality of intergenerational disparities cannot be overlooked. We must explore the topic by accumulating productive discussions based on sophisticated generational accounting, such as that described in this chapter.

Chapter 7, "Social Security Finance in Japan: Trends, Issues, and Some Measures for Stabilization" by Masahito Abe, provides a valuable overview of Japan's complex public health insurance system, written in a way that makes it relatively easy for foreign readers to grasp the overall picture. As a leading country with declining birthrates and its aging population, Japan will inevitably attract increasing international attention. We are confident that this chapter serves as a reliable guide in this regard. Chapter 7 discusses the difficult situation of the Japanese system, mainly from the perspective of fiscal theory, and examines the consumption tax issue as a source of revenue, focusing on the recent integrated reforms of social security and taxation. Moreover, the chapter also highlights the importance of preventive medicine and health and productivity management from the perspective of securing productive workers and social security bearers in a declining population. These issues may provide new perspectives for developing fiscal debates related to social security systems. For a long time, there have been advocates of the need for fundamental reform of the social security system in Japan; however, progress has been far from satisfactory. The issues highlighted in this chapter are important for deconstructing the malady and enhancing the system's reliability for people now and future generations.

Chapter 8, "The Effect of Political Uncertainty and Political Lobbying" by Eriko Aihara and Tsuyoshi Shinozaki, presents an econometric analysis of the topic of political economy, which has been accumulating interesting results in recent years. Specifically, this chapter tackles important issues related to the political process, beginning with a theoretical discussion of public investment under the consideration of political uncertainty and lobbying based on previous studies. The main theoretical consequence is that public investment increases with the strength of special interest politics and decreases with the strength of political uncertainty. Next, this theoretical hypothesis was tested using Japanese data. Results show that increased political uncertainty and size of special interest groups may have opposite effects on public investment. Essentially, presence of both factors can lead to desirable public policies. It is worth listening to the implication that political institutions are the most fundamental "institutions" of a nation and that the way they constitute determines the qualitative aspects of public investment.

Chapter 9, "A Historical Perspective on the Role of Public Electric Utility in Modern City Formation in Japan" by Sachiko Kumoshikari, examines the fiscal management of local governments during the modernization process and how this affects the economic development of the nation in detail. This ambitious study takes a historical approach to local fiscal management and attempts to draw macro-level implications. Taking Japan as an example, under the centralized system of government, local regions and major regional cities were important cogs for economic development. However, the development of local regions often occurred in a manner that did not promote interindustry labor mobility. Therefore, in this respect, their contribution to the increase in national income and economic growth was limited. This is an important point raised in Chap. 9. Moreover, the same implication can be drawn from the analysis of modern regional economic history, where the metabolism of firms and smooth labor mobility are key factors in developing the macroeconomy. The highlight of this chapter is that the above assertion is supported by an examination of local fiscal management in Sendai City, Japan. If the facts highlighted here are taken slightly more broadly, they may provide an opportunity to discuss the relationship between modern economic growth and institutional organizations.

Chapter 10, "Concentration and Agglomeration in Spatial Monopoly, Spatial Duopoly, and Spatial Competition" by Tohru Wako and Shuetsu Takahashi, tackles spatial economics, a field that has been rapidly developing in recent years. Specifically, it discusses the issue of urban growth in the context of different structures of urban economies. Through this analysis, we observed differences in the impact on key economic variables. For example, for any given external utility level, wage rate is higher for spatial duopoly and lower for dispersed spatial competition. The rent profile is determined by the maximum commuting distance. Furthermore, perhaps the most important results of this chapter are the clear conditioning on the sustained point of dispersed spatial competition and the breaking point of concentration in the city center. These conditions depend on the level of external utility and labor productivity in urban spaces. A spatial duopoly, rather than a spatial monopoly in a centralized city, leads to agglomeration. Countries at a mature stage of economic development are undergoing major changes in their demographic and industrial structures compared to the past, which may be forcing an undeniable change in the nature of urban cities. Analyses such as those in this chapter may be useful as basic knowledge for designing urban restructurings responding to the demands of the times.

Finally, we would like to express our sincere gratitude to Professor Emeritus Yoshiro Higano, the Editor-in-Chief of the *New Frontiers in Regional Science: Asian Perspectives book series*, and editorial board members for accepting our book in the series.[1]

Nagoya, Japan — Mitsuyoshi Yanagihara
Tokyo, Japan — Kei Hosoya
Sendai, Japan — Tsuyoshi Shinozaki

References

Acemoglu D, Robinson JA (2006) Economic origins of dictatorship and democracy. Cambridge University Press, Cambridge, UK

Acemoglu D, Robinson J (2012) Why nations fail: origins of power, poverty, and prosperity. Crown Publishers (Random House), New York

Aoki M (2001) Toward a comparative institutional analysis. MIT Press, Cambridge, MA

[1] This preface was written by Hosoya on behalf of the editors, and contents were reviewed by all members of the editorial board.

Contents

1 **Declining Population Growth and the Serendipity Theorem** 1
Shuetsu Takahashi

2 **Consumption of Leisure Goods, Leisure Time, and Inheritance of Tastes for Leisure in an Overlapping Generations Model** 33
Mitsuyoshi Yanagihara and Weizhen Hu

3 **Overlapping Generations Model with Relative Preference for Children's Human Capital** 55
Hideya Kato

4 **The Impact of Life Insurance on Human Capital Investment During the Steady Growth Period in Japan: Simulation Analysis in an Overlapping Generations Model with Endogenous Growth** 71
Yuko Shindo

5 **The Effects of Patience in a Growth Model with Infrastructure and a Related Externality** 87
Kei Hosoya

6 **Intergenerational Inequalities and Policy Options for Achieving Generational Balance in Japan** 107
Yasuhito Sato

7 **Social Security Finance in Japan: Trends, Issues, and Some Measures for Stabilization** 129
Masahito Abe

8 **The Effect of Political Uncertainty and Political Lobbying** 151
Eriko Aihara and Tsuyoshi Shinozaki

9 **A Historical Perspective on the Role of Public Electric Utility in Modern City Formation in Japan** 165
Sachiko Kumoshikari

10 **Concentration and Agglomeration in Spatial Monopoly, Spatial Duopoly, and Spatial Competition** 183
Tohru Wako and Shuetsu Takahashi

Contributors

Masahito Abe School of Social Welfare, Hokusei Gakuen University, Sapporo, Japan

Eriko Aihara Toyota Tsusho America Inc., Houston, Texas, USA

Kei Hosoya Faculty of Economics, Kokugakuin University, Tokyo, Japan

Weizhen Hu Department of Economy and Trade, Business School, Central South University, Changsha, Hunan, China

Hideya Kato Faculty of Economics, Ryukoku University, Kyoto, Japan

Sachiko Kumoshikari Miyako Junior College, Iwate Prefectural University, Miyako, Japan

Yashuhito Sato Faculty of Economics, Tohoku Gakuin University, Sendai, Japan

Yuko Shindo Faculty of Intercultural Studies, Yamaguchi Prefectural University, Yamaguchi, Japan

Tsuyoshi Shinozaki Faculty of Economics, Tohoku Gakuin University, Sendai, Japan

Shuetsu Takahashi Tohoku Gakuin University, Sendai, Japan

Tohru Wako Faculty of Economics, Tohoku Gakuin University, Sendai, Japan

Mitsuyoshi Yanagihara Graduate School of Economics, Nagoya University, Nagoya, Japan

Chapter 1
Declining Population Growth and the Serendipity Theorem

Shuetsu Takahashi

Abstract This chapter focuses on the Serendipity Theorem of Samuelson (Int Econ Rev 16(3):531–538, 1975a) to investigate the optimum population growth rate for a society with a declining population. First, this chapter shows that, for the Serendipity Theorem to hold, a decrease of capital per capita in a stable laissez-faire steady state needs to be larger than the one in golden-rule steady state when population growth rate increases slightly in the neighborhood of Samuelson's solution. This is an interpretation in economics of the first-order and second-order conditions for the existence of the Theorem shown by Jaeger and Kuhle (J Popul Econ 22:23–41, 2009). Second, this chapter algebraically derives the optimum population growth rate given Cobb–Douglas preference and CES technology. The theorem holds if the elasticity of substitution is less than unity. There exists a negative optimum population growth rate if the capital share to income is less than the adequate value determined by structural parameters. Technical innovation which decreases the elasticity of substitution is required to improve the negative optimum rate. Third, the deepening of ICT&AI has a significant effect on population decline. Using a two-level, three-factor production technology of both the ICT&AI-producing and ICT&AI-using sectors, labor movement from the latter to the former decreases the positive or negative optimum population rate.

Keywords Negative optimum population growth rate · Samuelson's Serendipity Theorem · Capital accumulation

JEL Classification: E13, E21, E22, H55

S. Takahashi (✉)
Tohoku Gakuin University, Sendai, Miyagi, Japan
e-mail: shu@mail.tohoku-gakuin.ac.jp

S. Takahashi et al. (eds.), *Modern Macroeconomics with Historical Perspectives*, New Frontiers in Regional Science: Asian Perspectives 67,
https://doi.org/10.1007/978-981-99-1067-0_1

1.1 Introduction

This chapter focuses on the optimum population growth rate for the Serendipity Theorem of Samuelson (1975a) to hold. The problem of the optimum population growth rate is an important one that has to be solved for a society, whether it be decreasing or increasing.

Almost 220 years ago, Thomas Robert Malthus argued that an ever-increasing population would continually strain society's ability to provide for itself, and predicted mankind would live in poverty forever. Recent international research has found countries with high rates of population growth tend to be associated with low per-capita income levels. This relationship is known as a trade-off between population growth rates and per-capita income. Accordingly, high population growth is still an urgent problem in some developing countries.

On the other hand, some developed countries are having to deal with the problem of population decline. The natural rate of population growth (i.e., the crude births minus the crude deaths) is already negative in Japan, Germany, and Italy (United Nations 2019). In the long run, a total fertility rate slightly greater than 2 is required in order to sustain a constant population. The total fertility rates are 1.37 for Japan, 1.60 for Germany, and 1.31 for Italy. And even though their population is still increasing, many developed countries' total fertility rates have already fallen below replacement levels. For example, the total fertility rates are 1.65 for Eastern Asia, 1.66 for Europe and North America, and 1.83 for Australia and New Zealand. This indicates many developed countries will have negative population growth in the future (see Chap. 7 for the Japanese population structure).

Various economic and social problems arise due a declining birthrate. Sweden and other Scandinavian countries have implemented with some success a variety of policies to increase the birthrate. These countries have been able to increase and maintain their birthrate by implementing policies that take the burden off the shoulders of working women through developing and enhancing comprehensive policies that help families balance the demands of child care and work, such as the system for paid maternity and child-care leave.

To date, research has mostly focused on the effect high population growth rates have had on economic growth and incomes. Solow (1956) shows that there is a trade-off between population growth and per-capita income. The Solow model highlights the interaction between population growth and capital accumulation. Rapid growth in the number of workers forces the capital stock to spread more thinly. Accordingly, high population growth is associated with lower per-capita output as each worker is equipped with less capital.

Studies that explicitly consider negative population growth are few. Ritschl (1985) and Sasaki (2019) introduce negative population into the Solow growth model. Sasaki (2019) finds that when the rate of technological progress is zero and the elasticity of substitution between capital and labor is less than unity, the long-run growth rate of per-capita output is zero. Christianns (2011), Sasaki and Hoshida (2017), and Jones (2020) assuming semi-endogenous or endogenous growth study the economic effects of negative population growth. Using a model that allows for exogenous population growth and endogenous fertility, Jones (2020) shows that gradual population decline results in knowledge and living standards stagnating.

However, "what is the population optimum growth rate for the economy?" is an important question that needs to be addressed. Combining the Solow growth model with Samuelson' (1958) overlapping generations model, Diamond (1965) sets up a two-period overlapping generations model to examine the feasibility of using internal debt to shift the burden of public expenditures to future generations. Using Diamond (1965) framework, Samuelson (1975a) derives the optimum rate for population growth, resulting in his Serendipity Theorem, that is, a rate of population growth which leads a competitive economy to "the most-golden golden-rule (MGG) lifetime state" is optimal. Deardorff (1976) using a class of counterexamples with both utility and production functions of Cobb–Douglas type shows the first-order conditions lead to a minimum, not to a maximum. He also shows that the unbounded production function rules out global optimality of Samuelson's solution, and predicts Samuelson's optimal rate of growth of population may be optimal for sufficiently inelastic CES production functions.

The discussion is generalized to include utility and production functions of CES type by Michel and Pestieau (1993). They show that for the Serendipity Theorem to hold, it is sufficient that the factors of production have low substitutability and the intertemporal elasticity of substitution to be small. Jaeger and Kuhle (2009) extend the Serendipity Theorem to show that the first-order and second-order conditions for the existence of the Theorem in a planned and in a laissez-faire economy are identical. Momota et al. (2019) reexamine the Serendipity Theorem from the stability viewpoint for the Cobb–Douglas preference and CES technology. They show that, assuming the elasticity of substitution in production less than unity, the Serendipity Theorem holds if and only if a stability condition for the laissez-faire steady-state equilibria is satisfied.

In this chapter, we show that, for the Serendipity Theorem of Samuelson (1975a) to hold, a decrease of capital per capita in a stable laissez-faire steady state needs to be larger than the one in golden-rule steady state when population growth rate increases slightly in the neighborhood of Samuelson's solution. This is an interpretation in economics of the first-order and second-order conditions for the existence of the Serendipity Theorem shown by Jaeger and Kuhle (2009).

Second, we investigate the conditions for optimum population growth rate in the context of the Serendipity Theorem. We algebraically derive the optimum population growth rate, assuming Cobb–Douglas preference and CES technology. For the negative optimum rate, it is sufficient that the capital share to income to be less than an adequate value determined by structural parameters. When structural changes occur in the economy, technical innovation which decreases the elasticity of substitution in production is needed to raise the negative optimum population rate. This has important policy implications for developed countries with declining populations.

Third, the relationship between a population decrease and ICT&AI (Information and Communication Technology and Artificial Intelligence) is investigated.

Demographic changes promote the development and adoption of ICT&AI, and thus the deepening of ICT&AI has a significant effect on population growth. We use a two-level, three-factor production technology which allows for both an ICT&AI-producing sector and an ICT&AI-using sector as an extension of the above single CES production technology. We find that the Serendipity Theorem holds when there is an increase in the ratio of laborers in the ICT&AI-producing sector, resulting in an increase in productivity and a decrease in the optimum population growth rate. Thus, if the current estimated population growth rate is less than the optimum one, then economic policies that encourage the deepening of ICT&AI and increase productivity are necessary.

In the next section, we set up the basic overlapping generations model and review Samuelson's Serendipity Theorem. Section 1.3 discusses the relationship between population growth and social welfare in the golden rule, and utility in the laissez-faire steady state from a per-capita capital point of view. We confirm Jaeger and Kuhle (2009) results from this unique point of view. In Sect. 1.4, assuming Cobb–Douglas preference and CES technology, we confirm Momota et al. (2019) results using our extended model. Section 1.5 algebraically derives the positive or negative optimum population growth rate for the Serendipity Theorem to hold, and examine the effects of structural changes on the optimum population growth rate. Section 1.6 focuses on ICT&AI sectors to show the effects of change in employment structures on the declining population. Finally, Sect. 1.7 presents concluding remarks.

1.2 The Basic Overlapping Generations Model and the Serendipity Theorem

The basic overlapping generations model with capital accumulation is due to Diamond (1965).

In each period t, population of L_t are born and live for two periods. At each point in time, two generations are alive and overlap. The number in each generation grows at a constant rate n:

$$L_t = (1+n)\,L_{t-1}. \tag{1.1}$$

Consequently, the total population $L_t + L_{t-1}$ grows at the same rate. Note that the model represents economies where population decreases at a constant rate in the case of $0 > n > -1$.

Each generation works when they are young in their first period of life t, and retire when they are old in their second period of life $t+1$. The income of the young generation is equal to the real wage w_t. They allocate their income between current consumption c_t and savings s_t. We assume perfect foresight. Accordingly, the real rental price r_{t+1} that is expected in period $t+1$ is the one that occurs at that date.

The income of the old generation comes from real rental price r_{t+1} on savings s_t made at period t. As they do not care about their bequest after their death, they consume their income entirely.

The budget constraint of a representative individual born in period t is

$$c_t + \frac{e_{t+1}}{1 + r_{t+1}} = w_t, \tag{1.2}$$

where e_{t+1} is consumption in their old age.

We assume that each individual can be represented by a life-cycle utility function $u(c_t, e_{t+1})$. They maximize their utility function $u(c_t, e_{t+1})$ subject to budget constraint (1.2). The necessary condition for a maximum is

$$\frac{u_c}{u_e} = (1 + r_{t+1}). \tag{1.3}$$

Supposing $u(c_t, e_{t+1})$ is quasi-concave, consumption and savings are given as follows:

$$c_t = c_t (w_t, r_{t+1}), \tag{1.4}$$

$$\frac{e_{t+1}}{1 + r_{t+1}} = s_t = s_t (w_t, r_{t+1}). \tag{1.5}$$

The production technology is represented by the neoclassical well-behaved production function $F(K_t, L_t)$. The function F is homogeneous of degree one with respect to its arguments: capital K_t and labor L_t. It can be expressed by the mean of one variable $k_t = K_t/L_t$:

$$F(K_t, L_t) = f(k_t)L_t. \tag{1.6}$$

During the production process, the capital stock depreciates physically at a constant rate δ with $0 \leq \delta \leq 1$. Accordingly, the necessary conditions for a profit maximum are

$$w_t = f(k_t) - k_t f'(k_t), \tag{1.7}$$

$$r_t + \delta = f'(k_t). \tag{1.8}$$

We assume savings s_t made at period t become the productive capital used in the production process at period $t + 1$:

$$K_{t+1} = s_t L_t. \tag{1.9}$$

Using the above equations, the capital market equilibrium condition is given by

$$(1+n)\,k_{t+1} = s_t\,(w_t, r_{t+1}) = \frac{e_{t+1}}{1+r_{t+1}}. \tag{1.10}$$

This equation is identical to the equation of Diamond (1965).

Now we consider the effect of a resource constraint at period t. For simplicity, we assume that the part of capital, $(1-\delta)K_t$, which is not depreciated is identical to the good produced, $f(k_t)L_t$. These are used for consumption by both generations alive at period t and capital stock in the next period. Hence, the resource constraint at period t can be written as

$$c_t L_t + e_t L_{t-1} + K_{t+1} = f\,(k_t)\,L_t + (1-\delta)\,K_t,$$

or

$$c_t + \frac{e_t}{1+n} + (1+n)\,k_{t+1} = f\,(k_t) + (1-\delta)\,k_t. \tag{1.11}$$

This equation is identical to those of Samuelson (1975a) and Deardorff (1976). Substituting (1.7), (1.8), (1.10) into (1.2) and replacing $(1 + r_t)k_t$ for $e_t/(1 + n)$, we obtain (1.11) again; thus, a laissez-faire capital market equilibrium implies the above resource constraint is satisfied.

An appropriate convergence condition in (1.10) as discussed in the next section leads to the laissez-faire steady state. In the steady state, as variables per capita are constant over time, we drop subscript t in our notation.

The following equations are required for further discussion in the laissez-faire steady state for a given n:

$$\frac{u_c}{u_e} = (1+r), \tag{1.12}$$

$$f'(k) = r + \delta, \tag{1.13}$$

$$c + \frac{e}{1+r} = f(k) - kf'(k), \tag{1.14}$$

$$(1+n)\,k = \frac{e}{1+r} = s\,(w, r)\,. \tag{1.15}$$

Given the above steady-state conditions, the resource constraint is given by

$$c + \frac{e}{1+n} + (1+n)\,k = f(k) + (1-\delta)\,k. \tag{1.16}$$

Now we consider the social planning problem developed by Diamond (1965), Samuelson (1975a, b), Takahashi (1979), and Jaeger and Kuhle (2009). The constraint in this case is the resource constraint (1.11), *not* (1.2) of the competitive market. In a steady state, we directly maximize social welfare, $u(c, e)$ subject to

(1.16) with respect to c, e, and k. Assuming an interior maximum, we obtain the following optimality conditions for a given n:

$$\frac{u_c}{u_e} = (1+n), \tag{1.17}$$

$$f'(k^*) = n + \delta, \tag{1.18}$$

$$c^* + \frac{e^*}{1+n} + (1+n)k^* = f(k^*) + (1-\delta)k^*, \tag{1.19}$$

where c^*, e^*, and k^* are the golden-rule values of c, e, and k for each given n. Equation (1.17) is the biological interest rate relation of Samuelson (1958); and (1.18) is the familiar golden-rule production relation, which implies a maximum of consumption per capita. Note the above golden-rule conditions satisfy the following constraint as a result:

$$c^* + \frac{e^*}{1+n} = f(k^*) - k^* f'(k^*). \tag{1.20}$$

Given an arbitrary population rate n, private savings in the laissez-faire will *not* generally lead to the golden-rule steady state. Therefore, if n is a given and society insists upon achieving the golden-rule optimum, governments must resort to public debt or to some form of compulsory social security to achieve it. For example, when private savings become excessive, pay-as-you-go social security that taxes the young to provide for the old will serve to displace enough capital formation from the private savings. In the case of a government with perfect information about preference and production technology, the government may set up a transfer, τ, from the younger to the older generation as

$$\tau = \frac{e^*}{1+n} - (1+n)k^*, \tag{1.21}$$

where e^* and k^* come from solutions of Eqs. (1.17)–(1.19). It may also use an inverse transfer ($\tau < 0$) from the older to the younger generation when private savings are insufficient. In the case of a government without perfect information, it may adopt a heuristic adjustment of transfer such as

$$\tau_{t+1} = \theta (n - r_t) k_t + \tau_t, \tag{1.22}$$

where θ is adjustment coefficient ($\theta > 0$). In either case of (1.21) and (1.22), a planned economy achieves the golden rule. In the golden rule, a representative person pays τ to the government when they are young and receives $(1+n)\tau$ from the government when they are old. When the budget constraints in the golden rule are changed to $c^* + s^*_{\text{priv}} = w^* - \tau$ and $e^* = (1+n)\left(s^*_{\text{priv}} + \tau\right)$, where s^*_{priv} represents their private savings. As they still maintain $c^* + e^*/(1+n) = w^*$ as in

(1.2), they decide an optimal consumption pattern c^* and e^* as in the laissez-faire. In other words, their gross savings are $s^* = s^*_{\text{priv}} + \tau$ given $s^* = w^* - c^*$. However, private savings in the planned economy are

$$s^*_{\text{priv}} = \frac{e^*}{1+n} - \tau = (1+n)\,k^*. \tag{1.23}$$

(See Appendix for an additional explanation.)

As we will discuss in detail in the following sections, we vary n to find the optimum population rate n_M for all of the golden-rule states. The highest social welfare of all the golden-rule states, the so-called most-golden golden-rule (MGG) steady state, is achieved at $n = n_M$.

Formally, the MGG allocation (c_M, e_M, k_M, n_M) must satisfy the above golden-rule Eqs. (1.17–1.19) and (1.23). Comparing these equations, substituting the MGG allocation into the equations that describe the competitive market equilibrium, we observe that the latter coincides with the former when the competitive equilibrium without any government intervention achieves the golden-rule steady state, that is, $r = n_M$ and $\tau = 0$. This remarkable result is the Serendipity Theorem of Samuelson (1975a), that is, *at the optimum population rate n_M, the laissez-faire steady state will just support the MGG steady state.*

Returning to the competitive market conditions (1.13), (1.14), and (1.16), we can obtain the following equation:

$$\left[\,(1+n)\,k - \frac{e}{1+r}\,\right]\left[\,n + \delta - f'(k)\,\right] = 0, \tag{1.24}$$

which shows either the capital market equilibrium condition (1.15) or the golden-rule condition of $f' = n + \delta$ (Takahashi 1979). The Serendipity Theorem implies the above two conditions hold simultaneously.

1.3 Population Growth, Social Welfare, and Capital Accumulation

This section is a preliminary section to find the optimum population growth rate n_M. We begin with making a distinction between the utility level in the laissez-faire steady state and social welfare level in the golden-rule steady state achieved by a planned economy. Here we express the former as $V = u(c, e)$ and the latter as $W = u(c^*, e^*)$.

It is clear under plausible conditions that, for a given n,

$$W \geq V.$$

Now we consider V and W as indirect functions of n. We vary n to find n_M. The problem amounts to finding the maximum of the indirect functions of n.

We can derive $V(n)$ from (1.12) to (1.15) and $W(n)$ from (1.17) to (1.19). Applying the envelope theorem, we obtain:

$$\frac{\mathrm{d}V}{\mathrm{d}n} = \lambda\left[n + \delta - f'(k)\right]\frac{kf''(k)}{1+r}\frac{\mathrm{d}k}{\mathrm{d}n}, \tag{1.25}$$

$$\frac{\mathrm{d}W}{\mathrm{d}n} = \mu\left[\frac{e^*}{(1+n)^2} - k^*\right] = \mu\left(\tilde{k} - k^*\right) = \mu\frac{\tau}{1+n}, \tag{1.26}$$

where λ and μ represent the marginal utility of income, respectively. $\tilde{k}$ is defined as

$$\tilde{k} \equiv \frac{e^*}{(1+n)^2}. \tag{1.27}$$

In the economy with the pay-as-you-go social security system as in the previous section, we obtain $(1+n)\tilde{k} = e^*/(1+n) = s^*_{\text{priv}} + \tau = s^*$ and $(1+n)k^* = s^*_{\text{priv}}$ from (1.23) and (1.27). $\tilde{k}$ is the imaginary per-capita capital corresponding to gross savings s^*.

In (1.25), V has the extremum when the laissez-faire achieves the golden rule, $f'(k) = n + \delta$. In (1.26), W has the extremum when the golden rule of $n = r$ is achieved by either the laissez-faire $(1+n)k^* = e^*/(1+r)$ or the planned economy with $\tau = 0$. The optimum population rate n_M satisfies both $f'(k^*) = n + \delta$ and $(1+n)k^* = e^*/(1+n)$. This is the Serendipity Theorem, which we refer in the previous section. In the following, we attach the subscript $_E$ to denote the extremum of variables which satisfy $\mathrm{d}V/\mathrm{d}n = 0$ and $\mathrm{d}W/\mathrm{d}n = 0$.

The second-order conditions for the optimum in the neighborhood of $n = n_E$ are given by the following two equations respectively:

$$\left.\frac{\mathrm{d}^2V}{\mathrm{d}n^2}\right|_{n=n_E} = \lambda\left[1 - f''\frac{\mathrm{d}k}{\mathrm{d}n}\right]\frac{kf''}{1+r}\frac{\mathrm{d}k}{\mathrm{d}n} < 0, \tag{1.28}$$

$$\left.\frac{\mathrm{d}^2W}{\mathrm{d}n^2}\right|_{n=n_E} = \mu\left[\frac{\mathrm{d}\tilde{k}}{\mathrm{d}n} - \frac{\mathrm{d}k^*}{\mathrm{d}n}\right] = \frac{\mu}{1+n}\frac{\mathrm{d}\tau}{\mathrm{d}n} < 0. \tag{1.29}$$

Jaeger and Kuhle (2009) Extended Serendipity Theorem proves that the second-order condition for the optimum for V and W depends upon an identical condition (1.34) which will be explained later when examining the case of $\mathrm{d}k/\mathrm{d}n < 0$.

In the following, we examine the conditions for optimum from the perspective of capital per capita to obtain Proposition 1.1 and Proposition 1.2.

First, we focus on the relationship between population growth and capital per capita. As population growth dilutes the capital-labor ratio, positive population growth requires a larger fraction of output to be devoted to physical or human capital if a given capital-labor ratio is to be maintained. In the golden-rule steady state, it is clear $\mathrm{d}k^*/\mathrm{d}n = 1/f'' < 0$ from (1.18) given the property of diminishing marginal product.

However, the sign of $\mathrm{d}k/\mathrm{d}n$ is ambiguous. From the capital accumulation dynamic equation of (1.10), the convergence condition to the laissez-faire steady state in the neighborhood of $k_t = k$ for a given n is

$$A \equiv 1 + n + kf'' \frac{\partial s}{\partial w} - f'' \frac{\partial s}{\partial r} > 0. \tag{1.30}$$

(For the convergence condition, see Diamond 1965; Takahashi 1979, 2008; Jaeger and Kuhle 2009 and Momota et al. 2019.) Differentiating (1.15) with respect to n, we derive $\mathrm{d}k/\mathrm{d}n$ as

$$\mathrm{d}k/\mathrm{d}n = -k/A. \tag{1.31}$$

If $A > 0$, then $\mathrm{d}k/\mathrm{d}n < 0$ and capital-dilution effect occurs; if $A < 0$, then the capital-enrichment effect occurs.

Therefore, we obtain the following lemma.

Lemma 1.1 *The convergence condition to the laissez-faire steady state in the neighborhood of k for each n is satisfied if and only if population growth dilutes capital per capita in the steady state. The laissez-faire steady state is unstable if and only if population growth implies capital enrichment.*

Here defining $B \equiv A + kf'$, we rewrite (1.28) and (1.29) as

$$\left.\frac{\mathrm{d}^2 V}{\mathrm{d}n^2}\right|_{n=n_E} = -\lambda \frac{B}{A^2} \frac{k^2 f''}{1+r} < 0, \tag{1.32}$$

$$\left.\frac{\mathrm{d}^2 W}{\mathrm{d}n^2}\right|_{n=n_E} = -\mu \frac{B}{(1+n)\, f''} < 0. \tag{1.33}$$

[See Appendix for the proof of (1.32) and (1.33).]

Clearly, the second-order optimum condition for V and W is satisfied if

$$B \equiv A + kf'' < 0. \tag{1.34}$$

This is the Extended Serendipity Theorem of Jaeger and Kuhle (2009).

Now we return to our main topic. In the stable case of $A > 0$, $\mathrm{d}k/\mathrm{d}n < 0$ and the local maximum for V in (1.28) requires the condition $\mathrm{d}k/\mathrm{d}n < 1/f''$ in the neighborhood of n_E, which implies $\mathrm{d}k/\mathrm{d}n < \mathrm{d}k^*/\mathrm{d}n = 1/f'' < 0$. As (1.28) and (1.32) are equivalent, we have $B < 0$, which makes $\left.\frac{\mathrm{d}^2 W}{\mathrm{d}n^2}\right|_{n=n_E} < 0$ in (1.33) and $\mathrm{d}\tilde{k}/\mathrm{d}n < \mathrm{d}k^*/\mathrm{d}n$ in (1.29). Similarly, $\mathrm{d}\tilde{k}/\mathrm{d}n < \mathrm{d}k^*/\mathrm{d}n$ in (1.29) leads to $B < 0$ and $\left.\frac{\mathrm{d}^2 V}{\mathrm{d}n^2}\right|_{n=n_E} < 0$, which makes $\mathrm{d}k/\mathrm{d}n < \mathrm{d}k^*/\mathrm{d}n$. Therefore, in the capital-dilution or the stable laissez-faire steady state, the first-order optimum solution n_E becomes the optimum population growth rate n_M in $dk/dn < dk^*/dn < 0$ and $d\tilde{k}/dn < dk^*/dn$.

As mentioned above, $dk/dn < dk^*/dn < 0$ implies $B < 0$, that is, the Extended Serendipity Theorem of Jaeger and Kuhle (2009) holds. Therefore, n_E becomes n_M if a decrease of capital per capita in the stable laissez-faire steady state is larger than the one in golden-rule steady state when n increases slightly in the neighborhood of n_E. This is an interpretation in economics of Proposition 1.1 that will be referred later.

With a minor assumption, $dk/dn < d\tilde{k}/dn < dk^*/dn < 0$ in the neighborhood of $n = n_M$ (see Appendix for the proof). These inequalities show that $k \gtreqless \tilde{k} \gtreqless k^* \gtreqless k_M$ for each $n \lesseqgtr n_M$ in the neighborhood of $n = n_M$, where k_M corresponds to n_M. Figure 1.1 shows the Serendipity Theorem in relation to capital per capita.

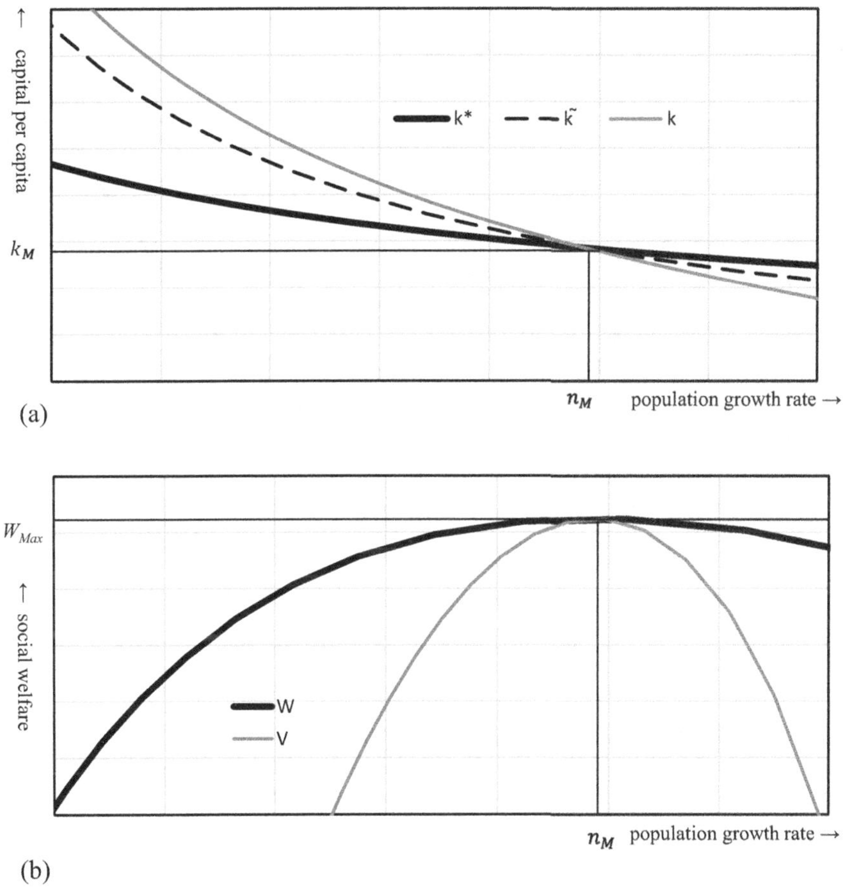

Fig. 1.1 The Serendipity Theorem. (**a**) Capital per capita. (**b**) Social welfare

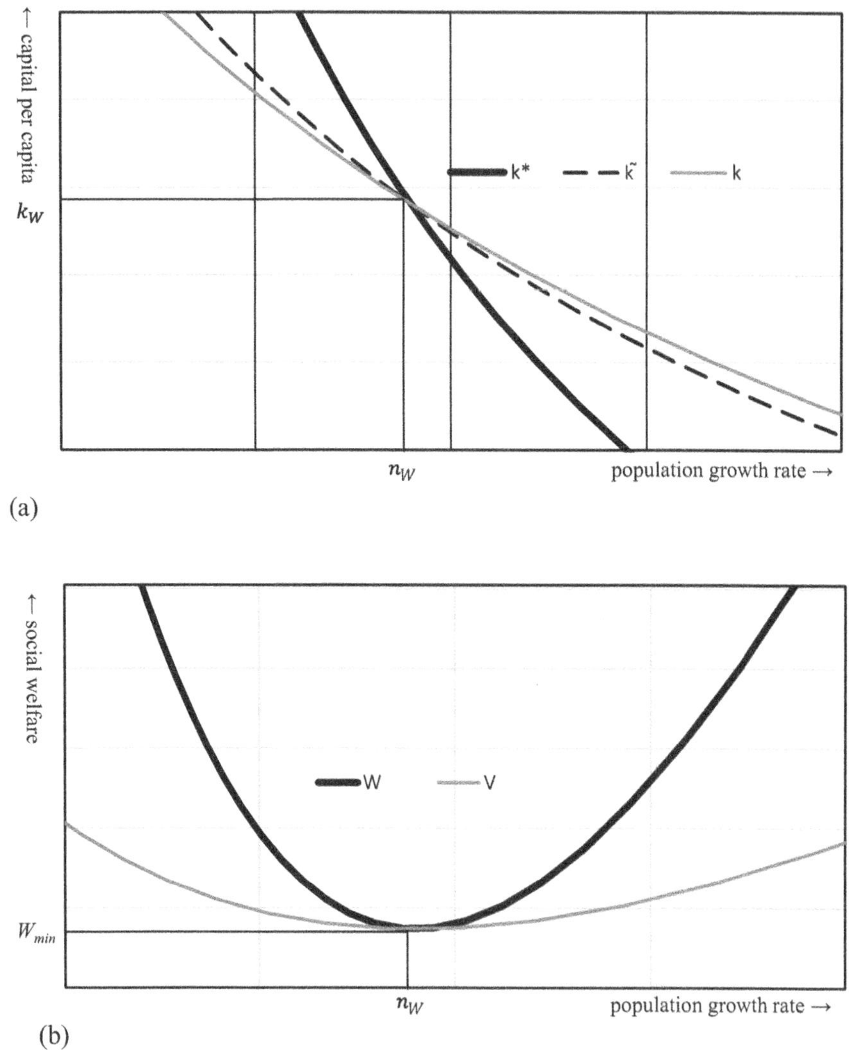

Fig. 1.2 The Deardorff case. (**a**) Capital per capita. (**b**) Social welfare

In the unstable case of $A < 0$, we have $\mathrm{d}k/\mathrm{d}n > 0$ and therefore $B < 0$, which is the local maximum for V and W in (1.32) and (1.33). In other words, n_E becomes n_M in capital-enrichment or the unstable laissez-faire steady state, and we definitely have $\mathrm{d}\tilde{k}/\mathrm{d}n < \mathrm{d}k^*/\mathrm{d}n < 0 < \mathrm{d}k/\mathrm{d}n$ in the neighborhood of $n = n_M$ (see Appendix for the proof).

Figure 1.2 shows that the Serendipity Theorem fails to hold. In the case of $A > 0$ and $B > 0$, the second-order optimum condition for V and W is not satisfied in (1.32)

and (1.33). The first-order optimum solution n_E is the worst population growth rate n_W. As dk/dn < 0, we obtain dk^*/dn <dk/dn < 0 in (1.28) and $\mathrm{d}k^*/\mathrm{d}n < \mathrm{d}\tilde{k}/\mathrm{d}n$ in (1.29). From the proof in Appendix, we have dk^*/dn < $\mathrm{d}\tilde{k}/\mathrm{d}n$ < dk/dn < 0 in the neighborhood of $n = n_E$. These inequalities imply that we have $k^* \gtreqless \tilde{k} \gtreqless k \gtreqless k_W$ for each $n \lesseqgtr n_W$ in the neighborhood of $n = n_W$, where k_W corresponds to n_W.

Summing up, we have the following propositions.

Proposition 1.1 *Suppose the stable laissez-faire steady state achieves the golden rule at* $n = n_E$. *The Serendipity Theorem holds in* $n = n_E$ *if and only if* $k \gtreqless \tilde{k} \gtreqless k^* \gtreqless k_E$ *for each* $n \lesseqgtr n_E$. *The population growth rate* n_E *is the optimum population growth rate* n_M.

Proposition 1.2 *Suppose the stable laissez-faire steady state achieves the golden rule at* $n = n_E$. *The Serendipity Theorem fails to hold in* $n = n_E$ *if and only if* $k^* \gtreqless \tilde{k} \gtreqless k \gtreqless k_E$ *for each* $n \lesseqgtr n_E$. *The population growth rate* n_E *is the worst population growth rate* n_W.

Finally, we will briefly discuss the multiple root problem. Takahashi (2008) uses Cobb–Douglas preference and CES technology and assumes zero capital depreciation $\delta = 0$ and the elasticity of substitution in production $\sigma = 0.5$. Figure 1.3, assuming $\alpha = 0.4$, $\beta = 0.05$, $\sigma = 0.5$ and $\delta = 0$, shows that the stable steady state k for each n leads to two distinct real roots of n_E, with the larger one supporting the Serendipity Theorem. (An explanation of parameters, α and β, is provided in the next section.)

1.4 Cobb–Douglas Preference and CES Technology

One period represents 20 or 30 years in an overlapping generations model. It is often assumed that the depreciation rate δ is one (de la Croix and Michel 2002; Michel and Pestieau 1993; Momota et al. 2019), that is, total depreciation of capital after a period length. We also assume $\delta = 1$.

We suppose well-behaved general functions of V, W, and $f(k)$ as in the previous section. Here our analysis focuses on the case of Cobb–Douglas preference and CES technology. This is a special case of Michel and Pestieau (1993), and also the same case as Momota et al. (2019).

We express the Cobb–Douglas preference as a linear-logarithmic utility:

$$u(c, e) = \alpha \ln c + (1 - \alpha) \ln e, \tag{1.35}$$

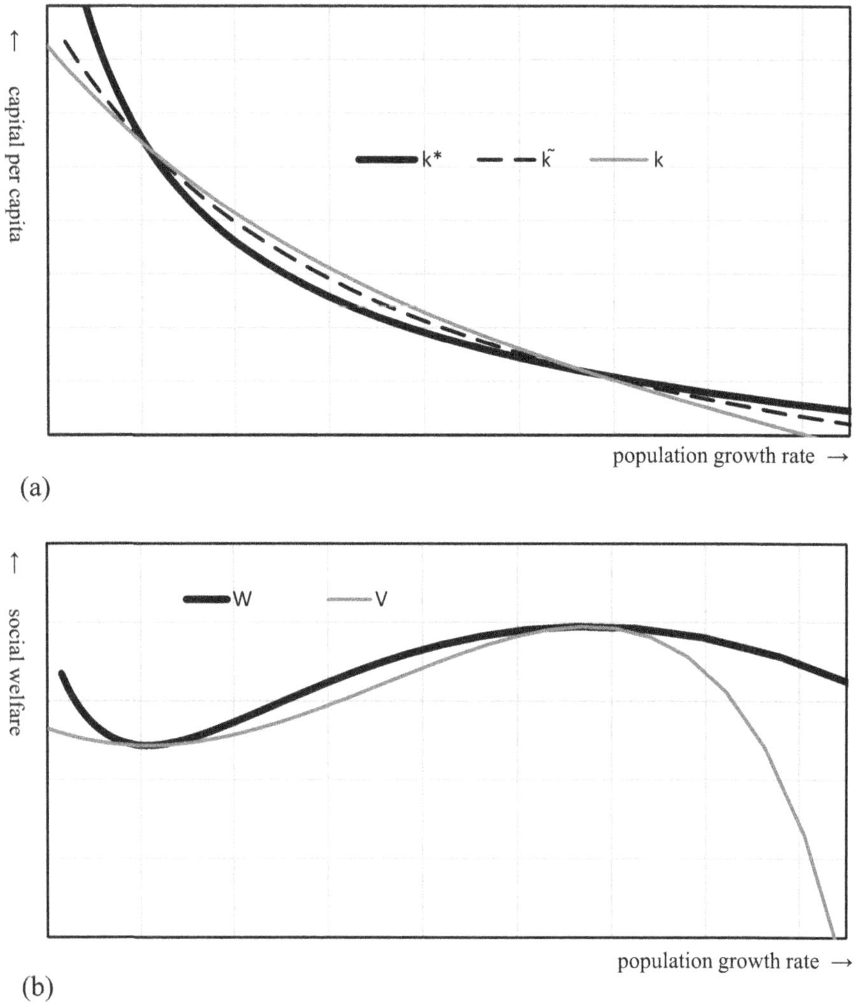

Fig. 1.3 Multiple solutions in $\delta = 0$. (**a**) Capital per capita. (**b**) Social welfare

where α is a consumption allocation parameter ($0 < \alpha < 1$). We also consider the CES technology:

$$f(k) = \left(\beta k^{-\rho} + 1 - \beta\right)^{-\frac{1}{\rho}}, \tag{1.36}$$

where β is a parameter of income distribution ($0 < \beta < 1$) and ρ is a substitution parameter ($\rho > -1$). The elasticity of substitution between capital and labor, σ, is equal to $1/(1 + \rho)$.

Given the above specifications, the optimal consumption allocations in the laissez-faire steady state for a given n are

$$c = \alpha\left[f(k) - kf'(k)\right], \tag{1.37}$$

$$\frac{e}{1+r} = (1+n)k = (1-\alpha)\left[f(k) - kf'(k)\right], \tag{1.38}$$

$$f(k) - kf'(k) = (1-\beta)\left(\beta k^{-\rho} + 1 - \beta\right)^{-\frac{1}{\rho}-1}. \tag{1.39}$$

To confirm the relationship between n and k in the laissez-faire steady state, we calculate the slope of (n, k)-curve from (1.38) and (1.39) to obtain

$$(1-\alpha)(1-\beta)\left(\beta k^{-\rho} + 1 - \beta\right)^{-\frac{1}{\rho}-2}\left(\rho\beta k^{-\rho} - (1-\beta)\right)\mathrm{d}k/\mathrm{d}n = k^2. \tag{1.40}$$

Therefore, if $\rho < 0$, then $\mathrm{d}k/\mathrm{d}n < 0$, that is, (n, k)-curve is a downward-sloping curve.

Defining $\check{k}$ as

$$\check{k} \equiv \left[(1-\beta)/\rho\beta\right]^{-\frac{1}{\rho}}, \tag{1.41}$$

we obtain

if $\rho > 0$ and $k > \check{k}$, then $\mathrm{d}k/\mathrm{d}n < 0$,

if $\rho > 0$ and $k < \check{k}$, then $\mathrm{d}k/\mathrm{d}n > 0$,

if $\rho > 0$ and $k = \check{k}$, then $\mathrm{d}k/\mathrm{d}n = +\infty$.

These imply that if $\rho > 0$, the (n, k)-curve becomes a backward-bending curve at $\left(\check{n}, \check{k}\right)$,where $\check{n}$ is the highest population growth rate under which a steady-state equilibrium exists, that is,

$$\check{n} = (1-\alpha)\beta^{-\frac{1}{\rho}}(1+\rho)^{-\frac{1}{\rho}}\frac{\rho}{1+\rho} - 1. \tag{1.42}$$

From Lemma 1.1, if $\mathrm{d}k/\mathrm{d}n < 0$, k is stable, and if $\mathrm{d}k/\mathrm{d}n > 0$, k is unstable. Denoting these as k^s and k^u respectively, we obtain $k^s > \check{k} > k^u$, $\mathrm{d}k^s/\mathrm{d}n < 0$ and $\mathrm{d}k^u/\mathrm{d}n > 0$. This is the same result of Momota et al. (2019). Using the above simple method, we have verified Momota et al. (2019).

Summing up, we have the following lemma.

Lemma 1.2 *Assume $\rho > 0$ and $\delta = 1$. Given $\check{n}$ is the highest population growth rate under which a steady-state equilibrium exists, then it follows that there exist two kinds of steady-state equilibria k for each given n in $-1 < n < \check{n}$, with stable equilibria k^s larger than unstable one k^u, and also with $dk^s/dn < 0$ and $dk^u/dn > 0$.*

Lemma 1.2 together with Proposition 1.1 results in Proposition 1.3, which is also the same result of Momota et al. (2019). This is easily verified by using the following alternative proof.

First, we calculate the shape of (n, k)-curve and (n, k^*)-curve. We can rewrite the golden-rule condition (1.18) as follows:

$$f'\left(k^*\right) = \beta\left(\beta k^{*-\rho} + 1 - \beta\right)^{-\frac{1}{\rho}-1} k^{*-\rho-1} = 1 + n, \tag{1.43}$$

or

$$(1 + n)\, k^* = \beta\left(\beta k^{*-\rho} + 1 - \beta\right)^{-\frac{1}{\rho}-1} k^{*-\rho}. \tag{1.44}$$

Thus, the slope of (n, k^*)-curve is

$$-(1 + \rho)(1 - \beta)\left(\beta k^{*-\rho} + 1 - \beta\right)^{-\frac{1}{\rho}-2} \beta k^{*-\rho}\, \mathrm{d}k^*/\mathrm{d}n = k^{*2}. \tag{1.45}$$

Accordingly, $\mathrm{d}k^*/\mathrm{d}n < 0$ as $0 < \beta < 1$ and $\rho > -1$. (n, k^*)-curve is a downward sloping. As mentioned above, (n, k)-curve is a downward sloping if $\rho < 0$ and a backward-bending at $\left(\check{n}, \check{k}\right)$ if $\rho > 0$.

Next, assuming that the laissez-faire steady state achieves the golden rule at (n_E, k_E), we have from (1.38), (1.39), and (1.44):

$$k_E = \left[(1 - \alpha)\frac{1 - \beta}{\beta}\right]^{-\frac{1}{\rho}}, \tag{1.46}$$

$$n_E = \beta^{-\frac{1}{\rho}}\left[\frac{1 - \alpha}{2 - \alpha}\right]^{\frac{1}{\rho}+1} - 1. \tag{1.47}$$

Finally, we derive the slope of (n, k)-curve and (n, k^*)-curve at (n_E, k_E). From (1.40), (1.45) and (1.46), we obtain

$$\left.\frac{\mathrm{d}k}{\mathrm{d}n}\right|_{n=n_E} = \frac{C}{[\rho(1 - \alpha) - 1]}, \tag{1.48}$$

$$\left.\frac{\mathrm{d}k^*}{\mathrm{d}n}\right|_{n=n_E} = -\frac{C}{1 + \rho}, \tag{1.49}$$

where

$$C = \frac{k_E^2}{(1 - \alpha)(1 - \beta)^{-\frac{1}{\rho}}(2 - \alpha)^{-\frac{1}{\rho}-2}} > 0. \tag{1.50}$$

Accordingly,

$$\left.\frac{dk}{dn}\right|_{n=n_E} - \left.\frac{dk^*}{dn}\right|_{n=n_E} = C\frac{\rho}{1+\rho}\frac{2-\alpha}{[\rho(1-\alpha)-1]}, \tag{1.51}$$

If $0 < \rho < 1/(1-\alpha)$, we obtain $\left.\frac{dk^s}{dn}\right|_{n=n_E} < \left.\frac{dk^*}{dn}\right|_{n=n_E} < 0$ from (1.48), (1.51) and Lemma 1.2. The discussion in the previous section leads to $A > 0$ and $B < 0$; thus $\left.\frac{d^2V}{dn^2}\right|_{n=n_E} < 0$ and $\left.\frac{d^2W}{dn^2}\right|_{n=n_E} < 0$. Now n_E is the optimum population rate n_M.

$\left.\frac{dk^*}{dn}\right|_{n=n_E} < 0$ shows (n, k^*)-curve is a downward sloping and $\left.\frac{dk^s}{dn}\right|_{n=n_E} < 0$ shows that (n_M, k_M) is a stable equilibrium on the downward part of the backward-bending (n, k)-curve. From the discussion in the previous section, we attain $\frac{dk^s}{dn} < \frac{d\tilde{k}}{dn} < \frac{dk^*}{dn} < 0$ in the neighborhood of $n = n_M$. These inequalities imply $k^s \gtreqless \tilde{k} \gtreqless k^* \gtreqless k_M$for each $n \lesseqgtr n_M$ in the neighborhood of $n = n_M$, where $n_M \le \check{n}$ and $n \le \check{n}$. Figure 1.4 depicts a pattern diagram of the Serendipity Theorem in the case of Cobb–Douglas preference and CES technology when $\delta = 1$. Here we specify the structural parameters as $\alpha = 0.7$, $\beta = 0.3$, and $\rho = 1.0$, though $n_M = -0.82$.

If $\rho > 1/(1-\alpha)$, we have $\left.\frac{dk^u}{dn}\right|_{n=n_E} > 0 > \left.\frac{dk^*}{dn}\right|_{n=n_E}$ from (1.48), (1.51) and Lemma 1.2, which leads to

$A < 0$ and $B < 0$, and thus $\left.\frac{d^2V}{dn^2}\right|_{n=n_E} < 0$ and $\left.\frac{d^2W}{dn^2}\right|_{n=n_E} < 0$. $\left.\frac{dk^u}{dn}\right|_{n=n_E} > 0$ shows that (n_E, k_E) is an unstable equilibrium on the upward part of the backward-bending (n, k)-curve. Figure 1.5 shows a pattern diagram of the unstable equilibrium in the case of $\alpha = 0.6$, $\beta = 0.3$, $\rho = 5.0$, and $\delta = 1$, which gives $n_E = -0.72$.

If $-1 < \rho < 0$, we have $\left.\frac{dk^*}{dn}\right|_{n=n_E} < \left.\frac{dk}{dn}\right|_{n=n_E} < 0$ from (1.40) and (1.51), which leads to $A > 0$ and $B > 0$; thus, $\left.\frac{d^2V}{dn^2}\right|_{n=n_E} > 0$ and $\left.\frac{d^2W}{dn^2}\right|_{n=n_E} > 0$. Now n_E is the worst population growth rate n_W.

The discussion in the previous section leads to $dk^*/dn < d\tilde{k}/dn < dk/dn < 0$ in the neighborhood of $n = n_W$. These inequalities imply $k^* \gtreqless \tilde{k} \gtreqless k \gtreqless k_W$ for each $n \lesseqgtr n_W$ in the neighborhood of $n = n_W$, where $n_W \le \check{n}$ and $n \le \check{n}$. Both the (n, k)-curve and the (n, k^*)-curve are downward sloping. These results lead us to Proposition 1.2 and Fig. 1.2.

In the case of the Cobb–Douglas preference, CES technology and $\delta = 1$, summing up together with Proposition 1.1 and Proposition 1.2, we have the following propositions.

Proposition 1.3 *Suppose the stable laissez-faire steady state achieves the golden rule at $n = n_E$. The Serendipity Theorem holds in $n = n_E$ if and only if $0 < \rho < 1/(1-\alpha)$. The population growth rate n_E is the optimum population growth rate n_M.*

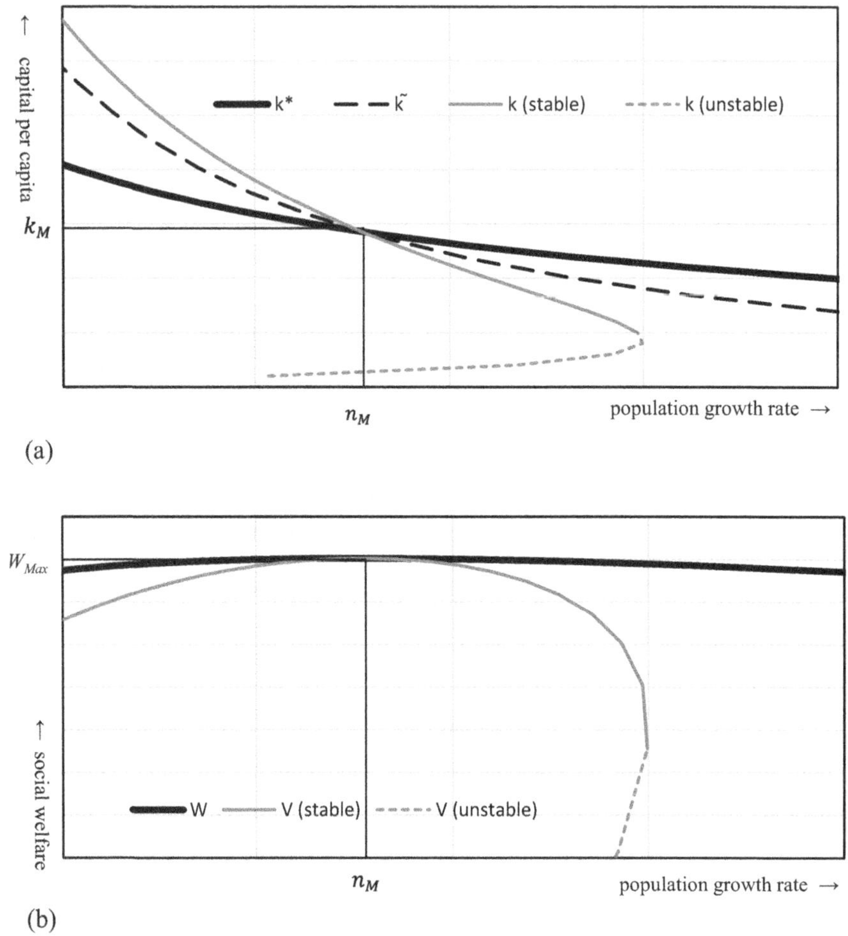

Fig. 1.4 A stable case with Cobb–Douglas preference and CES technology. (**a**) Capital per capita. (**b**) Social welfare

Proposition 1.4 *Suppose the stable laissez-faire steady state achieves the golden rule at* $n = n_E$. *The Serendipity Theorem fails to hold in* $n = n_E$ *if and only if* $-1 < \rho < 0$. *The population growth rate* n_E *is the worst population growth rate* n_W.

1.5 Optimum Population Growth Rate

This section focuses on the optimum population growth rate in a society with a decreasing population. First, we reconfirm the solutions in the previous section (1.46) and (1.47), from the point of view of the indirect social welfare maximization.

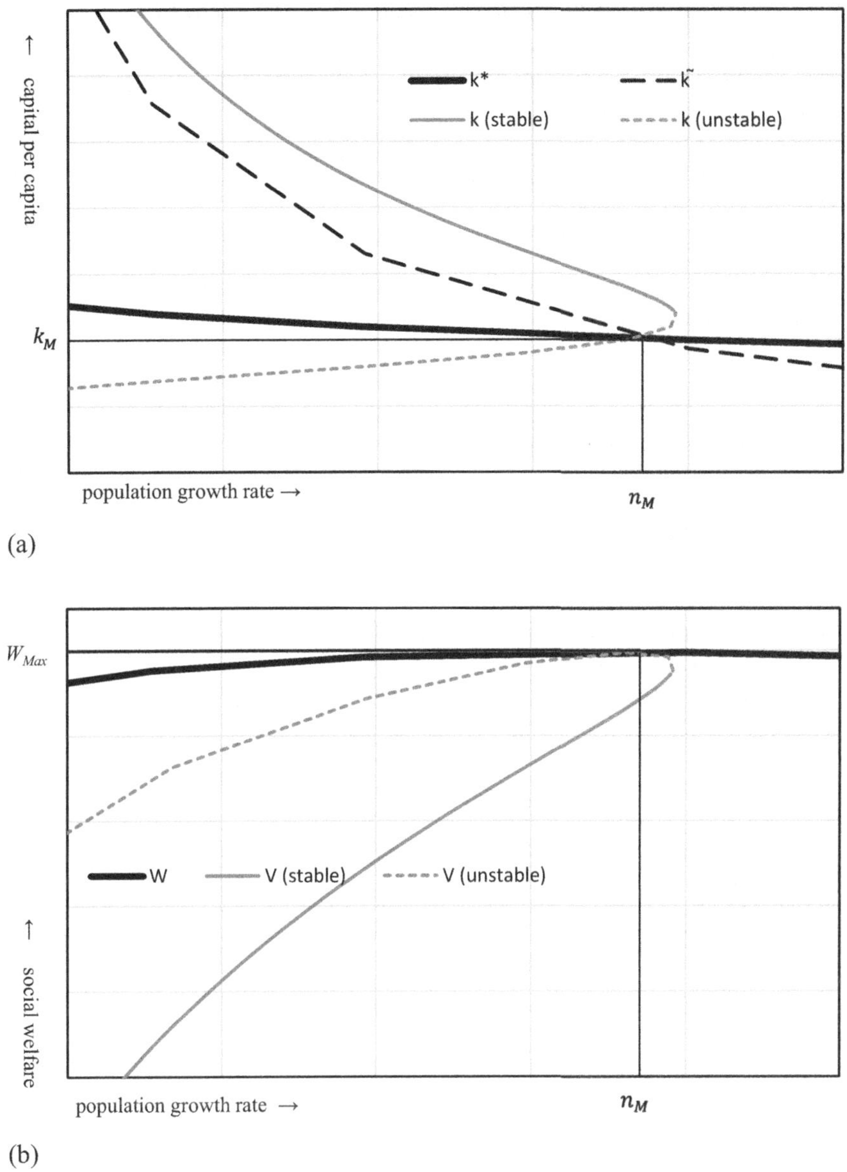

Fig. 1.5 An unstable case with Cobb–Douglas preference and CES technology. (**a**) Capital per capita. (**b**) Social welfare

Second, we examine the possibility of a negative optimum population growth rate. Third, we examine the effects of the parameters of α, β, and ρ on the optimum population rate n_M.

1.5.1 Maximization of Indirect Social Welfare Function

We begin with the linear-logarithmic utility function (1.35). This function gives the optimal consumption allocations in the laissez-faire steady state for a given n as

$$c = \alpha \left[f(k) - kf'(k) \right], \tag{1.52}$$

$$\frac{e}{1+r} = (1+n)\,k = (1-\alpha)\left[f(k) - kf'(k) \right]. \tag{1.53}$$

Hence, an indirect utility function in the laissez-faire is

$$V = \ln\left[f(k) - kf'(k) \right] + (1-\alpha)\ln(1+r) + D, \tag{1.54}$$

where $D = \alpha \ln \alpha + (1-\alpha)\ln(1-\alpha)$.

Similarly, the indirect social welfare function given the golden rule is

$$W = \ln\left[f\left(k^*\right) - (1+n)\,k^* \right] + (1-\alpha)\ln(1+n) + D, \tag{1.55}$$

where $k*$ satisfies the golden-rule condition (1.44). On the right-hand side in (1.55), population growth increases the second column and decreases the first column through the capital dilution-effect, $\mathrm{d}k^*/\mathrm{d}n = 1/f'' < 0$.

The familiar first-order condition for a maximum is $\mathrm{d}W/\mathrm{d}n = 0$, that is,

$$\frac{\mathrm{d}W}{\mathrm{d}n} = -\frac{k^*}{f\left(k^*\right) - (1+n)\,k^*} + \frac{1-\alpha}{1+n} = 0. \tag{1.56}$$

Considering the CES technology of (1.36), we derive:

$$f\left(k^*\right) = \left(\beta k^{*-\rho} + 1 - \beta\right)^{-\frac{1}{\rho}} = \frac{2-\alpha}{1-\alpha}(1+n)\,k^*. \tag{1.57}$$

Using (1.43) and (1.57), we obtain the following:

$$V = \ln\left[f(k) - kf'(k) \right] + (1-\alpha)\ln(1+r) + D, \tag{1.58}$$

$$V = \ln\left[f(k) - kf'(k) \right] + (1-\alpha)\ln(1+r) + D. \tag{1.59}$$

These results are the same as (1.46) and (1.47) respectively; and of course, the above k_E and n_E satisfy $\mathrm{d}V/\mathrm{d}n = 0$.

1.5.2 Optimum Population Rate

Next, we consider the second-order condition for maximization at the neighborhood of n_E. Calculating $\mathrm{d}^2W/\mathrm{d}n^2$ and then using (1.44) and Eqs. (1.56)–(1.58), we obtain:

$$\left.\frac{\mathrm{d}^2W}{\mathrm{d}n^2}\right|_{n=n_E} = -\frac{\rho}{1+\rho}\frac{(1-\alpha)(2-\alpha)}{(1+n_E)^2}, \tag{1.60}$$

in the neighborhood of n_E. If $\rho > 0$, $\left.\frac{\mathrm{d}^2W}{\mathrm{d}n^2}\right|_{n=n_E} < 0$, then n_E is the optimum population growth rate n_M. As mentioned in Sect. 1.3, the convergence condition to the laissez-faire steady state is given by (1.30). Rewriting (1.30), we obtain:

$$A \equiv (1+n_E)\,[1-(1-\alpha)\,\rho\,] > 0, \tag{1.61}$$

which implies $\rho < 1/(1-\alpha)$. Therefore, if $0 < \rho < 1/(1-\alpha)$, the laissez-faire steady state is stable and achieves the golden rule at $n = n_E$. The population growth rate n_E is the optimum one n_M. If $\rho > 1/(1-\alpha)$, the laissez-faire steady state is unstable even though the population growth rate n_E maximizes W as $\mathrm{d}^2W/\mathrm{d}n^2 < 0$. If $\rho < 0$, we have $\mathrm{d}^2W/\mathrm{d}n^2 > 0$ from (1.60). The population rate n_E is the worst one n_W. Proposition 1.3 and Proposition 1.4 in the previous section summarize these conclusions.

We will now numerically examine the relation between the optimum population rate and structural parameters. An imperceptible change in parameters shows that the results are highly sensitive to these changes. Relatively low values of parameters α, β, and ρ result in mild optimum population rates. For example, we obtain $n_M = -0.01375$ in the case of $\alpha = 0.55$, $\beta = 0.2$, and $\rho = 0.38$. We also attain $n_M = +0.01563$ when $\alpha = 0.52$, $\beta = 0.22$ and $\rho = 0.34$. Relatively high values of these parameters result in extreme optimum population rates. For example, supposing ρ within the range [0.4, 1.5] as in Momota et al. (2019), $\alpha = 0.77$ and $\beta = 0.4$, then the optimum population rates fall within the range [0.8874, –0.9721].

1.5.3 Negative Optimum Population Rates

We will now look at a society with a decreasing population to determine its optimum population growth rate. Clearly the optimum population growth rate in (1.59) is negative if $\beta^{-\frac{1}{\rho}}\left[\frac{1-\alpha}{2-\alpha}\right]^{\frac{1}{\rho}+1} < 1$ or $\frac{1-\alpha}{2-\alpha} < \beta^{\frac{1}{1+\rho}}$ when $\rho < 0$. Noting that the capital share to income in the MGG allocation, $\frac{k_M f'(k_M)}{f(k_M)}$, is equal to $\frac{1-\alpha}{2-\alpha}$, we obtain the negative optimum population rate when the capital share to income in the MGG allocation is less than β^{σ} with $\sigma = \frac{1}{1+\rho}$.

Summing up, we have the following proposition as an expression of the elasticity of substitution.

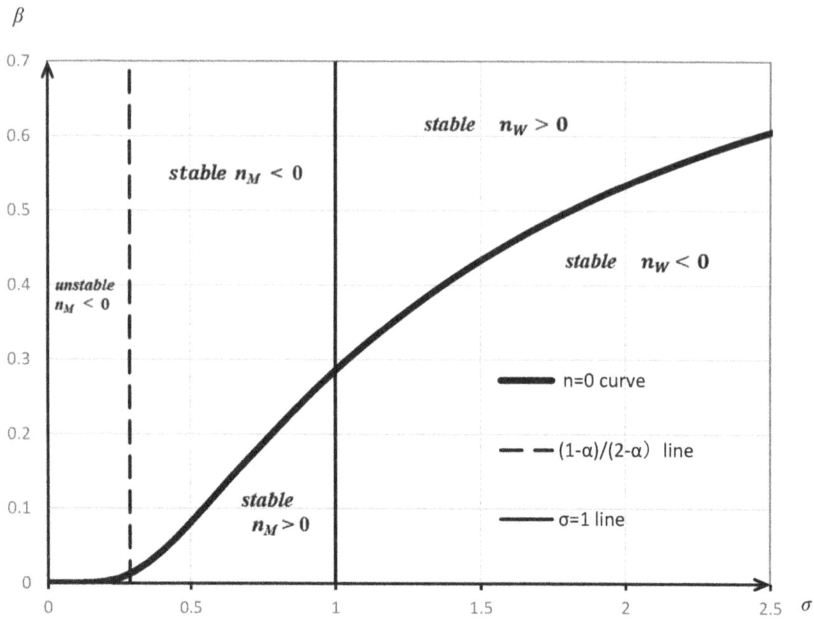

Fig. 1.6 The zero population growth rate in $\alpha = 0.6$

Proposition 1.5 *If* $(1 - \alpha)/(2 - \alpha) < \sigma < 1$, *the Serendipity Theorem holds. The optimum population growth rate* n_M *is a negative optimum one when* $(1 - \alpha)/(2 - \alpha) < \beta^{\sigma}$.

Figure 1.6 shows the relation between β and σ satisfying the population growth rate curve of $n = 0$ in (1.59). Assuming $\alpha = 0.6$, then this implies $\frac{1-\alpha}{2-\alpha} \cong 0.286$ which is the capital share to income in the MGG allocation. The Serendipity Theorem holds for $0.286 < \sigma < 1$. We calculate the negative optimum growth rate to be $0.286 < \beta^{\sigma}$. The laissez-faire steady state is unstable for $0 < \sigma < 0.286$, and the positive optimum growth rate nearly disappears when $0.286 > \beta^{\sigma}$. The worst population growth rate area is for $1 < \sigma$.

1.5.4 Effects of Parameter Changes

To confirm the effects of the parameters α, β, and ρ on the optimum population rate n_M, we derive the following from (1.59) assuming $\rho > 0$:

$$\frac{\partial n_M}{\partial \alpha} = -\frac{\left(\frac{1}{\rho} + 1\right)(1 + n_M)}{(1 - \alpha)(2 - \alpha)} < 0, \tag{1.62}$$

$$\frac{\partial n_M}{\partial \beta} = -\frac{1+n_M}{\rho\beta} < 0, \tag{1.63}$$

$$\frac{\partial n_M}{\partial \rho} = \frac{1+n_M}{\rho^2} \ln \frac{\beta(2-\alpha)}{1-\alpha} \gtreqless 0 \text{ for } \beta \gtreqless \frac{1-\alpha}{2-\alpha}. \tag{1.64}$$

An increase in α and β always results in a decrease in the optimum population rate n_M.

We will look at the effects of the parameters on the optimum capital per capita k_M as a counterpart of n_M. The following are clear from (1.58):

$$\frac{\partial k_M}{\partial \alpha} = \frac{k_M}{\rho(1-\alpha)} > 0, \tag{1.65}$$

$$\frac{\partial k_M}{\partial \beta} = \frac{k_M}{\rho\beta(1-\beta)} > 0, \tag{1.66}$$

$$\frac{\partial k_M}{\partial \rho} = -\frac{k_M}{\rho} \ln k_M \lesseqgtr 0 \text{ for } \beta \gtreqless \frac{1-\alpha}{2-\alpha}. \tag{1.67}$$

The sign conditions $\beta \gtreqless (1-\alpha)/(2-\alpha)$ become $(1-\alpha)(1-\beta)/\beta \lesseqgtr 1$, which implies $k_M \gtreqless 1$ in (1.58) with $\rho > 0$ and in turn $\frac{\partial k_M}{\partial \rho} \lesseqgtr 0$ in (1.67).

Defining W_M as social welfare W corresponding to the MGG allocation, we examine the effects of the parameters on W_M. W_M indicates $W_{\max}$ in Figs. 1.4b and 1.5b. Using (1.56), we rewrite W in (1.55) to get

$$W_M = \ln k_M + (2-\alpha)\ln(1+n_M) + \alpha[\ln\alpha - \ln(1-\alpha)]. \tag{1.68}$$

Considering (1.58) and (1.59), we obtain the following:

$$\begin{aligned}\frac{\partial W_M}{\partial \alpha} &= \frac{1}{k_M}\frac{\partial k_M}{\partial \alpha} + \frac{2-\alpha}{1+n_M}\frac{\partial n_M}{\partial \alpha} - \ln(1+n_M) \\ &\quad + \ln\frac{\alpha}{1-\alpha} + \frac{1}{1-\alpha} = \ln\frac{\alpha}{(1-\alpha)(1+n_M)},\end{aligned} \tag{1.69}$$

$$\frac{\partial W_M}{\partial \beta} = \frac{1}{k_M}\frac{\partial k_M}{\partial \beta} + \frac{2-\alpha}{1+n_M}\frac{\partial n_M}{\partial \beta} = \frac{\beta(2-\alpha)-(1-\alpha)}{\rho\beta(1-\beta)} \gtreqless 0 \text{ for } \beta \gtreqless \frac{1-\alpha}{2-\alpha}, \tag{1.70}$$

$$\frac{\partial W_M}{\partial \rho} = \frac{1}{k_M}\frac{\partial k_M}{\partial \rho} + \frac{2-\alpha}{1+n_M}\frac{\partial n_M}{\partial \rho}. \tag{1.71}$$

From (1.69), we obtain $\frac{\partial W_M}{\partial \alpha} \gtreqless 0$ for $\frac{\alpha}{1-\alpha} \gtreqless 1+n_M$. The sign conditions of $\frac{\partial W_M}{\partial \rho}$ in (1.71) are ambiguous because $\frac{\partial k_M}{\partial \rho} \lesseqgtr 0$and $\frac{\partial n_M}{\partial \rho} \gtreqless 0$ for $\gtreqless \frac{1-\alpha}{2-\alpha}$.

Here we note that $\beta > (1-\alpha)/(2-\alpha)$ implies $\beta^\sigma > \beta > (1-\alpha)/(2-\alpha)$ for $\sigma < 1$, that is, $n_M < 0$ as in Proposition 1.5.

Summing up, we have the following propositions in the expression of the elasticity of substitution, $\sigma = 1/(1 + \rho)$.

Proposition 1.6 *Suppose the optimum population growth rate* n_M *with* $(1 - \alpha)/(2 - \alpha) < \sigma < 1$. *An increase in* α *decreases the positive or negative optimum population growth rate* n_M. *If* $\beta > (1 - \alpha)/(2 - \alpha)$, *then the optimum population growth rate* n_M *is a negative optimum one. An increase in* β *rises social welfare* W_M *in the MGG allocation though the negative optimum one decreases. If* $\beta < (1 - \alpha)/(2 - \alpha)$, *an increase in* β *decreases the optimum one* n_M *and social welfare* W_M.

Proposition 1.7 *Suppose the optimum population growth rate* n_M *with* $(1 - \alpha)/(2 - \alpha) < \sigma < 1$. *If* $\beta > (1 - \alpha)/(2 - \alpha)$, *a decrease in the elasticity of substitution is required to improve the negative optimum one. If* $\beta < (1 - \alpha)/(2 - \alpha)$, *a decrease in the elasticity of substitution is required to decrease the positive or negative optimum one* n_M.

Lawrence (2015) surveys a large number of studies in the USA and finds that the elasticity of substitution between capital and labor σ is less than unity. Mućk (2017) estimates the elasticity of substitution σ in 12 developed economies between 1980 and 2006 and finds that capital and labor are gross complements and the estimated σ is on average around 0.7. The estimated σ for Japan is around 0.5, and equals on average 0.49 and 0.55 for Germany and the USA. Hirakata and Koike (2018) estimate σ using a dynamic stochastic general equilibrium model and estimate σ to be 0.2 for Japan, though around 1.25 for the USA. Also, Lawrence (2015) estimates the elasticity of substitution in total manufacturing in the USA as $\sigma = 0.693$ in 1947–1979, $\sigma = 0.510$ in 1980–2010, and $\sigma = 0.417$ in 1999–2010. Broadly speaking, research suggests that the capital and labor elasticity is decreasing in the long run. Given these countries' population growth rates, our results suggest that a decreasing elasticity is associated with a decline in the optimum population rate.

1.6 Technological Innovation and Optimum Population Growth

Some developed countries face a population decline problem due to a declining birthrate and an aging population. In order to cope with the decline in the labor force population and to improve productivity, it is essential to promote labor-saving technological innovations. Information and Communication Technology (ICT) and Artificial Intelligence (AI) encourage the provision of techniques enabling easy utilization of technology and thus improving productivity.

Acemoglu and Restrepo (2022) argue that aging creates a shortage of workers and leads to greater industrial automation. They also argue that demographic changes in several countries, most notably Germany, Japan, and South Korea, promote the development and adoption of automation innovation. Moreover, Acemoglu and Restrepo (2018, 2020) show the displacement effect of automation and AI tends to reduce the demand for labor and wages.

However, it is naturally conceivable that reverse causal relationship also exists; that is, the deepening of ICT&AI results in a declining population. In this section, we examine the effect deepening ICT&AI has on the optimum population growth rate using a model that allows for two different production sectors: an ICT&AI-producing sector and an ICT&AI-using sector. The former develops new technology and provides the techniques enabling easy utilization of them. The latter produces final goods and services using ICT&AI technology and techniques. Population grows at a constant rate n ($n > -1$) as shown in the previous section. A constant fraction of the young generation works for the former. The remaining young generation works for the latter.

We use a two-level, three-factor production technology model, which was developed by Papageorgiou and Saam (2008). The ICT&AI-producing sector produces its products (X) with capital (K) and labor (L_{AI}) as inputs, and the ICT&AI-using sector produces final goods and services (Y) with ICT&AI products (X) and labor (L_T) as inputs. The first level of the two-level function is given by the CES production function:

$$X = \left[\beta K^{-\rho} + (1-\beta) L_{\mathrm{AI}}^{-\rho}\right]^{-\frac{1}{\rho}}, \tag{1.72}$$

where $0 < \beta < 1$ and $\rho > -1$ as well as (1.36). This CES function is then nested into another Cobb–Douglas function, representing the second level given by

$$Y = X^{\gamma} L_T^{1-\gamma}, \tag{1.73}$$

where $(1-\alpha)/(2-\alpha) < \gamma < 1$. If $\gamma = 1$, (1.72) and (1.73) become (1.36) in Sect. 1.5.

We denote the ratio of laborers in the ICT&AI-producing sector as h and the ratio of laborers in the ICT&AI-using sector as j ($h + j = 1$), where h and j are constants. Thus, (1.72) and (1.73) can be rewritten as an expression of per capita as follows:

$$x = \left[\beta k^{-\rho} + (1-\beta) h^{-\rho}\right]^{-\frac{1}{\rho}}, \tag{1.74}$$

$$y = x^{\gamma} (1-h)^{1-\gamma}. \tag{1.75}$$

Therefore, we have:

$$y = f(k) = \left[\beta k^{-\rho} + (1-\beta) h^{-\rho}\right]^{-\frac{\gamma}{\rho}} (1-h)^{1-\gamma}. \tag{1.76}$$

The wages of both sectors are denoted by w_{AI} and w_T, respectively. The young generation maximize their linear-logarithmic utility function (1.35) to determine their consumption and saving levels. The savings of workers in each sector are given by $(1 - \alpha)w_{\mathrm{AI}}$ and $(1 - \alpha)w_T$ respectively. Total savings are $(1 - \alpha)(w_{\mathrm{AI}}L_{\mathrm{AI}} + w_T L_T)$; and savings per capita are $(1 - \alpha)(hw_{\mathrm{AI}} + (1 - h)w_T)$. Given profit maximization in both sectors, we derive savings per capita as $(1 - \alpha)[f(k) - kf'(k)]$. Therefore, (1.38) holds in the laissez-faire steady state for a given n.

We now use the analysis method of Sects. 1.4 and 1.5 to examine the steady-state path in the golden rule. Assuming $\delta = 1$, we obtain the following from the golden-rule condition (1.43):

$$f'\left(k^*\right) = \beta\gamma\left[\beta k^{*-\rho} + (1-\beta)\, h^{-\rho}\right]^{-\frac{\gamma}{\rho}-1}(1-h)^{1-\gamma}k^{*-\rho-1} = 1+n. \qquad (1.77)$$

Given dW/dn= 0, from (1.56) with (1.76), and using the linear-logarithmic utility $u(c, e)$ in (1.35) and the indirect social welfare function W in (1.55), we obtain:

$$f\left(k^*\right) = \left[\beta k^{*-\rho} + (1-\beta)\, h^{-\rho}\right]^{-\frac{\gamma}{\rho}}(1-h)^{1-\gamma} = (1+n)\, k^* \frac{2-\alpha}{1-\alpha}. \qquad (1.78)$$

Using (1.77) and (1.78), we obtain:

$$k_E{}^{-\rho} = k^{*-\rho} = Dh^{-\rho}, \qquad (1.79)$$

where E= $(1 - \alpha)(1 - \beta)/(\beta H)$ and H= $\gamma(2 - \alpha) - (1 - \alpha)$, and $H > 0$ by the assumption of $(1 - \alpha)/(2 - \alpha) < \gamma < 1$. Further we have the following:

$$x_E = x = (1-\beta)^{-1/\rho}\left[\gamma\,(2-\alpha)\,/H\right]^{-1/\rho} h, \qquad (1.80)$$

$$y_E = y = (1-\beta)^{-\gamma/\rho}\left[\gamma\,(2-\alpha)\,/H\right]^{-\gamma/\rho} h^{\gamma}\,(1-h)^{1-\gamma}, \qquad (1.81)$$

$$n_E = n = E^{1/\rho} J^{-\gamma/\rho}[(1-h)\,/\,h]^{1-\gamma}\frac{1-\alpha}{2-\alpha} - 1, \qquad (1.82)$$

where $J = \beta E + (1 - \beta) > 0$. Here we attach the subscript $_E$ to variables which satisfy dW/d$n = 0$.

We can now derive the sufficient condition for the maximization. Calculating d^2W/dn^2 and then considering (1.77–1.79), we obtain:

$$\left.\frac{\mathrm{d}^2 W}{\mathrm{d}n^2}\right|_{n=n_E} = -\rho\frac{(1-\alpha)\,(2-\alpha)\,H}{(\gamma+\rho H)\,(1+n_E)^2}, \qquad (1.83)$$

in the neighborhood of n_E. As n_E in (1.82) is a unique solution, the population rate n_E is the optimum population growth rate n_M if $\rho > 0$ or $\sigma < 1$. In the following, we attach the subscript $_M$ to variables which satisfy the MGG allocation.

Next, we examine the effect of laborers shift to the ICT&AI-producing sector from the ICT&AI-using sector. Laborers shift to the former increases the ratio of laborers, h. Thus,

$$\frac{\partial k_M}{\partial h} = \frac{k_M}{h} > 0, \tag{1.84}$$

$$\frac{\partial x_M}{\partial h} = \frac{x_M}{h} > 0, \tag{1.85}$$

$$\frac{\partial y_M}{\partial h} = \frac{y_M(\gamma - h)}{h(1-h)} \gtrless 0 \text{ for } \gamma \gtrless h, \tag{1.86}$$

$$\frac{\partial n_M}{\partial h} = -\frac{(1+n_M)(1-\gamma)}{h(1-h)} < 0. \tag{1.87}$$

Accordingly, a shift of laborers to the ICT&AI-producing sector decreases the optimum population growth rate n_M.

We will now look at W_M, the level social welfare W corresponding to the MGG allocation. The indirect social welfare function (1.55) can be rewritten as (1.68) in the previous section by using $\mathrm{d}W/\mathrm{d}n = 0$. In this section, we rewrite (1.68) as (1.88), that is,

$$W_M = \ln k_M + (2-\alpha)\ln(1+n_M) + \alpha[\ln\alpha - \ln(1-\alpha)], \tag{1.88}$$

which satisfies (1.79) and (1.82). Thus, we obtain:

$$\frac{\partial W_M}{\partial h} = \frac{1}{k_M}\frac{\partial k_M}{\partial h} + \frac{2-\alpha}{1+n_M}\frac{\partial n_M}{\partial h} = \frac{H-h}{h(1-h)} \gtrless 0 \text{ for } H \gtrless h. \tag{1.89}$$

The condition of $H \gtrless h$ reduces to $\gamma \gtrless \frac{1-\alpha}{2-\alpha} + \frac{h}{2-\alpha}$.

We now summarize the above as the following two propositions.

Proposition 1.8 *Assuming a linear-logarithmic preference and a two-level, three-factor production technology, the Serendipity Theorem holds if* $\sigma < 1$. *The optimum population growth rate* n_M *is given by* (1.82).

Proposition 1.9 *Assuming Proposition 1.8 holds, labor movement from the ICT&AI-using sector to the ICT&AI-producing sector always decreases the optimum population growth rate* n_M. *It raises social welfare* W_M *in the MGG allocation if* $\gamma > \frac{1-\alpha}{2-\alpha} + \frac{h}{2-\alpha}$ *and reduces* W_M *if* $\frac{1-\alpha}{2-\alpha} + \frac{h}{2-\alpha} > \gamma > \frac{1-\alpha}{2-\alpha}$.

Similarly, we have $\partial k_M/\partial\alpha > 0$, $\partial k_M/\partial\beta > 0$, and $\partial k_M/\partial\gamma > 0$ from (1.79) which indicate that an increase in parameters is associated with an increase production in both the ICT&AI-producing and ICT&AI-using sectors. However, the effects of parameters on the optimum population rate n_M and social welfare W_M are ambiguous.

1.7 Concluding Remarks

The developed countries in Europe, North America, Eastern Asia, Australia, and New Zealand already have fertility rates that have fallen below replacement levels. In Eastern Asia, especially Japan, South Korea, and China, they face the problem of a rapidly declining birthrate and aging population. In an effort to prevent economic stagnation and contraction caused by these factors, they have introduced various economic policies to increase the birthrate, but they have not been successful. Although it is necessary to improve labor productivity through ITC&AI and factor-augmenting technology as well as to develop human resources, it is not easy to substitute ITC&AI and factor-augmenting technology to solve labor shortages.

We extended the basic overlapping generations model to include Cobb–Douglas preference and CES technology. We derived the optimum population growth rate n_M from the viewpoint of the Serendipity Theorem. We showed the optimum population growth rate exists if the elasticity of substitution is less than unity. A negative optimum population growth rate also exists if the capital share to income in the MGG allocation is less than an adequate value determined by the structural parameters. A decrease in the elasticity of substitution is required to improve the negative optimum population growth rate. The developed countries need to implement a variety of policies to increase the birthrate. Labor movement from the ICT&AI-using sector to the ICT&AI-producing sector decreases the positive or negative optimum population growth rate, lowering the optimum population rate. Thus, the deepening of ICT&AI is needed given the current low fertility rates.

We believe our results have significant policy implications for a society with a declining population.

Acknowledgements I would like to thank Professors Mitsuyoshi Yanagihara, Kei Hosoya, Tsuyoshi Shinozaki, and Wilson Alley for their valuable comments and suggestions. I also would like to thank seminar participants at several online meetings on *modern macroeconomics with historical perspectives* for their helpful comments and suggestions.

Appendix

Proof of $\mathrm{d}\tilde{k}/\mathrm{d}n < 0$

We already know that $\mathrm{d}k^*/\mathrm{d}n = 1/f''(k^*) < 0$ from (1.18) and $\mathrm{d}k/\mathrm{d}n = -k/A$ from (1.31).

Now we prepare the following discussion to derive $\mathrm{d}\tilde{k}/\mathrm{d}n$. First, we consider a government which has the aim to achieve the golden rule with pay-as-you-go social security. The government sets up a transfer τ from the younger to the older generation; therefore, budget constraint (1.2) in the laissez-faire has been changed to $c_t + s_{\text{priv},t} = w_t - \tau$ and $e_{t+1} = (1 + r_{t+1})s_{\text{priv},t} + (1 + n)\tau$;, thus,

$c_t + e_{t+1}/(1 + r_{t+1}) = w_t + (n - r_{t+1})\tau/(1 + r_{t+1})$. Also, the capital market equilibrium condition (1.10) has been changed to $(1 + n)k_{t+1} = s_{\text{priv},t} = e_{t+1}/(1 + r_{t+1}) - (1 + n)\tau/(1 + r_{t+1})$. If the convergence condition in this equation is satisfied and a smart government assigns a proper value to τ, the golden-rule steady state is $n + \delta = r^* + \delta = f'(k^*)$ with $\delta = 1$, $(1+n)k^* = s^*_{\text{priv}}$, and $w^* = f(k^*) - (1 + n)k^*$. The budget constraint in the golden rule becomes $c^* + e^*/(1 + n) = w^*$ in (1.2). Hence a representative individual chooses an optimal consumption pattern c^* and e^* as under the constraint in the laissez-faire. In other words, their gross savings are $s^* = s^*_{\text{priv}} + \tau$ as $s^* = w^* - c^*$.

In the golden rule achieved by the above economy, $(1+n)\tilde{k} = e^*/(1+n) = s^*$ from the above discussion and the definition of $\tilde{k}$. Having $s^* = s(w^*, r^*)$, we obtain $\mathrm{d}\tilde{k}/\mathrm{d}n$ as

$$\begin{aligned}\frac{\mathrm{d}\tilde{k}}{\mathrm{d}n} &= \frac{\frac{\partial s}{\partial w}\frac{\mathrm{d}w^*}{\mathrm{d}n} + \frac{\partial s}{\partial r}\frac{\mathrm{d}r^*}{\mathrm{d}n}}{1+n} - \frac{s^*}{(1+n)^2} = -k^*\frac{\frac{\partial s}{\partial w}}{1+n} + \frac{\frac{\partial s}{\partial r}}{1+n} - \frac{\tilde{k}}{1+n} \\ &= -\frac{1}{1+n}\left(k^*\frac{\partial s}{\partial w} - \frac{\partial s}{\partial r} + \tilde{k}\right).\end{aligned} \tag{1.90}$$

If $\partial s/\partial r$ is low or negative, we have $k^* \partial s/\partial w - \partial s/\partial r > 0$ and thus $\mathrm{d}\tilde{k}/\mathrm{d}n < 0$. In the case of a linear-logarithmic utility, $\partial s/\partial r = 0$ and clearly $\mathrm{d}\tilde{k}/\mathrm{d}n < 0$.

Derivation of (1.32) and (1.33)

Substituting (1.31) into (1.28) leads to (1.32). From (1.90) and $\mathrm{d}k^*/\mathrm{d}n = 1/f'$, we immediately have

$$\begin{aligned}\frac{\mathrm{d}\tilde{k}}{\mathrm{d}n} - \frac{\mathrm{d}k^*}{\mathrm{d}n} &= -\frac{1}{(1+n)f''}\left(1 + n + k^* f''\frac{\partial s}{\partial w} - f''\frac{\partial s}{\partial r} + k^* f''\right) \\ &= -\frac{B}{(1+n)f''}.\end{aligned} \tag{1.91}$$

Thus, we obtain (1.33).

Proof of $\mathrm{d}k/\mathrm{d}n < \mathrm{d}\tilde{k}/\mathrm{d}n < \mathrm{d}k^*/\mathrm{d}n < 0$ *in Fig. 1.1a*

In the stable case of $A > 0$, the second-order condition for a maximum of V and W is satisfied if $B < 0$. If so, it is clear that $\mathrm{d}k/\mathrm{d}n < \mathrm{d}k^*/\mathrm{d}n = 1/f' < 0$ from (1.28) and $\mathrm{d}\tilde{k}/\mathrm{d}n < \mathrm{d}k^*/\mathrm{d}n < 0$ from (1.29) or (1.91).

Now we look at the relationship between dk/dn and d$\tilde{k}$/dn in the neighborhood of $n = n_M$ (i.e., in $k = \tilde{k}$). From (1.31) and (1.90), we obtain:

$$\frac{\mathrm{d}k}{\mathrm{d}n} - \frac{\mathrm{d}\tilde{k}}{\mathrm{d}n} = \frac{1}{1+n}\left(k^*\frac{\partial s}{\partial w} - \frac{\partial s}{\partial r}\right)\frac{B}{A}. \tag{1.92}$$

As $A > 0$ and $B < 0$, then dk/dn < d$\tilde{k}$/dn < 0 when $\partial s/\partial r$ is a low or a negative.

Thus, we obtain dk/dn < d$\tilde{k}$/dn < dk^*/dn < 0 in the neighborhood of $n = n_M$, which implies $k \gtreqless \tilde{k} \gtreqless k^* \gtreqless k_M$ for each $n \lesseqgtr n_M$.

Proof of d$\tilde{k}$/dn < dk^*/dn < 0 < dk/dn *in the Unstable Case*

In the unstable case of $A < 0$, dk/dn > 0, which also means $B < 0$. Therefore, the second-order condition is satisfied in (1.32) and (1.33). Thus, dk/dn > 0 > dk^*/dn from (1.28) and dk^*/dn > d$\tilde{k}$/dn from (1.29). Hence, we have dk/dn > 0 > dk^*/dn > d$\tilde{k}$/dn in the neighborhood of $n = n_M$, which shows $\tilde{k} \gtreqless k^* \gtreqless k_M \gtreqless k$ for each $n \lesseqgtr n_M$.

Proof of dk^*/dn < d$\tilde{k}$/dn < dk/dn < 0 *in Fig. 1.2a*

In the stable case of $A > 0$, the second-order condition is not satisfied in (1.32) and (1.33) if $B > 0$. Thus, 0 > dk/dn >dk^*/dn from (1.28), d$\tilde{k}$/dn > dk^*/dn from (1.29) or (1.91), and dk/dn > d$\tilde{k}$/dn from (1.92). Therefore, we have 0 > dk/dn > d$\tilde{k}$/dn > dk^*/dn in the neighborhood of $n = n_M$, which shows $k^* \gtreqless \tilde{k} \gtreqless k \gtreqless k_W$ for each $n \gtreqless n_W$.

References

Acemoglu D, Restrepo P (2018) Artificial intelligence, automation and work, NBER Working Paper, No. 24196, 1–41

Acemoglu D, Restrepo P (2020) Robots and jobs: evidence from US labor markets. J Polit Econ 128(6):2188–2244

Acemoglu D, Restrepo P (2022) Demographics and automation. Rev Econ Stud 89(1):1–44

Christianns T (2011) Semi-endogenous growth when population is decreasing. Econ Bull 31(3):2667–2673

de la Croix D, Michel P (2002) A theory of economic growth: dynamics and policy in overlapping generations. Cambridge University Press, Cambridge

Deardorff A (1976) The optimum rate for population: comment. Int Econ Rev 17(2):510–515

Diamond PA (1965) National debt in a neoclassical growth model. Am Econ Rev 55(5):1126–1150

Hirakata N, Koike Y (2018) The labor share, capital-labor substitution, and factor augmenting technologies, Bank of Japan Working Paper, No. 18-E-20, 1–48

Jaeger K, Kuhle W (2009) The optimum growth rate for population reconsidered. J Popul Econ 22:23–41

Jones C (2020) The end of economic growth? Unintended consequences of a declining population, NBER Working Paper, No. 26651, 1–44

Lawrence R (2015) Recent declines in labor's share in US income: a preliminary neoclassical account, NBER Working Paper, No. 21292, 1–69

Michel P, Pestieau P (1993) Population growth and optimality: when does serendipity hold? J Popul Econ 6(4):353–362

Momota A, Sakagami T, Shibata A (2019) Reexamination of the serendipity theorem from the stability viewpoint. J Demogr Econ 85:43–70

Mućk J (2017) Elasticity of substitution between labor and capital: robust evidence from developed economies, NBP Working Paper, No. 271, 1–50

Papageorgiou C, Saam M (2008) Two-level CES production technology in the Solow and Diamond growth models. Scand J Econ 110(1):119–143

Ritschl A (1985) On the stability of the steady state when population is decreasing. J Econ 45(2):161–170

Samuelson P (1958) An exact consumption-loan model of interest with or without the social contrivance of money. J Polit Econ 66(6):467–482

Samuelson P (1975a) The optimum rate for population. Int Econ Rev 16(3):531–538

Samuelson P (1975b) Optimum social security in a life-cycle growth model. Int Econ Rev 16(3):539–544

Samuelson P (1976) The optimum rate for population: agreement and evaluations. Int Econ Rev 17(2):516–525

Sasaki H (2019) The Solow growth model with a CES production function and declining population. Econ Bull 39(3):1979–1988

Sasaki H, Hoshida K (2017) The effect of negative population growth: an analysis using a semi-endogenous R&D growth model. Macroecon Dyn 21(7):1545–1560

Solow R (1956) A contribution to the theory of economic growth. Q J Econ 70(1):65–94

Takahashi S (1979) Capital accumulation and income redistribution between two generations. Tohoku Gakuin Rev Econ 81:135–168

Takahashi S (2008) The optimum rate for population and a CES production function. Tohoku Gakuin Rev Econ 167:81–100

United Nations (2019) World population prospects 2019 volume II: demographic profiles. United Nations, New York

Chapter 2
Consumption of Leisure Goods, Leisure Time, and Inheritance of Tastes for Leisure in an Overlapping Generations Model

Mitsuyoshi Yanagihara and Weizhen Hu

Abstract This chapter considers an overlapping generations (OLG) model where leisure is a composite of time and consumption, the taste for leisure is inherited from parents, and a production externality exists. We investigate the existence and the feature of the steady-state equilibrium and the transitional dynamics of the economy. Then, we investigate how the preference for leisure and capital intensity affect individuals' consumption choice on leisure and the accumulation of capital.

The results of this chapter are as follows. First, although the production function exhibits an AK type, the economy has unique nontrivial and trivial steady states. Second, the nontrivial steady state of this economy is always periodic. In other words, the equilibrium is cyclical. Third, on the one hand, an increase in either the preference for leisure or capital intensity will reduce the levels of capital stock and the consumption of leisure goods in the long run. On the other hand, in the short run, the effects of a larger preference for leisure are ambiguous, while those brought about by a higher productivity of capital are negative.

Keywords Leisure time · Leisure goods · Inheritance of leisure · Overlapping generations model · Periodic equilibrium

JEL Classification: C61, C62, E21, J22

M. Yanagihara (✉)
Graduate School of Economics, Nagoya University, Nagoya, Japan
e-mail: yanagi@soec.nagoya-u.ac.jp

W. Hu
Department of Economy and Trade, Business School, Central South University, Changsha, China
e-mail: hu.weizhen@csu.edu.cn

S. Takahashi et al. (eds.), *Modern Macroeconomics with Historical Perspectives*,
New Frontiers in Regional Science: Asian Perspectives 67,
https://doi.org/10.1007/978-981-99-1067-0_2

2.1 Introduction

This chapter incorporates the leisure and inheritance of the taste for leisure from parents into an overlapping generations (OLG) model with a production externality. Similar to the usual OLG models, the individual obtains their utility from consumption in both young and old periods. Additionally, as distinct assumptions, (1) they obtain utility from leisure by integrating the consumption of leisure goods and the time spent on leisure, and (2) the utility from leisure is affected by the tastes of leisure inherited from the previous generation.

As is well known, in dynamic frameworks, especially in OLG models, leisure is captured as an opposing element for other activities that require time when incorporated into the utility function. The most representative is the trade-off between leisure and labor. Maoz (2010) incorporates leisure time into utility and shows that the different dynamic patterns between the US and European countries can be explained by the differences in the valuation of leisure. In other words, Maoz's (2010) interest lies in the role of leisure as a source of economic dynamics. Qiao and Wang (2019) consider leisure time an element of utility in an old period, as well as fertility rate in a young period, to investigate how relaxing fertility control affects the steady state. They examine the changes in leisure time in the old period brought about by the change in fertility rate in the young period. Liu and Thogersen (2020) note a trade-off between leisure time and retirement in the old period.

Some studies have investigated the effects of fiscal policies based on frameworks incorporating the trade-off between leisure and labor. Fanti and Spataro (2006) and Lopez-Garcia (2008) argue that the introduction of leisure time into the utility function into Diamond (1965) OLG model affects capital accumulation. More concretely, Fanti and Spataro (2006) indicate that the results obtained in Diamond (1965) stating that government debt necessarily crowds out capital accumulation are modified when leisure becomes an element of utility; however, Lopez-Garcia (2008) proves that their claim does not hold. To investigate the optimal nonlinear tax schedule, Brett (2012) assumes that the utility function is quasi-linear in leisure.

There are also some studies that consider time to be used for either leisure or human capital accumulation. Regarding health, on the one hand, Gori and Sodini (2020), using an OLG model, consider leisure time as an element of utility and endogenous lifetime, which is determined by both private and public health inputs. Regarding education, on the other hand, Futagami and Yanagihara (2008) consider the allocation of time between leisure and education to compare the growth rates of public education and private education schemes.

None of the above theoretical literature considers leisure consumption, that is, the input of goods for leisure, nor captures leisure as a composite of time and consumption. In other words, leisure has been considered a time-consuming activity in most theoretical literature. However, both Becker (1965) and De Serpa (1971) propose that consumption activities, including leisure, should be considered an integration of time and goods. From a real economic point of view, Bittman (2002) affirms that leisure can be considered a product of both leisure goods and services and leisure time. Abe et al. (2018) empirically investigated how Japanese households determine the input of leisure time and the consumption of leisure goods and services from the viewpoint of household production.

In addition to considering the integration of leisure time and leisure consumption, this chapter also sheds light on the existence of the inheritance of taste or preference for leisure, that is, aspiration for leisure. In an OLG model, De la Croix (1996) and De la Croix and Michel (1999) first incorporated the standard of living aspirations that children inherit from their parents. De la Croix (2001) considers human capital accumulation through education. In contrast to these three studies, all of which examine the stability of the equilibrium, some investigate how aspiration affects the economy. Caballé and Moro-Egido (2014) consider the introduction of habits and aspirations when individuals' labor productivity is subject to idiosyncratic shocks and when bequests arise from a joy-of-giving motive to confirm that the distribution of wealth is determined by these elements differently. Fanti et al. (2018) incorporate inherited tastes into an OLG model to show that the interaction between the intensity of inherited tastes and the elasticity of the substitution of effective consumption affect the qualitative and quantitative long-term dynamics. Fanti et al. (2019) further incorporate endogenous longevity and inherited tastes into an OLG model. In their model, individuals' health conditions depend on public investment in health, which is inherited by subsequent generations. Gori and Michetti (2016) indicate that endogenous fertility prevents endogenous fluctuations in a general equilibrium economy when aspirations exist.

Therefore, in our model, the following two featured elements are incorporated into an OLG model: the first is that the (utility of) leisure is captured as the composite of time and consumption, and the other is that the preference for leisure is inherited from the previous generation. Additionally, to describe the dynamics clearly, we introduce a production externality so that the production function exhibits an AK type. We further investigate the dynamics brought about by composite leisure and the inheritance of taste for leisure.

This study's results are as follows. First, although the production function exhibits an AK type, the economy has unique nontrivial and trivial steady states. Second, the nontrivial steady state of this economy is always periodic. In other words, the equilibrium is necessarily cyclical. Third, on the one hand, an increase in either the preference of leisure or capital intensity will reduce the levels of capital stock and the consumption of leisure goods in the long run. On the other hand, in the short run, the effects of a larger preference for leisure are ambiguous, while those brought about by a higher productivity of capital are negative.

This study proceeds as follows: Sect. 2.2 introduces the model and shows the features of the dynamics and the steady state. Section 2.3 describes the comparative statistics. Section 2.4 presents numerical examples. Section 2.5 further concludes the study.

2.2 The Model

2.2.1 Framework

We consider a closed, one-sector, overlapping-generations economy. Time is discrete and starts from period 1, and the economy lasts forever, $t = 1, 2, \ldots$ There is no population growth, and the number of populations is set to unity for analytical convenience. There are two types of goods in this economy, namely, leisure goods, which are used to enjoy leisure, and general goods, which can be used either for consumption or savings and are converted into capital stock.[1]

2.2.2 An Individual

An individual lives for two periods. In the first period of their life, they are young, and in the second period of life, they are old. The young in period t, generation t, allocate one unit of time for leisure, l_t, or for work, $1 - l_t$. They earn a wage income, w_t, for one unit of time by working so as to consume a general good, c_t, to buy a leisure good, y_t, or to save, s_t. Therefore, the budget constraint for the young can be written as

$$(1 - l_t)\, w_t = y_t + c_t + s_t. \tag{2.1}$$

The left- and right-hand sides represent their wage income and expenditure when young, respectively. It is important to note that the prices of consumption, savings, and leisure goods are set to 1.

When getting old, in period $t + 1$, the old makes a consumption, d_{t+1}, using the return from savings. Therefore, the budget constraint for the old can be given as

$$(1 + r_{t+1})\, s_t = d_{t+1}, \tag{2.2}$$

where r_{t+1} represents the net interest rate or the return on savings from the production in period $t + 1$. Similar to the budget constraint for the young, the left-hand side represents the income side, which encompasses the return from savings, and the right-hand side represents the expenditure side, which includes consumption only.

Similar to the usual OLG model, the individual obtains their utility from consumption in both young and old periods. Additionally, as distinct assumptions on utility, (1) they obtain utility from leisure by integrating the consumption of leisure

[1] As we assume that the economy has only one good production sector, the produced goods can be used for consumption, savings, and leisure. Therefore, the prices of consumption, savings, and leisure goods are equal, which are all unity.

goods and the time spent on leisure, and (2) the utility from leisure is affected by the taste inherited from the previous generation.

From the above settings, a utility function with a log-linear form is formulated as follows:

$$U\left(c_t, d_{t+1}, y_t, l_t\right) = \alpha_1 \ln c_t + \alpha_2 \ln d_{t+1} + \sigma y_{t-1} \ln\left(y_t l_t^{\theta}\right), \tag{2.3}$$

where α_1, α_2, and σy_{t-1} (σ is a constant, strictly positive value) represent the weights of the subutilities for consumption in the young, that in the old, and leisure in the young period, respectively. From the third term on the right-hand side of (2.3), we can acknowledge that the utility from leisure is expressed as the product of the amount of leisure goods and the time for leisure to the θ th power [assumption (1)]. Moreover, the weight on the subutility for leisure in the young period depends on the amount of leisure goods in period $t-1$, that is, the amount of leisure goods consumed by their parent [assumption (2)].

In conclusion, individuals' utility-maximization problem can be defined by maximizing the utility, (2.3), subject to budget constraints for the young and the old, (2.1) and (2.2). By solving this problem, we obtain:

$$c_t = \frac{\alpha_1 w_t}{\alpha_1 + \alpha_2 + \sigma\left(1+\theta\right) y_{t-1}}, \tag{2.4}$$

$$s_t = \frac{\alpha_2 w_t}{\alpha_1 + \alpha_2 + \sigma\left(1+\theta\right) y_{t-1}}, \tag{2.5}$$

$$d_{t+1} = \frac{\alpha_2\left(1+r_{t+1}\right) w_t}{\alpha_1 + \alpha_2 + \sigma\left(1+\theta\right) y_{t-1}}, \tag{2.6}$$

$$y_t = \frac{\sigma y_{t-1} w_t}{\alpha_1 + \alpha_2 + \sigma\left(1+\theta\right) y_{t-1}}, \tag{2.7}$$

$$l_t = \frac{\theta \sigma y_{t-1}}{\alpha_1 + \alpha_2 + \sigma\left(1+\theta\right) y_{t-1}}. \tag{2.8}$$

The assumption of the log-linear utility function provides the specific forms of the above solutions. It is well known that these solutions can be expressed as a weighted average of the weights of subutilities for the endowment. For instance, (2.4) clearly shows that consumption in the young period is the product of the weighted average ($\frac{\alpha_1}{\alpha_1+\alpha_2+\sigma(1+\theta)y_{t-1}}$) and the endowment ($w_t$).[2] Here, it should be noted that the amount of leisure goods in period t-1 is included in the denominator of the weight. Furthermore, (2.7) clearly shows that it is not only included in the denominator of the weight on the amount of leisure good consumption in period t but also in

[2] In this model, an individual is endowed with one unit of time, whose value in goods is w_t.

the numerator. This feature can also be observed in the time spent on leisure (2.8). These findings indicate that the weights on the subutility for the consumption of leisure goods and for leisure time in period t increase as the amount of leisure good consumption increases in the previous period. This expresses inherited tastes for leisure. Moreover, this effect brought about by inherited tastes is powerful in this formation.

2.2.3 Firms

Firms produce outputs by utilizing (aggregate) capital K_t and labor L_t when they compete perfectly in the markets of capital, labor, and output. The production function is given by a Cobb–Douglas form with an externality incurred by the average level of capital per labor, which was originally developed by Romer (1986).[3] By denoting capital stock in a per capita term by $k_t \equiv K_t/L_t$ and total factor productivity by $A > 0$, we express the aggregate production function as[4]

$$F\left(K_t, L_t, \overline{k}_t\right) = AK_t^{\beta} L_t^{1-\beta} \overline{k}_t^{1-\beta}, \tag{2.9}$$

where $\overline{k}_t$ represents the average level of capital per labor in the whole economy in period t. By dividing both sides of (2.9) by L_t, we can obtain the following production function in per capita terms:

$$f\left(k_t, \overline{k}_t\right) = Ak_t^{\beta} \overline{k}_t^{1-\beta}. \tag{2.10}$$

For each firm, $\overline{k}_t$ is exogenously given. Hence, the profit maximization for each firm gives the equivalence of the marginal productivities of the inputs and their prices as

$$r_t = \beta Ak_t^{\beta-1} \overline{k}_t^{1-\beta}, \tag{2.11}$$

$$w_t = (1-\beta) Ak_t^{\beta} \overline{k}_t^{1-\beta}. \tag{2.12}$$

[3] For a detailed explanation on the externality brought about by the average level of physical capital in a per capita term, see Romer (1986).

[4] This Romer-type externality for the average level of physical capital has been widely accepted as one of the sources of economic growth. This is applied, for example, in Kohn and Marion (1993), Caballé and Manresa (1994), Bhattacharya et al. (2009), Ono (2010), Ueda (2013), and Chen and Guo (2018).

As we will consider the equilibrium just below, in the equilibrium, $\overline{k}_t = k_t$ is realized ex post. Therefore, in the equilibrium, we have:

$$r_t = \beta A, \tag{2.13}$$

$$w_t = (1 - \beta) A k_t. \tag{2.14}$$

2.2.4 Equilibrium

In each period, the labor, capital, and goods markets should be clear to achieve a temporary equilibrium. Specifically, the following three equilibrium conditions must be satisfied:

$$L_t = 1 - l_t, \tag{2.15}$$

$$(1 - l_{t+1}) k_{t+1} = s_t, \tag{2.16}$$

$$A k_t = y_t + c_t + d_t + s_t. \tag{2.17}$$

(2.16) and (2.17) are expressed in a per capita term.[5]

Substituting the solutions for subjective maximization, (2.5), (2.8), (2.13), and (2.14) into (2.15) and (2.16), we can obtain a set of dynamic equations for physical capital accumulation and the evolution of the consumption of leisure goods as follows:

$$k_{t+1} = \frac{\alpha_2 (1 - \beta) A k_t}{\alpha_1 + \alpha_2 + \sigma (1 + \theta) y_{t-1}} \frac{\alpha_1 + \alpha_2 + \sigma (1 + \theta) y_t}{\alpha_1 + \alpha_2 + \sigma y_t}, \tag{2.18}$$

$$y_t = \frac{\sigma (1 - \beta) A k_t y_{t-1}}{\alpha_1 + \alpha_2 + \sigma (1 + \theta) y_{t-1}}. \tag{2.19}$$

It is interesting to note that both the amount of leisure goods in the present period and the capital stock in the next period depend on the amount of leisure goods in the previous period. This implies that the consumption of leisure or leisure activities directly affect leisure across generations within a household as well as the capital accumulation over time in an economy as a whole.

---

[5] From Walras's law, one of the equilibrium conditions of (2.15), (2.16), and (2.17) can automatically hold in equilibrium.

By setting $k_t = k_{t+1} = k^*$ and $y_{t-1} = y_t = y^*$ in (2.18) and (2.19), the physical capital and the consumption of leisure goods in the steady state can be obtained as

$$k^* = \frac{(1+\theta)\,\alpha_2\,(1-\beta)\,A - \theta\,(\alpha_1+\alpha_2)}{\sigma\,(1-\beta)\,A}, \tag{2.20}$$

$$y^* = \frac{\alpha_2\,(1-\beta)\,A - (\alpha_1+\alpha_2)}{\sigma}. \tag{2.21}$$

Although we incorporate the externality of physical capital, which often brings about endogenous growth, in contrast to many previous studies, the economy achieves a steady state where the growth rate is zero. Therefore, we make the following proposition.

Proposition 2.1 *The economy with a production externality has a unique nontrivial steady state.*

It can be easily verified that this economy has another steady state, which is trivial, with $k^* = y^* = 0$. We have excluded this situation from our analysis. Additionally, to guarantee that the above nontrivial steady state is meaningful, the following two inequalities must hold:

$$(1+\theta)\,\alpha_2\,(1-\beta)\,A - \theta\,(\alpha_1+\alpha_2) > 0, \tag{2.22}$$

$$\alpha_2\,(1-\beta)\,A - (\alpha_1+\alpha_2) > 0. \tag{2.23}$$

It is easily confirmed that, if the assumption of (2.23) holds, then the equality of (2.22) also holds. Therefore, we assume the following.

Assumption 2.1

$$\alpha_2\,(1-\beta)\,A - (\alpha_1+\alpha_2) > 0.$$

This assumption intuitively implies that (1) total factor productivity is sufficiently large, (2) capital intensity is sufficiently small, and (3) the weight on the subutility for consumption in the young period is sufficiently small.

Regarding the solutions for the individual, we can obtain the consumption in the young period, savings, the consumption in the old period, and the time spent on leisure in the steady state as

$$c^* = \frac{\alpha_1}{\sigma}, \tag{2.24}$$

$$s^* = \frac{\alpha_2}{\sigma}, \tag{2.25}$$

$$d^* = \frac{\alpha_2 (1 + A\beta)}{\sigma}, \tag{2.26}$$

$$l^* = \frac{[A\alpha_2 (1 - \beta) - (\alpha_1 + \alpha_2)]\theta}{A\alpha_2 (1 - \beta)(1 + \theta) - (\alpha_1 + \alpha_2)\theta}. \tag{2.27}$$

Consequently, substituting (2.21), (2.24), (2.26), and (2.27) into (2.3) yields the utility level in the steady state as follows:

$$\begin{aligned} &\alpha_1 \text{In}\left[\frac{\alpha_1}{\sigma}\right] + \alpha_2 \text{In}\left[\frac{\alpha_2 (1 + A\beta)}{\sigma}\right] + \{\alpha_2 (1 - \beta) A - (\alpha_1 + \alpha_2)\} \\ &\times \text{In}\left[\frac{\{\alpha_2 (1 - \beta) A - (\alpha_1 + \alpha_2)\}\left\{\frac{(\alpha_2(1-\beta)A - (\alpha_1+\alpha_2))\theta}{(1+\theta)\alpha_2(1-\beta)A - \theta(\alpha_1+\alpha_2)}\right\}^{\theta}}{\sigma}\right]. \end{aligned} \tag{2.28}$$

In conclusion, the nontrivial steady state has the following feature.

Proposition 2.2 *The steady state of this economy is periodic.*

Proof See Appendix.

Proposition 2.2 means that if the initial levels of capital and a leisure good differ from the steady state, the economy may circulate around its steady state.

2.3 Comparative Statics: Effects of Preference and Productivity

To understand how capital stock and leisure consumption develop in both the short and long run, we evaluate the effects of the preference for leisure, σ, and capital intensity, β, on the economy, respectively. We discuss how a change in σ or β affects individuals' choices, production, and capital market equilibrium. Particularly, we show that because of inherited tastes for the consumption of leisure goods, the effects on leisure consumption, y_t, will further amplify those on capital accumulation and the dynamics of the economy as a whole.

2.3.1 Effects of Preference for Leisure

First, we consider a change in the preference for leisure in the short run. When the preference for leisure increases, individuals allocate more of their time for leisure and thus less for work, which can be easily verified by differentiating (2.8) by σ:

$$\frac{\mathrm{d}l_t}{\mathrm{d}\sigma} = \frac{(\alpha_1 + \alpha_2)\, l_t}{[\alpha_1 + \alpha_2 + \sigma\,(1+\theta)\, y_{t-1}]\,\sigma} > 0. \tag{2.29}$$

Further, by differentiating (2.5) and (2.19) by σ, we obtain:

$$\frac{\mathrm{d}s_t}{\mathrm{d}\sigma} = s_t \left\{ \frac{1}{1-l_t}\frac{\mathrm{d}l_t}{\mathrm{d}\sigma} - \frac{(1+\theta)\, y_{t-1}}{\alpha_1 + \alpha_2 + \sigma\,(1+\theta)\, y_{t-1}} \right\} = -\frac{y_{t-1} s_t}{\alpha_1 + \alpha_2 + \sigma y_{t-1}} < 0, \tag{2.30}$$

$$\frac{\mathrm{d}y_t}{\mathrm{d}\sigma} = y_t \left\{ \frac{1}{1-l_t}\frac{\mathrm{d}l_t}{\mathrm{d}\sigma} + \frac{\alpha_1 + \alpha_2}{[\alpha_1 + \alpha_2 + \sigma\,(1+\theta)\, y_{t-1}]\,\sigma} \right\} = \frac{(\alpha_1 + \alpha_2)\, y_t}{[\alpha_1 + \alpha_2 + \sigma y_{t-1}]\,\sigma} > 0. \tag{2.31}$$

Regarding the effect on savings, s_t, the first term in the bracket of (2.30) represents a positive effect through the change in l_t. The increases in k_t and thus in the wage rate w_t increase the opportunity cost of leisure time, which encourages individuals to work and save more (①).[6] The second term in the bracket is a direct effect, simply because individuals save less under a larger preference for leisure (②). The total effects on s_t can be calculated as negative. The effects on y_t are similar. The first term in the bracket of (2.31) is also a positive effect through the change in l_t (③), while the second term shows a positive direct effect (④). The total effect on y_t is positive.

Further, we use (2.8), (2.16), and (2.19) to determine how leisure time, capital stock, and leisure consumption in period $t+1$ are affected:

$$\frac{\mathrm{d}l_{t+1}}{\mathrm{d}\sigma} = \frac{(\alpha_1 + \alpha_2)\, l_{t+1}}{[\alpha_1 + \alpha_2 + \sigma\,(1+\theta)\, y_t]\, y_t}\frac{\mathrm{d}y_t}{\mathrm{d}\sigma} + \frac{(\alpha_1 + \alpha_2)\, l_{t+1}}{[\alpha_1 + \alpha_2 + \sigma y_t]\,\sigma} > 0, \tag{2.32}$$

$$\frac{\mathrm{d}k_{t+1}}{\mathrm{d}\sigma} = \frac{1}{1-l_{t+1}}\left(\frac{\mathrm{d}s_t}{\mathrm{d}\sigma} + k_{t+1}\frac{\mathrm{d}l_{t+1}}{\mathrm{d}\sigma}\right), \tag{2.33}$$

[6] It is worthwhile to note that, from the capital market equilibrium (2.16) in period $t-1$, we can confirm that $\frac{\mathrm{d}k_t}{\mathrm{d}\sigma} = \frac{s_{t-1}}{(1-l_t)^2}\frac{\mathrm{d}l_t}{\mathrm{d}\sigma} = \frac{k_t}{1-l_t}\frac{\mathrm{d}l_t}{\mathrm{d}\sigma}$. This shows that a change in the leisure time in period t brought about by a change in the preference results in a change in the capital per labor, which further results in a change in the wage rate. This brings about the result that the income of individuals will not change, that is, $\frac{\mathrm{d}(1-l_t)w_t}{\mathrm{d}\sigma} = 0$. This is because $\frac{\mathrm{d}(1-l_t)w_t}{\mathrm{d}\sigma} = -\frac{w_t \mathrm{d}l_t}{\mathrm{d}\sigma} + \frac{(1-l_t)\mathrm{d}w_t}{\mathrm{d}\sigma} = -\frac{(1-\beta)Ak_t \mathrm{d}l_t}{\mathrm{d}\sigma} + \frac{(1-l_t)(1-\beta)Ak_t}{1-l_t}\frac{\mathrm{d}l_t}{\mathrm{d}\sigma} = 0$.

$$\frac{dy_{t+1}}{d\sigma} = y_{t+1}\left\{\frac{\alpha_1+\alpha_2}{[\alpha_1+\alpha_2+\sigma(1+\theta)y_t]\,y_t}\frac{dy_t}{d\sigma}+\frac{ds_t}{d\sigma}\right.$$
$$\left.+k_{t+1}\frac{dl_{t+1}}{d\sigma}+\frac{\alpha_1+\alpha_2}{[\alpha_1+\alpha_2+\sigma y_t]\,\sigma}\right\}. \tag{2.34}$$

Regarding the effect on l_{t+1}, there is also a direct effect, as shown in (2.29), ①. The first term in (2.32) expresses the intertemporal effect through y_t. Along with the change in σ, the change in y_t further affects individuals' preferences in the subsequent period. Because $\frac{dy_t}{d\sigma}$ is positive, the preference for leisure is amplified in period $t+1$, which encourages individuals to spend more time on leisure and consume more leisure goods (⑤). The increase in σ affects the accumulation of capital per labor through changes in capital and labor supplies, s_t and $(1-l_{t+1})$. Therefore, the total effects on k_{t+1} can be decomposed into five parts, resulting from ① to ⑤, as described above. The total effect on y_{t+1} can also be interpreted using a similar procedure.

To consider the long-run effects, that is, the effects in the steady state, by differentiating (2.20), (2.21), and (2.27), we have:

$$\frac{dk^*}{d\sigma} = -\frac{k^*}{\sigma} < 0, \tag{2.35}$$

$$\frac{dy^*}{d\sigma} = -\frac{y^*}{\sigma} < 0, \tag{2.36}$$

$$\frac{dl^*}{d\sigma} = 0. \tag{2.37}$$

Evidently the steady-state levels of capital stock and leisure consumption decrease with a larger σ. In the long run, the amplified preference for leisure reduces individuals savings, therefore hindering the accumulation of capital stock. Although individuals tend to consume more leisure goods, their disposable incomes decrease. Consequently, leisure consumption decreases. Regarding the change in leisure time, the effect on the preference brought about directly by the larger σ is perfectly canceled out by the effect on the preference brought about by a decrease in y^* under a log-linear utility function. Therefore, l^* is unaffected by σ.

2.3.2 *Effects of Capital Intensity*

We further investigate the effects of a change in capital intensity β. It is important to note that in this model, this β represents not only capital intensity but also production externality. This feature indicates that from the definition of AK-type production, the increase in β does not affect the production level; however, as seen in (2.14), the wage level decreases. Therefore, in the short run, that is, in period t, when β becomes larger, as l_t and k_t are unaffected, there emerges negative income effects on individuals' choices of saving and leisure goods consumption:

$$\frac{ds_t}{d\beta} = -\frac{A\alpha_2 k_t}{\alpha_1 + \alpha_2 + \sigma(1+\theta)y_{t-1}} < 0, \tag{2.38}$$

$$\frac{dy_t}{d\beta} = -\frac{A\sigma y_{t-1} k_t}{\alpha_1 + \alpha_2 + \sigma(1+\theta)y_{t-1}} < 0. \tag{2.39}$$

A decrease in y_t lowers the preference for leisure of generation $t+1$, which has a negative effect on l_{t+1}, k_{t+1} and y_{t+1}:

$$\frac{dl_{t+1}}{d\beta} = \frac{(\alpha_1+\alpha_2)\, l_{t+1}}{[\alpha_1 + \alpha_2 + \sigma(1+\theta)y_t]\, y_t}\frac{dy_t}{d\beta} < 0, \tag{2.40}$$

$$\frac{dk_{t+1}}{d\beta} = \frac{1}{1-l_{t+1}}\left(\frac{ds_t}{d\beta} + k_{t+1}\frac{dl_{t+1}}{d\beta}\right) < 0, \tag{2.41}$$

$$\frac{dy_{t+1}}{d\beta} = y_{t+1}\left\{\frac{\alpha_1+\alpha_2}{[\alpha_1 + \alpha_2 + \sigma(1+\theta)y_t]\, y_t}\frac{dy_t}{d\beta} + \frac{ds_t}{d\beta} + k_{t+1}\frac{dl_{t+1}}{d\sigma} - \frac{1}{1-\beta}\right\} < 0. \tag{2.42}$$

Specifically, similar to the discussion in Sect. 2.3.1, it is clear that the effects on capital per labor consist of two parts: the effect through savings and the effect through labor supply. Regarding y_{t+1}, the first term in the bracket of (2.42) is the effect of a change in preference. The second and third terms are the effects of the change in the wage rate caused by the change in capital stock. The last term represents the direct effect, that is, β's direct effect on the wage rate, as mentioned above.

Applying the same approach as in the short run, in the long run, we can confirm that a lager β reduces the steady-state levels of all k^*, y^*, and l^*:

$$\frac{dk^*}{d\beta} = -\frac{\theta(\alpha_1+\alpha_2)}{\sigma(1-\beta)^2 A} < 0, \tag{2.43}$$

$$\frac{dy^*}{d\beta} = -\frac{\alpha_2 A}{\sigma} < 0, \tag{2.44}$$

$$\frac{dl^*}{d\beta} = -\frac{A\alpha_2(\alpha_1+\alpha_2)\theta}{[A\alpha_2(1-\beta)(1+\theta) - (\alpha_1+\alpha_2)\theta]^2} < 0. \tag{2.45}$$

We only examine the intertemporal effects across periods t and $t + 1$ in the short run and the effects in the long run (or in the steady state) for both Sects. 2.3.1 and 2.3.2. In other words, we have not discussed the equilibria along the transition path, including the peak values and cycle length, which calls for a rigorous mathematical proof. Therefore, we take a simple look at how the shape of the cyclical transition path varies under different σ and β by numerical simulations in the next section to understand the dynamics of the economy.

2.4 Numerical Example

To clearly understand the features of the equilibrium, we show the following three cases of numerical simulations: Case (A) a base case, where we set $\alpha_1 = 0.2$, $\alpha_2 = 0.4$, $\theta = 0.5$, $\sigma = 0.4$, $A = 10$, and $\beta = 0.4$ as parameters, and $k_1 = 1.6$ and $y_0 = 4.0$ as the initial values; Case (B) a case with a larger $\sigma(=0.6)$; and Case (C) a case with a larger $\beta(=0.6)$.

First, in the base case, we execute a simulation from period 1 to period 41. Assumption 2.1, the inequality in (2.23), is satisfied, because $\alpha_2(1 - \beta)A - (\alpha_1 + \alpha_2) = 1.8$. In this numerical example, the steady-state values for k, y, and l are 1.375, 4.5, and 0.2727, respectively. The steady-state equilibrium values for all cases are summarized in Table 2.1.

Figure 2.1 presents the results for the base case, Case (A). The values of k and y are presented in Fig. 2.1a. Fixed points are represented by horizontal (dotted) lines at 1.375 for capital and 4.5 for leisure goods, and the cyclical solutions are represented by waved lines. The solutions show a seven-period cycle centered on straight lines. We can acknowledge that the change in the leisure good follows the movement of capital, that is, when the level of capital, which corresponds to the level of production, is increased, then the consumption of leisure goods also increases following the increase in the wage level.

Table 2.1 Parameters and steady-state values

	Case (A): base	Case (B)	Case (C)
α_1	0.2		
α_2	0.4		
θ	0.5		
A	10.0		
σ	0.4	0.6	0.4
β	0.4	0.4	0.6
k	1.375	0.917	1.313
y	4.5	3.0	2.5
l	0.2727	0.2727	0.2381

*With initial values of $k_1 = 1.6$ and $y_0 = 4.0$

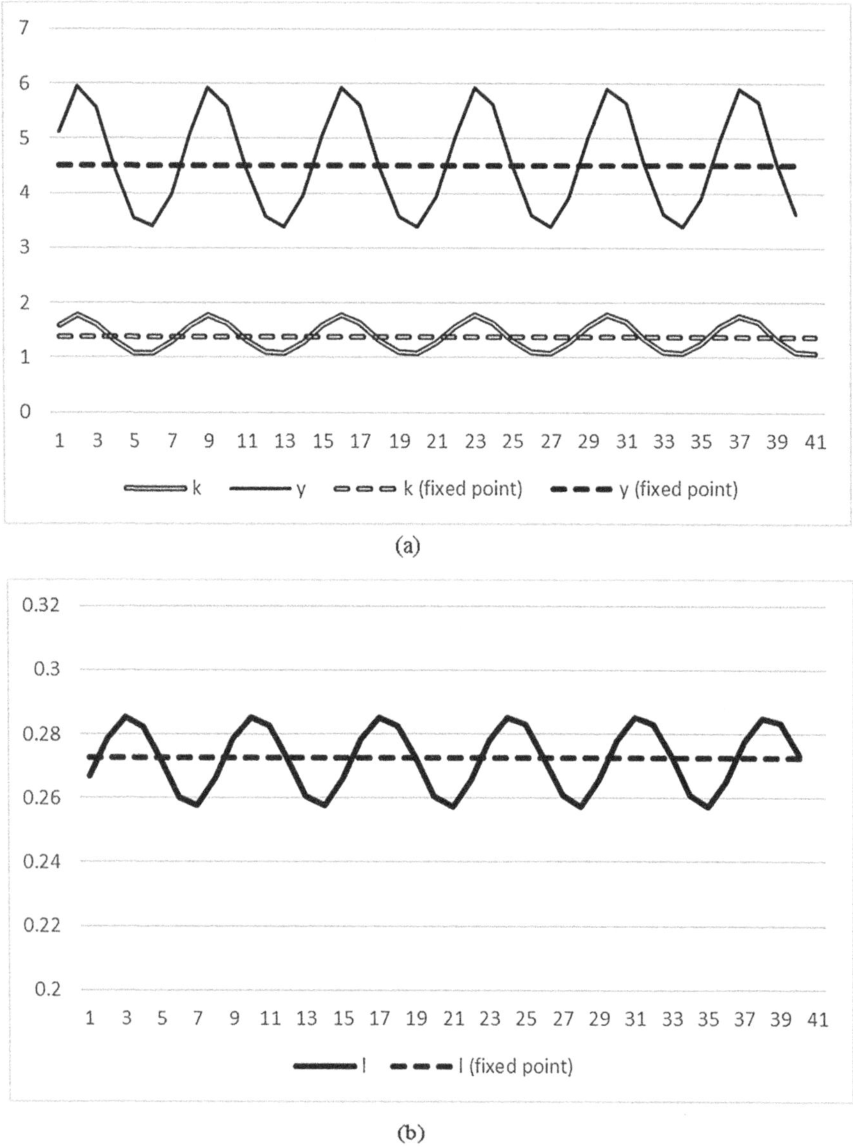

Fig. 2.1 Base case (A): $\alpha_1 = 0.2$, $\alpha_2 = 0.4$, $\theta = 0.5$, $\sigma = 0.4$, $A = 10$, and $\beta = 0.4$. (**a**) Periodic equilibrium (capital and leisure goods). (**b**) Periodic equilibrium (leisure time)

More specifically, (2.18) and (2.19) clearly show that because k_t, which has already been determined in the previous period, determines w_t and therefore, y_t, the movements of k_t and y_t synchronize. In contrast, the feature of utility function (2.3) indicates that because the weight on the subutility for the (composite) leisure, $y_t l_t^{\theta}$, encompasses the leisure consumption in the previous period, y_{t-1},the movement of leisure time, with a fixed point of 0.2727, is one period behind the movement of k_t and y_t, as shown in Fig. 2.1b. In other words, the inherited tastes for the consumption of leisure goods bring about such a delay in the movement of leisure time. This delay further results in an adverse effect on the movement of k_t and y_t. Therefore, we can confirm from this numerical simulation that inherited tastes are the main source of cyclical equilibrium.

Compared to the base case, Case (A), we assign $\sigma = 0.6$, which is more than 0.2, with the other parameters unchanged in Case (B). The results show that (1) the steady-state values of k^* and y^* become smaller, from 1.375 to 0.917 and from 4.5 to 3.0, respectively, while that of l^* is unchanged, which perfectly confirms the results in Eqs. (2.35)–(2.37), and (2) as shown in Fig. 2.2, k_t, y_t, and l_t fluctuate more significantly, cycling around the steady state. These results can be interpreted as follows. First, when σ increases, the weight on leisure increases; thus, more resources are allocated to leisure (both consumption and time) and less to savings. This consequently reduces capital accumulation and results in a lower level of capital in the steady state. Second, the more resources are allocated to leisure goods consumption, the stronger the inheritance of the taste for leisure. This brings about fluctuations in not only the consumption of leisure goods but also capital levels.

Regarding Case (C), we assign $\beta = 0.6$, which is more than 0.2 than the base case, with other parameters unchanged. In this case, we can acknowledge that the steady-state values of k^*, y^*, and l^* are all smaller, from 1.375 to 1.313, from 4.5 to 2.5, and from 0.2727 to 0.2381, respectively. These results correspond to those in Eqs. (2.43)–(2.45). These results can be interpreted as follows: the rise in β in this model implies both an increase in capital intensity and a decrease in the distribution of labor (or wage level), as seen in (2.14), owing to the existence of production externality. Therefore, the level of capital and, consequently, the consumption of leisure goods in the steady state will decrease. This decrease in the consumption of leisure goods is accompanied by a decrease in leisure time (Fig. 2.3).

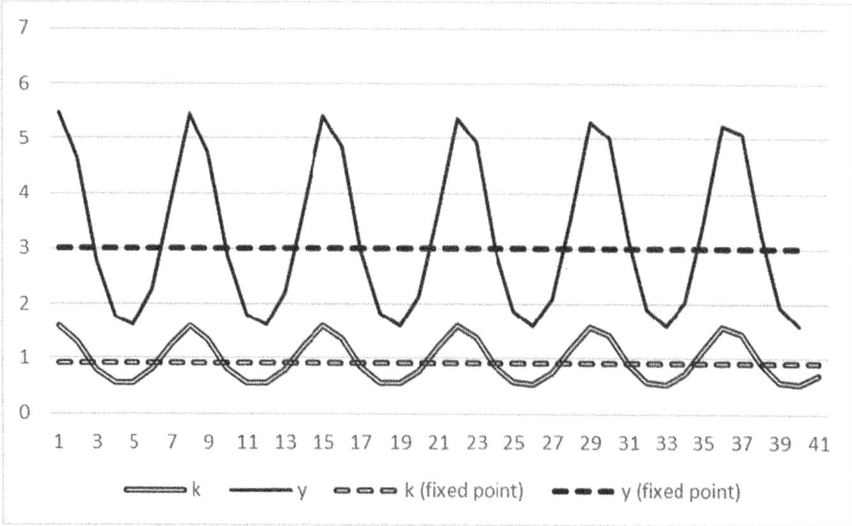

(a)

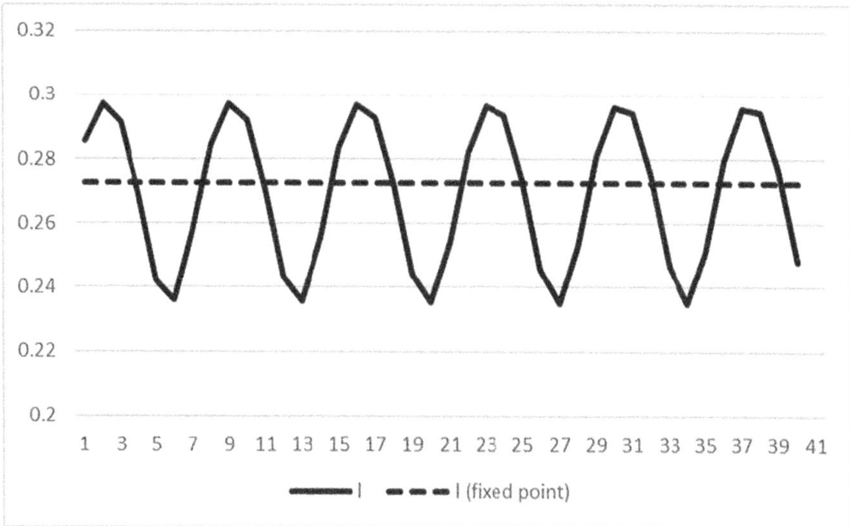

(b)

Fig. 2.2 Case (B): $\alpha_1 = 0.2$, $\alpha_2 = 0.4$, $\theta = 0.5$, $\sigma = 0.6$, $A = 10$, and $\beta = 0.4$. (**a**) Periodic equilibrium (capital and leisure goods). (**b**) Periodic equilibrium (leisure time)

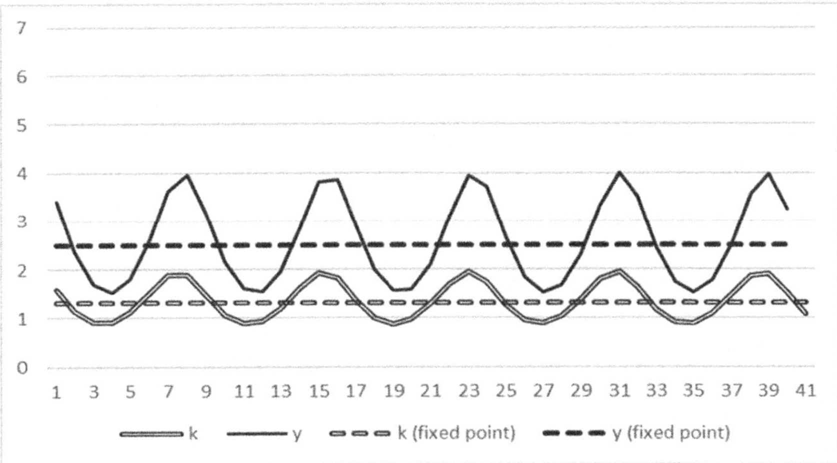

(a)

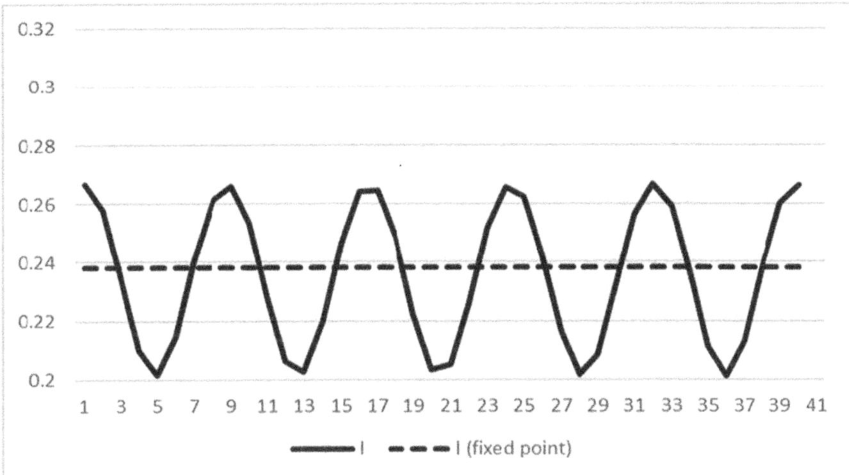

(b)

Fig. 2.3 Case (C): $\alpha_1 = 0.2$, $\alpha_2 = 0.4$, $\theta = 0.5$, $\sigma = 0.4$, $A = 10$, and $\beta = 0.6$. (**a**) Periodic equilibrium (capital and leisure goods). (**b**) Periodic equilibrium (leisure time)

2.5 Conclusion

This chapter considers leisure as a composite of time and consumption and the existence of the inheritance of the taste for leisure from the parents into an OLG model with a production externality.

As indicated in literature, leisure time, which is often considered a counterpart of working time, should be considered an integration of the consumption of leisure goods. Additionally, as we can acknowledge widely, tastes or preferences are inherited from previous generations. These two elements should be incorporated when considering individuals' lives within a dynamic framework.

Our analyses clearly show that although the production function exhibits an AK type, which often brings about endogenous growth in many previous studies, the economy has unique nontrivial and trivial steady states. This nontrivial steady state is necessarily periodic, which we show both quantitatively and qualitatively. In conclusion, we show that an increase in either preference for leisure or capital intensity reduces the level of capital stock and consumption of leisure goods in the steady state.

Our analyses indicate that the inheritance of taste, especially for leisure, brings about a business cycle. Therefore, when we consider the effect of fiscal policies, fluctuations in the economy might be amplified, which may cause instability in the economy. This indicates that individuals' preferences may become a source of such instability.

However, some of our analyses require further investigation. First, although there is a limit to evaluating fiscal policies in our model, these should be clarified to have clearer policy implications. Second, leisure services are often supplied by the labor-intensive production sector; therefore, the two-sector OLG model might be suitable for tackling the problem presented in this chapter. Third, although the result obtained in this chapter is clear regarding the features of the steady state, this is strongly dependent on the log-linear utility function. This assumption should be generalized.

Acknowledgements We thank Professor Emeritus Shuetsu Takahashi and Professors Kei Hosoya, Tsuyoshi Shinozaki, and Hideya Kato for their valuable comments and suggestions. We also thank the seminar participants at several online meetings on *modern macroeconomics with historical perspectives* and Pema Dorji, Mizue Ayukawa, and Mingzhu Li for their helpful comments and suggestions.

Appendix

Proof of Proposition 2

We prove that the steady state of the economy is periodic. We first linearize a dynamic equation for physical capital accumulation, (2.18), and one for the evolution of the consumption of leisure goods (2.19) around the neighborhood in the steady state, which gives

$$\begin{bmatrix} 1-\frac{\theta\sigma y_t}{\alpha_1+\alpha_2+(1+\theta)\sigma y_t} & k_{t+1}\left(\frac{\theta(1+\theta)\sigma^2 y_t}{(\alpha_1+\alpha_2+(1+\theta)\sigma y_t)^2}-\frac{\theta\sigma}{\alpha_1+\alpha_2+(1+\theta)\sigma y_t}\right) \\ 0 & \alpha_1+\alpha_2+(1+\theta)\,\sigma y_{t-1} \end{bmatrix}\begin{bmatrix} k_{t+1}-k^* \\ y_t-y^* \end{bmatrix}$$
$$=\begin{bmatrix} \frac{A\alpha_2(1-\beta)}{\alpha_1+\alpha_2+(1+\theta)\sigma y_{t-1}} & -\frac{A\alpha_2(1-\beta)(1+\theta)\sigma k_t}{(\alpha_1+\alpha_2+(1+\theta)\sigma y_{t-1})^2} \\ A\,(1-\beta)\,\sigma y_{t-1} & A\,(1-\beta)\,\sigma k_t-(1+\theta)\,\sigma y_t \end{bmatrix}\begin{bmatrix} k_t-k^* \\ y_{t-1}-y^* \end{bmatrix}. \tag{2.46}$$

Multiplying the inverted matrix of the matrix on the left-hand side of (2.46) on both sides of the (2.46), setting $k_t = k_{t+1} = k^*$ and $y_{t-1} = y_t = y^*$ and using (2.20) and (2.21), (2.46) can be rewritten as a dynamical system around the neighborhood of the steady state as

$$\begin{bmatrix} k_{t+1}-k^* \\ y_t-y^* \end{bmatrix}=\frac{\Gamma}{\Phi}\begin{bmatrix} k_t-k^* \\ y_{t-1}-y^* \end{bmatrix}, \tag{2.47}$$

where $\Phi \equiv A\alpha_2(1-\beta)(1+\theta)-(\alpha_1+\alpha_2)\theta$ and

$$\Gamma \equiv \begin{bmatrix} \frac{A^2{\alpha_2}^2(1-\beta)^2(1+\theta)-(\alpha_1+\alpha_2)^2\theta}{A\alpha_2(1-\beta)} & \frac{(\alpha_1+\alpha_2)^2\theta+A\alpha_2(\alpha_1+\alpha_2)(1-\beta)\theta(1+\theta)-A^2{\alpha_2}^2(1-\beta)^2(1+\theta)^2}{A^2\alpha_2(1-\beta)^2} \\ A\,(A\alpha_2\,(1-\beta)-(\alpha_1+\alpha_2))\,(1-\beta) & \alpha_1+\alpha_2 \end{bmatrix}. \tag{2.48}$$

The eigenvalues of the above matrix Γ can be obtained as

$$\lambda_1,\lambda_2=\frac{1}{2A^2\alpha_2(1-\beta)^2}\left\{A\,(1-\beta)\,[\alpha_1+\alpha_2\,(1+A-A\beta)] \pm\frac{\sqrt{\begin{array}{c}A^2\,[\alpha_1+\alpha_2-3A\alpha_2\,(-1+\beta)]\,[\alpha_1+\alpha_2+A\alpha_2\,(-1+\beta)] \\ (-1+\beta)^2[(\alpha_1+\alpha_2)\,\theta+A\alpha_2\,(-1+\beta)\,(1+\theta)]^2\end{array}}}{(\alpha_1+\alpha_2)\,\theta-A\alpha_2\,(1-\beta)\,(1+\theta)}\right\}. \tag{2.49}$$

We can confirm that, for the values of these two eigenvalues of the matrix Γ, (1) the eigenvalue is between 0 and 1, and the other one is more than 1, or (2) these eigenvalues are complex, with a modulus of one.

By defining the determinant and trace of matrix $\frac{\Gamma}{\Phi}$ as D and Tr, we can verify

$$D = 1 > 0, \tag{2.50}$$

$$D - Tr + 1 = \frac{A\alpha_2 (1-\beta) - (\alpha_1 + \alpha_2)}{A\alpha_2 (1-\beta)}, \tag{2.51}$$

$$Tr^2 - 4D = \frac{[\alpha_1 + \alpha_2 + 3A\alpha_2 (1-\beta)][\alpha_1 + \alpha_2 - A\alpha_2 (1-\beta)]}{A^2 {\alpha_2}^2 (1-\beta)^2}. \tag{2.52}$$

The assumption of Eq. (2.23) shows that because the sign of Eq. (2.52) is negative, the eigenvalues are complex. Additionally, (2.50) shows that its modulus is one, which implies that the steady-state values are periodic; in other words, the steady state is stable but not asymptotically stable.[7]

References

Abe N, Inakura N, Kohara M (2018) An empirical analysis on time and money expenditure on leisure. Econ Rev 69(4):289–313

Azariadis C (1993) Intertemporal macroeconomics. Blackwell, Cambridge

Becker GS (1965) A theory of the allocation of time. Econ J 75:493–517

Bhattacharya J, Haslag J, Martin A (2009) Optimal monetary policy and economic growth. Eur Econ Rev 53:210–221

Bittman M (2002) Social participation and family welfare: the money and time costs of leisure in Australia. Soc Policy Adm 36:408–425

Brett C (2012) The effects of population aging on optimal redistributive taxes in an overlapping generations model. Int Tax Public Financ 19:777–799

Caballé J, Manresa A (1994) Social rents, interest rates, and growth. Econ Lett 45:413–419

Caballé J, Moro-Egido AI (2014) Effects of aspirations and habits on the distribution of wealth. Scand J Econ 116(4):1012–1043

Chen SH, Guo JT (2018) On indeterminacy and growth under progressive taxation and utility-generating government spending. Pac Econ Rev 23:533–543

de la Croix D (1996) The dynamics of bequeathed tastes. Econ Lett 53:89–96

de la Croix D (2001) Growth dynamics and education spending: the role of inherited tastes and abilities. Eur Econ Rev 45:1415–1438

de la Croix D, Michel P (1999) Optimal growth when tastes are inherited. J Econ Dyn Control 23:519–537

de Serpa AC (1971) A theory of the economics of time. Econ J 81(3):828–846

Diamond PA (1965) National debt in a neoclassical growth model. Am Econ Rev 55:1126–1150

Fanti L, Gori L, Mammana C, Michetti E (2018) A model of growth with inherited tastes. Decis Econ Financ 41(2):163–186

Fanti L, Gori L, Mammana C, Michetti E (2019) Inherited tastes and endogenous longevity. Macroecon Dyn 23(2):674–698

[7] See Azariadis (1993) for the detailed discussion for the stability of the planar system.

Fanti L, Spataro L (2006) Endogenous labor supply in Diamond's (1965) OLG model: a reconsideration of the debt role. J Macroecon 28:428–438
Futagami K, Yanagihara M (2008) Private and public education: human capital accumulation under parental teaching. Jpn Econ Rev 59(3):275–291
Gori L, Michetti E (2016) The dynamics of bequeathed tastes with endogenous fertility. Econ Lett 149:79–82
Gori L, Sodini M (2020) Endogenous labour supply, endogenous lifetime and economic development. Struct Change Econ Dyn 52:238–259
Kohn M, Marion N (1993) On dynamic efficiency in a growth model with increasing returns. Econ Lett 41:93–98
Liu P, Thogersen J (2020) Pay-as-you-go pensions and endogenous retirement. Macroecon Dyn 24:1700–1719
Lopez-Garcia M-A (2008) On the role of public debt in an OLG model with endogenous labor supply. J Macroecon 30:1323–1328
Maoz YD (2010) Labor hours in the United States and Europe: the role of different leisure preferences. Macroecon Dyn 14:231–241
Ono T (2010) Growth and unemployment in an OLG economy with public pensions. J Popul Econ 23:737–767
Qiao X, Wang L (2019) Fertility and old-age labor supply in aging China. China Econ Rev 57:101261
Romer PM (1986) Increasing returns and long-run growth. J Polit Econ 94:1002–1037
Ueda K (2013) Banks as coordinators of economic growth and stability: microfoundation for macroeconomy with externality. J Econ Theory 148:322–352

Chapter 3
Overlapping Generations Model with Relative Preference for Children's Human Capital

Hideya Kato

Abstract This chapter considers altruistic preference for children's human capital relative to their own human capital in an overlapping generations model. Using this altruistic and relative preference, we can obtain an explicit equilibrium solution of the capital market in a steady state. This chapter also examines how the first-best outcomes can be achieved using policy instruments in the market economy in our model. Therefore, we focus on the education subsidy/tax and lump-sum taxes/transfers as policy instruments. The education subsidy/tax is used to adjust the human capital level (educational investment in children), and lump-sum taxes/transfers are used to adjust the physical capital level. If individuals emphasize the altruistic preference too heavily, the government should impose a tax on education expenditures for children and a lump tax on the older generation to achieve the first-best outcomes in our model. Interestingly, this result is contrary to the policy that has been adopted (i.e., education subsidy and old-age pension) in the real economy.

Keywords Overlapping generations model · Altruistic preference · Human capital · Intergenerational transfers

JEL Classification: D64, H21, O41

3.1 Introduction

In general, when parents invest in their children's education, they prefer for their children to have equal or higher educational backgrounds relative to their own:

H. Kato (✉)
Faculty of Economics, Ryukoku University, Kyoto, Japan
e-mail: hideyakato@econ.ryukoku.ac.jp

S. Takahashi et al. (eds.), *Modern Macroeconomics with Historical Perspectives*,
New Frontiers in Regional Science: Asian Perspectives 67,
https://doi.org/10.1007/978-981-99-1067-0_3

They compare children's human capital with their own human capital. This chapter incorporates this idea as an altruistic preference for children's human capital in the Diamond-type overlapping generations model (Diamond 1965).

From this perspective, Kato et al. (2020) considered parental aspiration for children's education by applying habit formation in an overlapping generations model.[1] They assume a linear-logarithmic utility function that consists not only of consumptions but also of the development of human capital, which is given by $\ln(H_{t+1} - \gamma H_t)$, where H_{t+1} and H_t are children's human capital and their own human capital, respectively, and $\gamma > 0$ is the aspiration parameter. That is, they introduced a subtractive form regarding altruistic preferences for children's human capital.

Our model assumes that parents care about their children's human capital relative to their own: H_{t+1}/H_t. Instead of using the subtractive form, illustrating this phenomenon in a proportional form has the following benefits. As seen in Kato et al. (2020), under the assumption of the linear–logarithmic utility function and Cobb–Douglas production function, using the subtractive form has the possibility of zero physical–human capital ratio in a steady state when γ is sufficiently high in the market economy. In addition, under the subtractive form preference, we cannot obtain an explicit solution of the physical–human capital ratio in the steady state. However, using the proportional form preference, we show that these two weaknesses do not occur in our model.

The other purpose of this chapter is to examine how the first-best outcomes can be achieved using policy instruments under the market economy in our model. Therefore, this chapter considers educational subsidy/tax and lump-sum taxes/transfers as policy instruments. The education subsidy/tax is used to adjust human capital (educational investment in children), and lump-sum taxes/transfers are used to adjust physical capital. If the individuals emphasize the altruistic preference too highly, the government should impose a tax on education expenditures for children and a lump-sum tax on the older generation to achieve the first-best outcomes. Interestingly, this result is contrary to the policy that is adopted (i.e., education subsidy and old-age pension) in the real economy.

The remainder of this chapter is organized as follows. Section 3.2 introduces the basic model and shows market equilibrium without policy instruments. In Sect. 3.3, we present the socially optimum conditions. Section 3.4 examines the optimal subsidy/tax rate for education expenditure and lump-sum taxes/transfers to achieve the socially optimum conditions. Finally, Sect. 3.5 concludes the chapter.

[1] There are many studies focusing on "aspiration" in an overlapping generations model (e.g., de la Croix 1996; de la Croix and Michel 1999; Kaneko et al. 2016; and Gori and Michetti 2016). However, these studies of inherited tastes focus on intergenerational taste externalities of consumption.

3.2 The Model

Consider an economy in a single-commodity world. Individuals live for three periods: childhood, adulthood, and old age. Individuals get an education in the childhood period, work in the adult period, and do not work and spend their golden years in the old-age period. All individuals make decisions during adulthood. For simplicity, we assume that the population of each generation is normalized to one: There is no population growth.

3.2.1 *Individuals*

We consider adult individuals in period t (generation t). Individuals derive utility not only from consumption in the adult and old-age periods (c_t and d_{t+1}, respectively) but also from children's human capital. We assume that individuals care not about children's absolute human capital level, H_{t+1}, but about children's human capital relative to their own human capital, H_{t+1}/H_t. The utility function of individuals of generation t is given by

$$u_t = \ln c_t + \alpha \ln d_{t+1} + \beta \ln \left(H_{t+1}/H_t \right), \tag{3.1}$$

where $\alpha > 0$ is a discount factor and $\beta > 0$ is an altruism parameter representing the strength of altruistic preference for children's human capital relative to their own human capital.

Parental educational investment in children affects their accumulation of human capital. Human capital of generation $t + 1$ is accumulated by the educational investment from the parent, e_t, and the parent's human capital, H_t:

$$H_{t+1} = e_t^{\gamma} H_t^{1-\gamma}, \tag{3.2}$$

where $0 < \gamma < 1$.

In the adult period, individuals are endowed with one unit of time and supply H_t unit of effective labor. In compensation for the labor supply, they receive labor income $w_t H_t$, where w_t is the wage per unit of human capital. They allocate this labor income to consumption in the adult period, savings, s_t, and educational investment in children, e_t. In the old-age period, they consume based on returns on savings. Thus, the budget constraints of the adult and old-age periods of generation t are given by

$$w_t H_t = c_t + s_t + e_t, \tag{3.3}$$

$$R_{t+1} s_t = d_{t+1}, \tag{3.4}$$

where R_{t+1} is the gross interest rate. From (3.3) and (3.4), the intertemporal budget constraint is given by

$$w_t H_t = c_t + \frac{d_{t+1}}{R_{t+1}} + e_t. \tag{3.5}$$

Individuals choose c_t, d_{t+1}, and e_t to maximize utility function (3.1), subject to (3.2) and (3.5). From the first-order conditions, we obtain the following conditions:

$$\frac{d_{t+1}}{\alpha c_t} = R_{t+1}, \tag{3.6}$$

$$\frac{e_t}{c_t} = \beta\gamma. \tag{3.7}$$

Using these conditions and (3.5), the consumption, savings, and educational investment are solved as follows:

$$c_t = \frac{1}{1+\alpha+\beta\gamma} w_t H_t, \tag{3.8}$$

$$d_{t+1} = \frac{\alpha R_{t+1}}{1+\alpha+\beta\gamma} w_t H_t, \tag{3.9}$$

$$s_t = \frac{\alpha}{1+\alpha+\beta\gamma} w_t H_t, \tag{3.10}$$

$$e_t = \frac{\beta\gamma}{1+\alpha+\beta\gamma} w_t H_t. \tag{3.11}$$

Note that while consumption in both periods and savings decrease with β, educational investment increases with β. If altruistic preference is strong, individuals have an incentive to invest in children's education more and to consume and save less.

3.2.2 Firms

We consider the production activities of firms in period t. The representative firm produces a homogeneous good by using physical and human capital. The production function is in the Cobb–Douglas form:

$$Y_t = A K_t^a H_t^{1-a}, \tag{3.12}$$

where $A > 0, 0 < a < 1$, and K_t is the aggregate physical capital in period t. Assuming that the goods and factor markets are perfectly competitive and capital depreciates fully after one period, the first-order conditions for profit maximization are

$$R_t = aAk_t^{a-1}, \tag{3.13}$$

$$w_t = (1-a)\,Ak_t^a, \tag{3.14}$$

where $k_t \equiv K_t/H_t$.

3.2.3 Equilibrium

The capital market equilibrium in period t can be described as

$$K_{t+1} = s_t. \tag{3.15}$$

Substituting (3.10) and (3.14) into (3.15) and then dividing both sides by H_{t+1}, the capital market equilibrium can be rewritten as

$$k_{t+1} = \frac{\alpha A\,(1-a)\,k_t^a}{(1+\alpha+\beta\gamma)\,g_{t+1}}, \tag{3.16}$$

where $g_{t+1} \equiv H_{t+1}/H_t$. From (3.2), (3.11), and (3.16), the dynamic sequence of the physical–human capital ratio is obtained as

$$k_{t+1} = \alpha\left(\frac{1}{\beta\gamma}\right)^{\gamma}\left(\frac{A\,(1-a)}{1+\alpha+\beta\gamma}\right)^{1-\gamma} k_t^{a(1-\gamma)} \equiv \varphi\,(k_t)\,. \tag{3.17}$$

The dynamics in our model are represented by the capital market equilibrium. Figure 3.1 shows the relationship between k_{t+1} and k_t with respect to $\varphi(k_t)$. The function $\varphi(k_t)$ passes through the origin and is an increasing and concave curve of k_t.[2] The function $\varphi(k_t)$ crosses the 45° line at the steady-state value, k. Given the initial level of the physical–human capital ratio $k_0(=K_0/H_0)$, the physical–human capital ratio monotonically converges to the unique steady-state level. For k_0 above k, the physical–human capital ratio decreases until a stable steady state k over time. In contrast, for k_0 below k, the physical–human capital ratio increases until k over

[2] In the model of Kato et al. (2020), though $\varphi(k_t)$ is increasing and concave in k_t, $\varphi(k_t)$ does not pass through the origin and cross the horizontal axis. Thus, there is some possibility that the 45° line and $\varphi(k_t)$ do not cross: There is no steady state equilibrium.

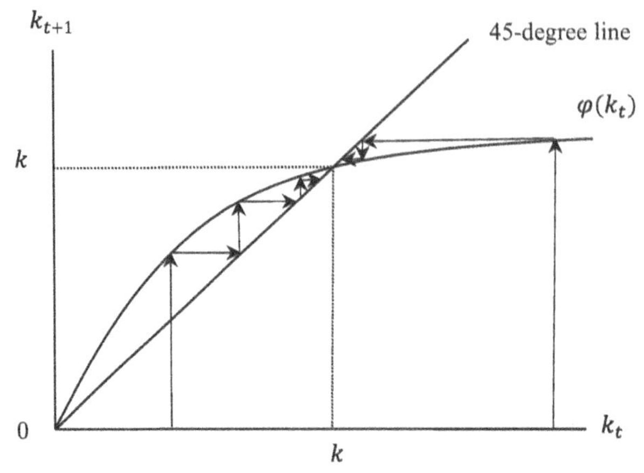

Fig. 3.1 The dynamic path of k

time. The physical–human capital ratio in the steady state can be obtained by setting $k_{t+1} = k_t = k$:

$$k = \left(\alpha \left(\frac{1}{\beta \gamma} \right)^{\gamma} \left(\frac{A(1-a)}{1+\alpha+\beta\gamma} \right)^{1-\gamma} \right)^{\frac{1}{1-a(1-\gamma)}}. \tag{3.18}$$

The growth rate of human capital is obtained as

$$\frac{H_{t+1}}{H_t} = \left(\frac{\beta \gamma A (1-a) k_t^a}{(1+\alpha+\beta\gamma)} \right)^{\gamma}. \tag{3.19}$$

Substituting (3.18) into (3.19), the growth rate in the steady state is expressed only by the parameters and becomes constant. Along a balanced growth path, the physical–human capital ratio, k_t, is constant, and the other endogenous variables c_t, d_t, e_t, and h_t grow at a constant rate g.

Lemma 3.1 *Under the assumption of the linear–logarithmic utility function and Cobb–Douglas production function, when altruistic preference is in the proportional form, the unique physical–human capital ratio in a steady state, k, is obtained. Therefore, the values of k and g can be solved explicitly.*

This result is different from Kato et al. (2020), who show that k and g are expressed by implicit functions, and there is the possibility of a zero physical–human capital ratio in the steady state. That is, the proportional form regarding altruistic preference for children's human capital is easier to handle than is the subtractive form in the sense that k and g can be expressed explicitly.

3.3 Social Optimum

In this section, we focus on the first-best socially optimum conditions, where the objective function of a social planner is the discounted sum of the life-cycle utilities of all the current and future generations. The objective function of a social planner is given by

$$\sum_{t=0}^{\infty} \rho^t \left[\ln c_t + \alpha \ln d_{t+1} + \beta \ln \left(H_{t+1}/H_t\right)\right], \tag{3.20}$$

where ρ $(0 < \rho < 1)$ is a discounted factor that reflects the social time preferences.[3] We assume that a social planner maximizes (3.20) subject to the human capital accumulation Eq. (3.2) and the following resource constraint:

$$AK_t^a H_t^{1-a} = c_t + d_t + e_t + K_{t+1}. \tag{3.21}$$

The social planner's maximization problem is given by

$$\underset{c_t, d_t, e_t, K_{t+1}, H_{t+1}}{\text{Max}} \quad \sum_{t=0}^{\infty} \rho^t \left[\ln c_t + \alpha \ln d_{t+1} + \beta \ln \left(H_{t+1}/H_t\right)\right],$$

$$s.t. AK_t^a H_t^{1-a} = c_t + d_t + e_t + K_{t+1},$$

$$H_{t+1} = e_t^{\gamma} H_t^{\gamma - 1},$$

$$K_0, H_0, \text{ and } c_{-1} \text{ given.}$$

As seen in Appendix, we derive the following conditions for the balanced growth path from the social planner's maximization problem:

$$\frac{\chi^*}{\alpha x^*} = aAk^{*a-1}, \tag{3.22}$$

$$g^* = \rho a A k^{*a-1}, \tag{3.23}$$

[3] Strictly speaking, utility of the old-age period in period 0, $\alpha \ln d_0$, should be included in the objective function of a social planner. However, because this utility does not depend on the endogenous variable, we do not consider the utility in the objective function. Of course, this assumption does not change the subsequent results.

$$\beta\left(\frac{1}{\rho}-1\right)+\frac{1}{x^*}\left[(1-a)\,Ak^{*a}+\frac{(1-\gamma)}{\gamma}\epsilon^*\right]-\frac{\epsilon^*}{\rho\gamma x^*}=0, \tag{3.24}$$

$$Ak^{*a}-x^*-\chi^*-gk^*+\epsilon^*=0, \tag{3.25}$$

$$g^*=\epsilon^{*\gamma}, \tag{3.26}$$

where $x_t \equiv c_t/H_t$, $\chi_t \equiv d_t/H_t$, $\epsilon_t \equiv e_t/H_t$, and x, χ, k, ϵ, and g are all constant along the balanced growth path.[4]

From (3.7), we can easily see that condition (3.24) is not satisfied in the competitive market equilibrium.[5] This is because the following two externalities occur in a market economy. First, when individuals choose educational investment in children, they ignore the positive intergenerational externality: Their educational investment increases the income of their children through human capital accumulation. From this positive externality effect, investment in education tends to be socially too low at market equilibrium. This externality is the standard positive externality in most of the overlapping generations models with human capital.

Second, individuals ignore the negative intergenerational externality: Educational investment decreases children's utility because children decrease utility from altruistic motivation in adulthood by increasing their own human capital. Due to this negative externality effect, educational investment tends to be socially too high at market equilibrium. This externality occurs when altruistic preference for children's human capital relative to their own human capital is considered.

In market equilibrium, neither externality is internalized without policy instruments: The first-best equilibrium cannot be attained. Therefore, in the next section, we consider optimal policy setting.

3.4 Optimal Policy

In this section, we investigate the conditions under which the first-best outcomes can be attained in market equilibrium with policy instruments. We consider subsidy/tax on education expenditures and lump-sum taxes/transfers in both the adult and old-age periods as policy instruments in the market economy.

---

[4] The superscript $*$ denotes the first-best outcomes.

[5] Equation (3.7) can be rewritten as $\frac{\epsilon}{x}=\beta\gamma$. Substituting this condition into (3.24), we obtain $-\beta+\frac{1}{x}\left[(1-a)\,Ak^a+\frac{(1-\gamma)}{\gamma}\epsilon\right]=0$. The first term, $-\beta$, represents the negative externality, and the remaining second term represents the positive externality.

First, we incorporate these policy instruments into the model. Let τ_e denote the subsidy/tax rate on education expenditures; T_t^A and T_{t+1}^O denote the lump-sum taxes/transfers in the adult and old-age periods of generation t, respectively. The government budget constraint in period t is

$$T_t^A + T_t^O = \tau_e e_t. \tag{3.27}$$

The budget constraints in the adult and old-age periods of generation t are

$$w_t H_t - T_t^A = c_t + s_t + (1 - \tau_e) e_t, \tag{3.28}$$

$$R_{t+1} s_t - T_{t+1}^O = d_{t+1}. \tag{3.29}$$

From (3.28) and (3.29), the intertemporal budget constraint is given by

$$w_t H_t - T_t^A - \frac{T_{t+1}^O}{R_{t+1}} = c_t + \frac{d_{t+1}}{R_{t+1}} + (1 - \tau_e) e_t. \tag{3.30}$$

Individuals choose c_t, d_{t+1}, and e_t to maximize the utility function (3.1), subject to (3.2) and (3.30). From the first-order conditions, we obtain the following conditions:

$$\frac{d_{t+1}}{\alpha c_t} = R_{t+1}, \tag{3.31}$$

$$\frac{e_t}{c_t} = \frac{\beta\gamma}{1 - \tau_e}. \tag{3.32}$$

Using these conditions together with budget constraints, consumption, savings, and educational investment are solved as follows:

$$c_t = \frac{w_t H_t - T_t^A}{1 + \alpha + \beta\gamma} - \frac{T_{t+1}^O}{(1 + \alpha + \beta\gamma) R_{t+1}}, \tag{3.33}$$

$$d_{t+1} = \frac{\alpha \left[R_{t+1} \left(w_t H_t - T_t^A\right) - T_{t+1}^O\right]}{1 + \alpha + \beta\gamma}, \tag{3.34}$$

$$s_t = \frac{\alpha \left(w_t H_t - T_t^A\right)}{1 + \alpha + \beta\gamma} + \frac{(1 + \beta\gamma) T_{t+1}^O}{(1 + \alpha + \beta\gamma) R_{t+1}}, \tag{3.35}$$

$$e_t = \frac{\beta\gamma \left(w_t H_t - T_t^A\right)}{(1 - \tau_e)(1 + \alpha + \beta\gamma)} - \frac{\beta\gamma T_{t+1}^O}{(1 - \tau_e)(1 + \alpha + \beta\gamma) R_{t+1}}. \tag{3.36}$$

Firms do not change their behavior even if policy instruments are introduced. Thus, from the profit maximization problem, (3.13) and (3.14) are derived. The capital market equilibrium in period t can be described as (3.15).

Here, we examine how policy instruments should be set to achieve socially optimum conditions on a balanced growth path. On such a path, the optimal values of the five key variables (x^*, χ^*, ϵ^*, k^*, g^*) satisfy conditions (3.22)–(3.26). At market equilibrium, conditions (3.22), (3.25), and (3.26) are satisfied. First, using (3.31) and (3.13), (3.22) is replicated. Second, using the individual budget constraints (3.28) and (3.29), the conditions of (3.13) and (3.14), and the government budget constraint (3.27), we can obtain the resource constraint (3.21), which is equivalent to (3.25). Third, (3.2) is equivalent to (3.26).

To achieve the first-best result, the government needs to satisfy conditions (3.23) and (3.24) by setting the appropriate choice of policy instruments. In Appendix, we derive the optimal subsidy/tax rate on education expenditure and the optimal intergenerational taxes/transfers:

$$\tau_e = \frac{\theta}{(1-a)(\alpha+\rho)+\beta(1-\rho)(1-a\rho)}, \tag{3.37}$$

$$\frac{T_t^A}{w_t^* H_t^*} = \frac{(1+\gamma\rho)\theta - \rho(1+\alpha)[1-\rho a(1-\gamma)]}{(1-a)\{(\alpha+\rho)[1-\rho(1-\gamma)]+\rho\beta\gamma(1-\rho)\}}, \tag{3.38}$$

$$\frac{T_t^O}{w_t^* H_t^*} = \frac{-\theta + \rho(1+\alpha)[1-\rho a(1-\gamma)]}{(1-a)\{(\alpha+\rho)[1-\rho(1-\gamma)]+\rho\beta\gamma(1-\rho)\}}, \tag{3.39}$$

where $\theta \equiv (1-a)(\alpha+\rho) - a\beta\gamma\rho(1-\rho)$.

The signs of the optimal subsidy/tax rate on education expenditure and lump-sum taxes/transfers are ambiguous. If $\beta > (<)[(1-a)(\alpha+\rho)]/[\gamma a\rho(1-\rho)] \equiv \psi$, then the optimal education subsidy rate is negative (positive). If $\beta > (<)\ \psi - \frac{(1+\alpha)[1-\rho a(1-\gamma)]}{\gamma a(1-\rho)(1+\rho\gamma)}$, then the sign of T_t^A is negative (positive). If $\beta > (<)\ \psi - \frac{(1+\alpha)[1-\rho a(1-\gamma)]}{\gamma a(1-\rho)}$, the sign of T_t^O is positive (negative). From $\psi > \psi - \frac{(1+\alpha)[1-\rho a(1-\gamma)]}{\gamma a(1-\rho)(1+\rho\gamma)} > \psi - \frac{(1+\alpha)[1-\rho a(1-\gamma)]}{\gamma a(1-\rho)}$, we obtain the following Proposition.

Proposition 3.1 *To achieve the first-best outcomes, the government should set optimal policy variables on the balanced growth path as follows:*

1. *If* $\beta > \psi$, $\tau_e < 0$, $T_t^A < 0$, *and* $T_t^O > 0$.
2. *If* $\psi > \beta > \psi - \frac{(1+\alpha)[1-\rho a(1-\gamma)]}{\gamma a(1-\rho)(1+\rho\gamma)}$, $\tau_e > 0$, $T_t^A < 0$, *and* $T_t^O > 0$.
3. *If* $\psi - \frac{(1+\alpha)[1-\rho a(1-\gamma)]}{\gamma a(1-\rho)(1+\rho\gamma)} > \beta > \psi - \frac{(1+\alpha)[1-\rho a(1-\gamma)]}{\gamma a(1-\rho)}$, $\tau_e > 0$, $T_t^A > 0$, *and* $T_t^O > 0$.
4. *If* $\beta < \psi - \frac{(1+\alpha)[1-\rho a(1-\gamma)]}{\gamma a(1-\rho)}$, $\tau_e > 0$, $T_t^A > 0$, *and* $T_t^O < 0$.

We see that the government sets the policy instruments as follows: First, the government must internalize the two externalities of education expenditures. When individuals care too much about their children's human capital relative to their own capital, the negative externality effect dominates the positive one. Therefore, the government should impose a tax on educational investment in children under market equilibrium if β is sufficiently large. By contrast, if β is sufficiently small, the government should subsidize educational investment, as seen in the standard overlapping generations model with human capital.

Next, we see that the government uses a lump-sum tax/transfer to achieve the optimal physical capital level. The sign of (3.39) depends on the overaccumulation or underaccumulation of physical capital; to determine this, we consider the case without a lump-sum tax/transfer in the old-age period, $T^o = 0$. As shown in Appendix, the interest rate in the case of $T^o = 0$ is given by

$$R_{T^o=0} = \frac{\gamma\theta}{\Omega} g, \tag{3.40}$$

where $\Omega \equiv (1+\alpha+\beta\gamma)(1-\rho)(1-a\rho)+(1+\alpha)(1-\rho)a\rho\gamma+\gamma(1-a)(\alpha+\rho)$. In contrast, from (3.23), the marginal return of physical capital on the balanced growth path under the first-best equilibrium yields

$$R^* = \frac{g}{\rho}. \tag{3.41}$$

This is the modified golden rule used in our endogenous growth model. Subtracting (3.40) from (3.41) yields

$$R^* - R_{T^o=0} = \frac{(1-a\rho)\{-\theta+\rho(1+\alpha)[1-\rho a(1-\gamma)]\}}{(1-a)\alpha(1-\rho)[1-a(1-\gamma)\rho]} g. \tag{3.42}$$

Comparing (3.42) to (3.39), the optimal T_t^O is negative (positive) if $R^* < (>)\ R_{T^o=0}$.

This result can be interpreted as follows. If $R_{T^o=0} < (>)\ R^*$, physical capital in the market economy is over-accumulated (under-accumulated). In a situation of overaccumulation (underaccumulation), the government needs to transfer to (tax) older individuals to decrease (increase) savings, and therefore physical capital, until the optimal accumulation level.

3.5 Conclusion

This chapter considers individuals' altruistic preference for children's human capital relative to their own human capital in an overlapping generations model. We can show that using the relative form of altruistic preference yields an explicit solution for equilibrium outcomes in a steady state.

In our model, the following two externalities arise in the market. First, as seen in the standard overlapping generations model with human capital, educational investment increases the productivity of human capital for future generations. Second, altruistic preference produces a negative externality because educational investment increases children's human capital, and, therefore, children's utility decreases based on altruistic preference. This negative externality occurs because of altruistic and relative preferences in our model. When the altruistic parameter is sufficiently large, the negative externality effect dominates the positive externality effect.

However, altruistic and relative preferences also influence the under- or overaccumulation of physical capital. When the altruistic parameter is large, individuals invest more in education and save less. Therefore, in this situation, there is underaccumulation of physical capital.

From the above effects, the government needs to impose a tax on education expenditure for children and a lump-sum tax on the older generation if the altruistic parameter is sufficiently large. In situations where parental enthusiasm for children's educational investment is excessive, the result of this chapter may cast doubt on the generally accepted common sense theory that the government has to subsidize education and pay the national pension for older generations.

Acknowledgements I would like to thank Shuetsu Takahashi and Kei Hosoya, Tsuyoshi Shinozaki and Mitsuyoshi Yanagihara for their valuable comments and suggestions. This paper is a research outcome of the 2022 Ryukoku University grant for domestic research.

Appendix

Derivation of the Socially Optimum Conditions for the Balanced Growth Path

The Lagrangian expression for socially optimum conditions can be written as

$$\mathcal{L} = \sum_{t=0}^{\infty} \rho^t \left[\ln c_t + \alpha \ln d_{t+1} + \beta \ln\left(H_{t+1}/H_t\right)\right] + \sum_{t=0}^{\infty} \rho^t \mu_t \left[AK_t^a H_t^{1-a} - c_t - d_t - e_t - K_{t+1}\right] + \sum_{t=0}^{\infty} \rho^t \nu_t \left[\phi e_t^\gamma H_t^{1-\gamma} - H_{t+1}\right],$$

where μ_t and ν_t are Lagrange multipliers with respect to the resource constraint and human capital accumulation equation, respectively.

Solving this maximization problem, we obtain the following first-order conditions:

$$\frac{\partial \mathcal{L}}{\partial c_t} = \frac{1}{c_t} - \mu_t = 0, \tag{3.43}$$

$$\frac{\partial \mathcal{L}}{\partial d_t} = \frac{\alpha}{\rho d_t} - \mu_t = 0, \tag{3.44}$$

$$\frac{\partial \mathcal{L}}{\partial e_t} = -\mu_t + \nu_t \gamma e_t^{\gamma-1} H_t^{1-\gamma} = 0, \tag{3.45}$$

$$\frac{\partial \mathcal{L}}{\partial K_{t+1}} = \rho \mu_{t+1} a A K_t^{a-1} H_t^{1-a} - \mu_t = 0, \tag{3.46}$$

$$\begin{aligned}\frac{\partial \mathcal{L}}{\partial H_{t+1}} = \frac{\beta}{H_{t+1}} \left(\frac{1}{\rho} - 1 \right) + \mu_{t+1} (1-a) A K_t^a H_t^{-a} \\ + \nu_{t+1} (1-\gamma) e_t^{\gamma} H_t^{-\gamma} - \frac{\nu_t}{\rho} = 0.\end{aligned} \tag{3.47}$$

From (3.43) and (3.44), we derive the optimal allocation between consumption in the adult and old-age periods of generation t:

$$\frac{\rho d_{t+1}}{\alpha c_t} = \frac{\mu_t}{\mu_{t+1}}. \tag{3.48}$$

Using (3.46) and (3.48), we get:

$$\frac{d_{t+1}}{\alpha c_t} = a A K_{t+1}^{a-1} H_{t+1}^{1-a}. \tag{3.49}$$

From (3.43), (3.45), and (3.2), the Lagrange multiplier associated with the human capital equation is given by

$$\nu_t = \frac{1}{\gamma c_t e_t^{\gamma-1} H_t^{1-\gamma}} = \frac{e_t}{\gamma c_t H_{t+1}}. \tag{3.50}$$

From (3.43) and (3.46), we obtain the Euler equation:

$$\frac{c_{t+1}}{c_t} = \frac{\mu_t}{\mu_{t+1}} = \rho a A K_{t+1}^{a-1} H_{t+1}^{1-a}. \tag{3.51}$$

Using (3.43) and (3.50), (3.47) is as follows:

$$\frac{\beta}{H_{t+1}} \left(\frac{1}{\rho} - 1 \right) + \frac{1}{c_{t+1}} \left[(1-a) A K_{t+1}^a H_{t+1}^{-a} + \frac{(1-\gamma) e_{t+1}}{\gamma H_{t+1}} \right] - \frac{e_t}{\rho \gamma c_t H_{t+1}} = 0. \tag{3.52}$$

By multiplying both sides of (3.52) by H_{t+1} and using (3.2), we obtain:

$$\beta\left(\frac{1}{\rho}-1\right)+\frac{H_{t+1}}{c_{t+1}}\left[(1-a)\,AK_{t+1}^{a}H_{t+1}^{-a}+\frac{(1-\gamma)\,e_{t+1}}{\gamma H_{t+1}}\right]-\frac{e_t}{\rho\gamma c_t}=0. \tag{3.53}$$

The conditions of (3.49), (3.51), and (3.53), together with the resource constraints of the economy and human capital accumulation, determine the dynamics of the economy.

Here, we define new variables, $x_t \equiv c_t/H_t$, $\chi_t \equiv d_t/h_t$, $k_t \equiv K_t/H_t$, $\epsilon_t \equiv e_t/h_t$. Along a balanced growth path, these per-unit human capital variables, x, χ, k, ϵ, are constant, and the per-capita variables c_t, d_t, e_t, K_t, and H_t grow at a constant rate g. From (3.49), (3.51), (3.53), (3.21), and (3.2), the following conditions for the balanced growth path are given by

$$\frac{\chi^*}{\alpha x^*}=aAk^{*a-1}, \tag{3.54}$$

$$g^*=\rho aAk^{*a-1}, \tag{3.55}$$

$$\beta\left(\frac{1}{\rho}-1\right)+\frac{1}{x^*}\left[(1-a)\,Ak^{*a}+\frac{(1-\gamma)}{\gamma}\epsilon^*\right]-\frac{\epsilon^*}{\rho\gamma x^*}=0, \tag{3.56}$$

$$Ak^{*a}-x^*-\chi^*-g^*k^*+\epsilon^*=0, \tag{3.57}$$

$$g^*=\epsilon^{*\gamma}, \tag{3.58}$$

where the superscript $*$ represents the first-best outcomes. These conditions correspond to conditions (3.22)–(3.26) in the text.

Derivation of the Optimal Subsidy/Tax Rate

This appendix solves the optimal education subsidy/tax rate and the optimal lump-sum taxes/transfers in market equilibrium with policy instruments. From (3.43) and (3.44), $d_t=\alpha c_t/\rho$. Using $\chi^*=\alpha x^*/\rho$ and (3.55), we can rewrite the condition in (3.57) as follows:

$$Ak^{*a}=\frac{\rho+\alpha}{\rho\,(1-\rho a)}x^*+\frac{1}{1-\rho a}\epsilon^*. \tag{3.59}$$

Substituting (3.59) into (3.56), we obtain:

$$\frac{\epsilon^*}{x^*} = \frac{\gamma\left[(1-a)(\rho+\alpha)+\beta(1-\rho)(1-a\rho)\right]}{(1-\rho)\left[1-\rho a(1-\gamma)\right]}. \tag{3.60}$$

First, we solve for the optimal education subsidy/tax to satisfy the socially optimum equilibrium condition. Substituting (3.60) into (3.32), the optimal education subsidy/tax rate is obtained as

$$\tau_e = \frac{(1-a)(\alpha+\rho)-\beta a\rho\gamma(1-\rho)}{(1-a)(\alpha+\rho)+\beta(1-\rho)(1-a\rho)}. \tag{3.61}$$

Next, we solve the optimal intergenerational taxes/transfers. To attain the first-best result, (3.15) must hold as follows:

$$K_{t+1}^* = s_t^*. \tag{3.62}$$

Setting the intergenerational taxes/transfers to satisfy the first-best condition, (3.28) and (3.29) are rewritten as

$$T_t^A = w_t^* H_t^* - c_t^* - s_t^* - (1-\tau_e)\, e_t^*, \tag{3.63}$$

$$T_t^O = R_t^* s_{t-1}^* - d_t^*. \tag{3.64}$$

Substituting (3.62) into (3.63) and (3.64), and then dividing both sides with respect to $w_t^* H_t^* \left(= (1-a)\, Ak_t^{*a} H_t^*\right)$, we obtain the following:

$$\frac{T_t^A}{w_t^* H_t^*} = 1 - \frac{x_t^*}{(1-a)\, Ak_t^{*a}} - \frac{k_{t+1}^*}{(1-a)\, Ak_t^{*a}} g - \frac{(1-\tau_e)\,\epsilon_t^*}{(1-a)\, Ak_t^{*a}}, \tag{3.65}$$

$$\frac{T_t^O}{w_t^* H_t^*} = \frac{a}{1-a} - \frac{\chi_t^*}{(1-a)\, Ak_t^{*a}}. \tag{3.66}$$

Using (3.55), (3.59), (3.60), and (3.61), we have rewritten (3.65) and (3.66) as follows:

$$\frac{T_t^A}{w_t^* H_t^*} = 1 - \frac{\rho a}{1-a} - \frac{\rho(1-\rho a)(1+\beta\gamma)}{(1-a)\left[(\rho+\alpha)+\rho\frac{\epsilon_t^*}{x_t^*}\right]}, \tag{3.67}$$

$$\frac{T_t^O}{w_t^* H_t^*} = \frac{a}{1-a} - \frac{\alpha(1-\rho a)}{(1-a)\left[(\rho+\alpha)+\rho\frac{\epsilon_t^*}{x_t^*}\right]}. \tag{3.68}$$

Substituting (3.60) into (3.67) and (3.68), we obtain the following optimal lump-sum taxes/transfers:

$$\frac{T_t^A}{w_t^* H_t^*} = \frac{(1+\gamma\rho)\theta - \rho(1+\alpha)[1-\rho a(1-\gamma)]}{(1-a)\{(\alpha+\rho)[1-\rho(1-\gamma)] + \rho\beta\gamma(1-\rho)\}}, \tag{3.69}$$

$$\frac{T_t^O}{w_t^* H_t^*} = \frac{-\theta + \rho(1+\alpha)[1-\rho a(1-\gamma)]}{(1-a)\{(\alpha+\rho)[1-\rho(1-\gamma)] + \beta\gamma\rho(1-\rho)\}}, \tag{3.70}$$

where $\theta \equiv (1-a)(\alpha+\rho) - a\beta\,\gamma\rho(1-\rho)$.

Derivation of the Interest Rate in the Case of $T^o = 0$

In the case of $T^o = 0$, the government budget constraint becomes

$$T_t^A = \tau_e e_t. \tag{3.71}$$

By substituting (3.36) and (3.61) into (3.71), the lump-sum tax/transfer in the adult period is given by

$$\frac{T_t^A}{w_t^* H_t^*} = \frac{\gamma\theta}{\Omega}, \tag{3.72}$$

where $\Omega \equiv (1+\alpha+\beta\gamma)(1-\rho)(1-a\rho) + (1+\alpha)(1-\rho)a\,\rho\gamma + \gamma(1-a)(\alpha+\rho)$.

Using (3.13), (3.15), (3.35), and (3.72), we obtain the interest rate on the balanced growth path for $T^o = 0$:

$$R_{T^o=0} = \frac{\gamma\theta}{\Omega} g. \tag{3.73}$$

References

de la Croix D (1996) The dynamics of bequeathed tastes. Econ Lett 53:89–96

de la Croix D, Michel P (1999) Optimal growth when tastes are inherited. J Econ Dyn Control 23:519–537

Diamond PA (1965) National debt in a neoclassical model. Am Econ Rev 55:1126–1150

Gori L, Michetti E (2016) The dynamics of bequeathed tastes with endogenous fertility. Econ Lett 149:79–82

Kaneko A, Kato H, Shinozaki T, Yanagihara M (2016) Bequeathed tastes and fertility in an endogenous growth model. Econ Bull 36:1422–1429

Kato H, Shinozaki T, Yanagihara M (2020) Economic growth and parental enthusiasm of education investment. Mimeo, Memphis

Chapter 4
The Impact of Life Insurance on Human Capital Investment During the Steady Growth Period in Japan: Simulation Analysis in an Overlapping Generations Model with Endogenous Growth

Yuko Shindo

Abstract We quantitatively estimate the effects of life insurance on human capital investment during the steady growth period (1975–1994) in Japan using a three-period overlapping generations model with endogenous growth fueled by human capital accumulation. Importantly, we use actual Japanese socioeconomic data from the sample period and calibrate the contribution of life insurance to the *actual* growth rate by comparing it with a counterfactual *artificial* growth rate, which was simulated without life insurance. With insurance, the results show a 0.262-million-yen larger physical capital per effective labor unit and 0.008 more years of education. Furthermore, the human capital accumulation (i.e., economic growth rate) is higher by approximately 0.167 percentage points per year on average, while government bonds are reduced by 0.3 million yen. These results indicate that life insurance plays a crucial role in ensuring economic growth during the period by accumulating both physical and human capital and reducing government bonds.

Keywords Computable general equilibrium model · Life insurance · Uncertainty · Human capital · Economic growth

JEL Classification: C68, D80, G52, J24, O40

Y. Shindo (✉)
Faculty of Intercultural Studies, Yamaguchi Prefectural University, Yamaguchi, Japan
e-mail: shindo@yamaguchi-pu.ac.jp

S. Takahashi et al. (eds.), *Modern Macroeconomics with Historical Perspectives*,
New Frontiers in Regional Science: Asian Perspectives 67,
https://doi.org/10.1007/978-981-99-1067-0_4

4.1 Introduction

This chapter investigates the effect of life insurance on both physical and human capital investment, and economic growth using the framework of the overlapping generations (OLG) model with endogenous growth fueled by human capital accumulation. Based on Yanagihara et al. (2012) model, we performed numerical analyses to compare two cases: when all individuals have life insurance and when no one has life insurance. Through this comparison, we show that the economy underestimates the importance of life insurance on both physical and human capital accumulation during the steady growth period in Japan.

Figure 4.1 shows Japan's real economic growth rate since 1956. Japan's economy is often categorized into three phases: rapid growth period from 1955 to 1974, stable economic growth period from 1975 to 1994, and the lost decades from 1995 to the present.

According to the triennial survey by the Japan Institute of Life Insurance (1965–2021), nearly 90% of households purchased life insurance by 1968 (Fig. 4.2). While the national pension system was established in 1961, the percentage of life insurance holders in the country rose quickly and peaked in 1994. The

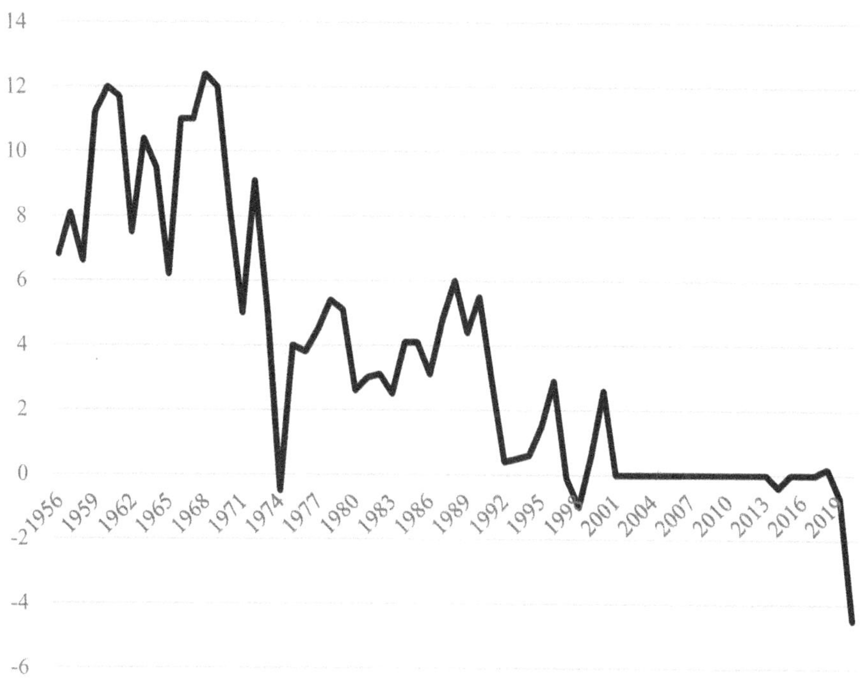

Fig. 4.1 Real economic growth rate (%). [Source: Cabinet Office, Government of Japan (1957–2021)]

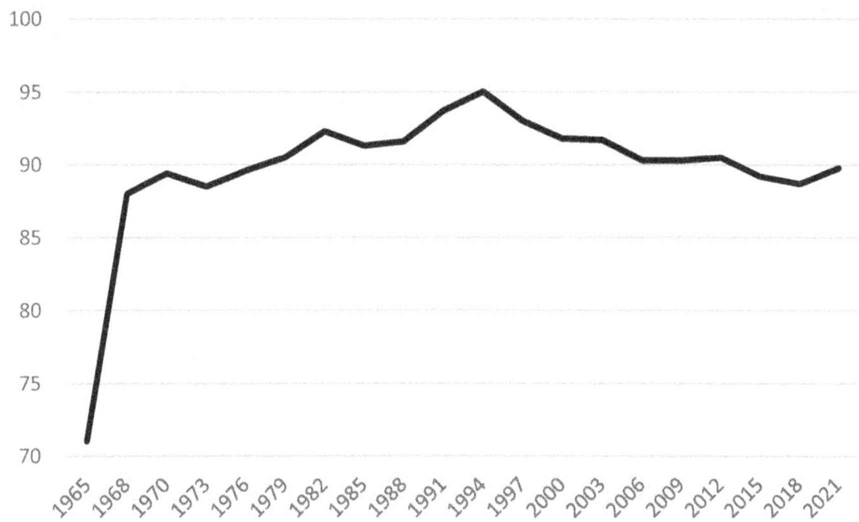

Fig. 4.2 Life insurance holders (%). [Source: Japan Institute of Life Insurance (1965–2021)]

recent reduction in the percentage of life insurance holders has been attributed to the economic slowdown, declining birthrate, and aging population.

Figure 4.3 shows the average years of schooling for 15–64 and for 15–24-year-olds. They are measured at all levels of education from primary to tertiary by age group. We can presume that upper secondary and higher education became popular during the rapid growth period, with a gradual increase in the average years of schooling. However, when we focus on the younger bracket (15–24-year-olds), this has stagnated lately.

Numerous studies, such as the early work by Yaari (1965), followed by Lewis (1989), show how life insurance reduces uncertainty and increases expected lifetime utility. Based on their theoretical framework, empirical studies provide some valuable results. Beck and Webb (2003) analyze aggregate data for 68 countries between 1961 and 2000. The authors find that income, inflation, banking sector development, and religion are important factors for life insurance consumption, whereas the influence of education, life expectancy, the young dependency ratio, and the size of the social security system is not robust. Li et al. (2007) use data on OECD countries from 1993 to 2000 to show that dependency ratio, education, life expectancy, social security expenditure, financial development, insurance market competitiveness, inflation, and real interest rates are related to life insurance consumption. Chuma and Asano (1993) examine the demand for life insurance using 1988 Japanese data. They show that income, assets, and education positively affect life insurance purchasing. Using long-term Japanese data from 1956 to 2007, Fukuchi (2014) reveals a positive income elasticity of life insurance demand, consistent with Chuma and Asano's study (1993).

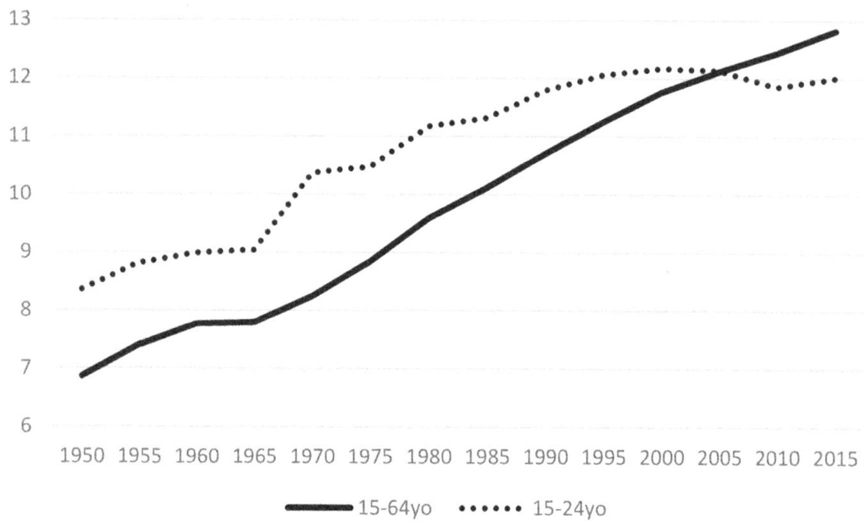

Fig. 4.3 Average years of total schooling (year). [Source: Barro Lee Data Set]

However, these studies used a partial equilibrium model that contained neither physical nor human capital accumulation. Ignoring the accumulation mechanisms under uncertain lifetimes may overestimate the economic impacts.[1] Investing in education is determined by the return on lifetime income; however, the return also depends on one's longevity. In line with these studies, we explore how life insurance helps accumulate physical and human capital to accelerate economic growth during the steady economic growth period in Japan.

We find that compared to the case without insurance, physical capital accumulation is higher by 0.262 million yen per effective labor unit, the number of years of education is higher by 0.008 years, and the economic growth rate is higher by approximately 0.167 percentage points per year on an average in the case with insurance. These figures indicate that life insurance contributed to achieving both higher educational levels and higher economic growth rates during the stable economic growth period.

The remainder of this chapter is organized as follows. First, we describe the framework of the model. We then explain the parameter settings for calibrating the steady growth paths of the two types of economies, with and without insurance based on Japanese data. Furthermore, we compare the impact of life insurance on educational levels and economic growth in the steady growth paths. Finally, we present the conclusions.

[1] See Yanagihara et al. (2012).

4.2 Model

We consider perfectly competitive markets in a closed economy, which starts from period 0 and continues forever.[2] Let t index the period. There are three types of economic agents in this economy: individuals, firms, and the government. The individuals who start acting as economic agents at the beginning of period t are called generation t. This generation lives for three periods. The first period is from 16 to 35 years of age, classified as age 1. The second period from 36 to 55 years is age 2, and the third period from 56 to 75 years is age 3.[3] To simplify the model, there is no population growth, and the size of each generation is normalized to unity. In addition, we assume that the individuals are identical and face the risk of asset loss at age 3 with the probability of longevity. Purchasing life insurance can mitigate this risk. There are two types of firms: goods-producing and life insurance firms.

4.2.1 Individuals

In age 1, individuals of generation t allocate their one unit of time between education, e_t, and work, $1 - e_t$ $(0 \leq e_t \leq 1)$.[4] At age 2, they supply labor inelastically. At age 3, they allocate their time between work, $1 - \zeta_{t+2}^3$, and retirement, ζ_{t+2}^3 $\left(0 \leq \zeta_{t+2}^3 \leq 1\right)$. In addition, at age 3, they face a risk of death with the probability of ρ $(0 \leq \rho \leq 1)$. If they die, they do not receive labor income and pension benefit. To avoid the risk of potential income loss, they have an incentive to purchase life insurance at age 2.[5] That is, they can have a fixed amount of labor income without uncertainty by purchasing life insurance.

The human capital of generation t at period t, h_t^1, is inherited from the previous generation without depreciation. Their human capital in the next period, $\overline{h}_{t+1}^2$, is accumulated over the length of education, e_t, through the human capital accumulation equation as follows:

$$\overline{h}_{t+1}^2 = \left(1 + \xi e_t^{\psi}\right) h_t^1, \tag{4.1}$$

---

[2] While our interest lies in the domestic economy, the setting of a closed economy may overvalue or undervalue the effect under the globalization of the economy.

[3] In Japan, the average lifespan for men was 74.6 years during the steady growth period from 1975 to 1994, while that for women was 80.2 years, according to the Ministry of Health, Labour, and Welfare (2021a).

[4] Since compulsory education is completed at the age of 15 in Japan, we do not analyze the lifetime under 15 years. In addition, we do not analyze the effect of lifelong education due to the lack of data.

[5] The average age at the time of first marriage was 28.3 for men and 25.5 for women from 1975 to 1994 (Ministry of Health, Labour, and Welfare, 2021b). People in Japan usually purchase life insurance after marriage or the birth of their first child.

where ξ (>0) and ψ ($0 < \psi < 1$) are the parameters of human capital productivity and education investment, respectively.[6] Based on this level of human capital, individuals further accumulate human capital through on-the-job training (OJT) so that their earning power becomes the following:

$$h_{t+1}^{2} = \theta^{2}\overline{h}_{t+1}^{2} = \theta^{2}\left(1 + \xi e_{t}^{\psi}\right) h_{t}^{1}, \tag{4.2}$$

where θ^2 (>1) is a given parameter accumulated through OJT at age 2 at period t +1. Successively, their human capital in period $t + 2$ is either accumulated or depreciated as follows:

$$h_{t+2}^{3} = \theta^{3}\left(1 + \xi e_{t}^{\psi}\right) h_{t}^{1}, \tag{4.3}$$

where θ^3 (>0) is a given parameter for the effectiveness of OJT in age 3 at period t +2, which is accumulated and then eventually depreciated over time.

Individuals earn income per effective labor. The disposable labor income of generation t in age j (=1, 2, 3) is represented as $(1 - \tau_t)\, w_t h_t^j$, where $w_t h_t^j$ and τ_t ($0 < \tau_t < 1$) represent the wage per capita of generation t in age j and the labor income tax rate at period t, respectively.[7] Besides disposable income, individuals of generation t receive an education subsidy at age 1 at period t, $\upsilon_t e_t (1 - \tau_t)\, w_t h_t^1$, where υ_t is the fraction of their disposable income, and per capita pension benefit at age 3 at period $t + 2$, $\zeta_{t+2}^3 p_{t+2}^3 h_{t+2}^3$. The amount of consumption per capita, c_t^j, and asset per capita, $a_t^j h_t^j$, at period t are determined depending on their lifetime income, which is given in ages 1, 2, and 3.[8,9] Their incomes are fully consumed at the end of their lives in age 3.[10]

In short, the individual budget constraint of generation t in age 1 is written as follows:

$$c_t^1 + a_t^1 h_t^1 = (1 - e_t)(1 - \tau_t)\, w_t h_t^1 + \upsilon_t e_t (1 - \tau_t)\, w_t h_t^1. \tag{4.4}$$

Because individuals pay the insurance fee in age 2 to cover the loss due to death in age 3, the budget constraint in age 2 is given as follows:

$$c_{t+1}^2 + a_{t+1}^2 h_{t+1}^2 = (1 - \tau_{t+1})\, w_{t+1} h_{t+1}^2 + (1 + r_{t+1})\, a_t^1 h_t^1 - \iota_{t+1}^2, \tag{4.5}$$

6 This is the extension of the framework created by Bouzahzah et al. (2002). This assumption follows Lucas (1988), whereby individuals spend on education for accumulating skills. While the equation can include the quality of education, a similar tendency is likely to be observed. See Shindo (2010a).

7 Mincer earnings function is applied in the context of economic growth.

8 Although h_t^j is not embedded in c_t^j, this represents per capita consumption.

9 Consumption tax was not included because it was not introduced until 1989 in Japan.

10 We assume that there is no motivation for inheritance.

where r_{t+1} and ι_{t+1}^2 are the interest rate and insurance payments of individuals of generation t at period $t + 1$. Because certain amounts of their income and, hence, their consumption in age 3 are guaranteed regardless of life expectancy, the budget constraint in age 3 becomes the following:

$$c_{t+2}^3 = \left(1 - \zeta_{t+2}^3\right)(1 - \tau_{t+2})\, w_{t+2} h_{t+2}^3 + (1 + r_{t+2})\ a_{t+1}^2 h_{t+1}^2 + \zeta_{t+2}^3 p_{t+2}^3 h_{t+2}^3. \tag{4.6}$$

In contrast, suppose that life insurance is unavailable. As insurance payment is not necessary, the budget constraint in age 2 becomes the following:

$$c_{t+1}^2 + a_{t+1}^2 h_{t+1}^2 = (1 - \tau_{t+1})\, w_{t+1} h_{t+1}^2 + (1 + r_{t+1})\ a_t^1 h_t^1. \tag{4.7}$$

In age 3, if the individuals live until the average life expectancy, with $1 - \rho$ percent having good health, the budget constraint is expressed as follows:

$$c_{t+2}^{3g} = \left(1 - \zeta_{t+2}^3\right)(1 - \tau_{t+2})\, w_{t+2} h_{t+2}^3 + (1 + r_{t+2})\ a_{t+1}^2 h_{t+1}^2 + \zeta_{t+2}^3 p_{t+2}^3 h_{t+2}^3, \tag{4.8a}$$

where c_{t+2}^{3g} indicates the amount of consumption per capita in good health.

By contrast, if ρ percent of them are in poor health and die in age 3, the budget constraint becomes the following:

$$c_{t+2}^{3b} = (1 + r_{t+2})\ a_{t+1}^2 h_{t+1}^2, \tag{4.8b}$$

where c_{t+2}^{3b} is the amount of per capita consumption in age 3.[11]

Individuals obtain utility from their consumption throughout their lives. Their utilities in ages 1 and 2 consist of the amount of consumption under certainty, whereas that in age 3 is an expected utility. The lifetime utility function is a constant relative risk aversion (CRRA) type and is additively separable in time with the time preference rate γ $(0 < \gamma < 1)$. This lifetime utility function is expressed as follows:

$$\begin{aligned} U_t = {} & \frac{1}{1 - 1/\sigma}\left(\left(c_t^1\right)^{1-1/\sigma} - 1\right) + \frac{\gamma}{1 - 1/\sigma}\left(\left(c_{t+1}^2\right)^{1-1/\sigma} - 1\right) \\ & + \frac{(1-\rho)\gamma^2}{1 - 1/\sigma}\left(\left(c_{t+2}^{3g}\right)^{1-1/\sigma} - 1\right) + \frac{\rho\gamma^2}{1 - 1/\sigma}\left(\left(c_{t+2}^{3b}\right)^{1-1/\sigma} - 1\right), \end{aligned} \tag{4.9}$$

where $\sigma \in \mathcal{R}$ is the coefficient of CRRA or the intertemporal elasticity of substitution.

[11] We use the selfish model rather than the altruism model which is more applicable for Japan. See Horioka (2002) for more details.

By contrast, if individuals purchase life insurance, the utility function assumes a normal form as their death risk can be eliminated. The lifetime utility can be then expressed as follows:

$$U_t = \frac{1}{1-1/\sigma}\left(\left(c_t^1\right)^{1-1/\sigma}-1\right)+\frac{\gamma}{1-1/\sigma}\left(\left(c_{t+1}^2\right)^{1-1/\sigma}-1\right) + \frac{\gamma^2}{1-1/\sigma}\left(\left(c_{t+2}^3\right)^{1-1/\sigma}-1\right). \tag{4.10}$$

4.2.2 Firms

The economy has two types of firms: goods-producing and life insurance firms. Goods-producing firms use skilled labor, H_t, and physical capital, K_t, to supply goods in each period according to a constant returns, Cobb–Douglas production function as follows:

$$Y_t = AK_t^\alpha H_t^{1-\alpha}, \tag{4.11}$$

where Y_t is the aggregate output at period t. A (>0) and α ($0 < \alpha < 1$) represent an exogenously given technology that explains unaccounted growth in the factors of production and the output elasticity of capital, respectively.

As explained in the previous subsection, the individuals supply their labor for $1 - e_t$ in age 1, 1 in age 2, and $(1-\rho)\left(1-\zeta_t^3\right)$ units of time on an average in age 3 at period t. Therefore, the average expected aggregate labor supply at period t is expressed as follows:

$$H_t = (1-e_t)\,h_t^1 + h_t^2 + (1-\rho)\left(1-\zeta_t^3\right)h_t^3. \tag{4.12}$$

Defining the capital stock and the output per effective labor unit as $k_t \equiv K_t/H_t$ and y_t, respectively, we can rewrite the aggregate production function in Eq. (4.11) as the one expressed as $y_t = Ak_t^\alpha$ in per effective labor unit term. In a perfectly competitive market, firms pay interest, r_t, to rent a unit of capital for one period and pay workers a wage, $w_t h_t^j$, per person. The goods-producing firms simply maximize their profits at present time. Therefore, the following equations hold:

$$\delta + r_t = A\alpha k_t^{\alpha-1}, \tag{4.13}$$

and

$$w_t = A(1-\alpha)\,k_t^\alpha, \tag{4.14}$$

where δ ($0 < \delta < 1$) is the constant physical capital depreciation rate.

However, insurance firms provide services by employing neither physical capital nor effective labor. Similar to goods-producing firms, they make zero profits because of the assumption of perfect competition.[12] Thus, insurance firms balance their budgets at each period as follows:

$$i_{t+1}^{2} = \left[(1-\rho)\,0 + \rho w_{t+2} h_{t+2}^{3}\right] / \left(1+r_{t+1}\right) = \rho w_{t+2} h_{t+2}^{3} / \left(1+r_{t+1}\right). \tag{4.15}$$

The left-hand side of Eq. (4.15) indicates the insurance payment by individuals per effective labor, and the right-hand side is the insurance disbursement by insurance firms in the effective labor unit. Here, we assume that insurance firms invest insurance payments in the capital market and obtain returns in the subsequent period to use for their insurance claim.

4.2.3 *Government*

In every period, the government balances its budget. When expenditure exceeds revenue, it issues government bonds. Thus, the government budget constraint at period t is written as follows:

$$\begin{aligned} \tau_t w_t H_t + \sum_{j=1}^{2} b_{t+1} h_{t+1}^{j} &= \upsilon_t e_t \left(1-\tau_t\right) w_t h_t^{1} + \zeta_t^{3} p_t^{3} w_t h_t^{3} \\ &+ \sum_{j=1}^{3} o_t h_t^{j} + \left(1+r_t\right) \sum_{j=1}^{2} b_t h_t^{j}, \end{aligned} \tag{4.16}$$

where $o_t h_t^j$ and $b_t h_t^j$ are exogenously given other government expenditure per capita, except for the pension and education subsidies, and the amount of government bonds per capita issued at period t which is repaid in period $t+1$, respectively.

The left-hand side of Eq. (4.16) represents the total government revenue consisting of the tax revenue and the bond issue, whereas the right-hand side is the total government expenditure, including the bond repayment issued in the previous period. There is no arbitrage between the return on capital and government bonds; the return rate for the bond is assumed to be equal to the interest rate.

---

[12] We assume a perfect insurance market since the data for service fees are not disclosed.

4.2.4 Equilibrium

The model describes two types of equilibria: one in which life insurance is available for an individual and one in which it is unavailable. In the former case, individuals maximize their lifetime utility in Eq. (4.10) subject to the budget constraint at each period, Eqs. (4.4), (4.5), and (4.6), under certainty. By contrast, in the latter case, they maximize their expected lifetime utility in Eq. (4.9) subject to the corresponding budget constraints in Eqs. (4.4), (4.7), (4.8a), and (4.8b). Human capital accumulation Eqs. (4.1), (4.2), and (4.3) apply to both cases.

Regarding the length of education, the optimal level is determined based on the condition that the ratio of marginal benefit to the length of education is equal to the marginal opportunity cost. Specifically, the marginal benefit from education results in an increase in income in ages 2 and 3 by the accumulation of human capital in age 1, whereas the marginal cost results in a decrease in income in age 1. Consequently, the optimal level of e_t is obtained as a function of the capital stock per effective labor unit, $e(k_t)$. Individuals who hold life insurance can invest more in education than those who face the risk of a reduced lifespan without insurance. Therefore, the growth rate of human capital with life insurance is greater than that without life insurance.

Further, the accumulation of physical capital from period t to period $t + 1$ is determined by the individual assets at period t. Their capital supply is used for production in the subsequent period. This process is expressed as the capital market equilibrium equation in aggregated terms as follows:

$$K_{t+1} + \sum_{j=1}^{2} b_{t+1} h_{t+1}^{j} = \sum_{j=1}^{2} a_t^j h_t^j + \frac{\rho w_{t+1} h_{t+1}^3}{1 + r_t}. \tag{4.17}$$

The left-hand side of Eq. (4.17) represents the capital demand by the goods-producing firms and the government. The right-hand side shows the total assets of individuals in period t and their insurance payments managed by insurance firms. Similar to asset management, insurance firms profit from insurance sales before payments in the next period. Thus, insurance payments contribute to physical capital accumulation and economic growth, as shown in the capital market.

When we rewrite the capital market equilibrium condition, which is in aggregate terms in Eq. (4.17) into effective labor unit term, we obtain the following:

$$k_{t+1} = \frac{\sum_{j=1}^{2} a_t^j h_t^j - \sum_{j=1}^{2} b_{t+1} h_{t+1}^j + \frac{\rho w_{t+1} h_{t+1}^3}{1+r_t}}{(1 - e_t)\, h_t^1 + h_t^2}. \tag{4.18}$$

Finally, the growth rate of human capital, namely, the economic growth rate, can be expressed as a function of physical capital per effective labor, k_t, from Eq. (4.1) as follows:

$$\frac{\overline{h}_{t+1}}{h_t} = 1 + \xi e(k_t)^{\psi}. \tag{4.19}$$

Therefore, the economic growth rate becomes constant, while the physical capital level per effective labor unit takes a constant value in the steady growth path.

4.3 Parameter Settings

Next, we calibrate the parameters of the model explained in the previous section based on actual socioeconomic data in Japan to replicate the economy from 1975 to 1994. All calibrated values and data sources are summarized in Table 4.1. These values are determined by using an annual average during the sample period, considering 20 years as one period in this model. Most parameters are calculated using statistical data published by the respective ministries indicated in the third column. Note that Japan experienced steady growth during this period, and the economy seesawed.

Table 4.1 Parameters

Parameters	Values	Sources
ξ: Human capital productivity	0.010	Barro Lee Data Set, Cabinet Office (1976–1995)
ψ:Education investment	0.738	
θ^2:OJT in age 2	1.800	Ministry of Health, Labour, and Welfare (1976–1995)
θ^3:OJT in age 3	1.265	
τ: Labor income tax rate	0.333	Ministry of Finance
ν: Education subsidy rate	1.133	Ministry of Education, Culture, Sports, Science, and Technology (1976–1995), Cabinet Office (1976–1995)
ι: Life insurance payment	0.138	Japan Institute of Life Insurance (1976–1994)
ζ^3: Retirement ratio	0.750	–
p: Pension benefit	1.407	Ministry of Health, Labour, and Welfare (2008)
ρ:Death ratio	0.341	Ministry of Health, Labour, and Welfare (2021a)
σ: CRRA	3.496	Kikkawa (2002)
γ: Time preference rate	0.093	Cabinet Office (1976–1995)
A: Technology	2.000	Cabinet Office (1976–1995)
α: Output elasticity of capital	0.319	
δ: Physical capital depreciation rate	0.057	
o:Other government expenditure	0.200	Ministry of Finance

The parameters relating to the human capital accumulation equation, human capital productivity, ξ, and education investment, ψ, in the first and second rows are obtained using the average years of total schooling from 15 to 64 and the average real economic growth rate of 3.5% per year, following Shindo (2010b). These data are obtained from the Barro Lee Data Set and the SNA (Cabinet Office, 1976–1995). For the data on OJT, θ,we derive the relative incomes using the wage data provided by the Ministry of Health, Labour, and Welfare (1976–1995).

The labor tax rate, τ, in the fifth row is not just the tax rate, but substitutes the national burden rate by the Ministry of Finance to fit the real economy. The education subsidy rate, ν, is adjusted to the ratio of public education expenditure per student to per capita income by the Ministry of Education, Culture, Sports, Science and Technology (1976–1995) and Cabinet Office (1976–1995). The life insurance payment, ι, is obtained from the statistics of the Japan Institute of Life Insurance (1976–1994). The retirement ratio, ζ^3, is set as people over 60 years of age receiving a pension during the period.[13] The pension benefit is calculated from Ministry of Health, Labour, and Welfare (2008). The death ratio, ρ, is determined by substituting the survival rate up to 75 years of age based on the data from the Ministry of Health, Labour, and Welfare (2021a).

The subjective value of CRRA, σ, is set based on Kikkawa (2002), who has estimated these values from 1970 to 2003 in Japan. Another subjective value of the time preference, γ, substitutes the real interest rate. Technology, output elasticity of capital, and physical capital depreciation rate are obtained from the SNA. Other government expenditure, o, is set to balance government revenue and the government debt issue minus public education expenditure minus pension payment, p.

4.4 Simulation Results

Here, we show the effect of life insurance on human capital investment (economic growth) by comparing the numerical solutions of the two cases in the steady growth paths. Table 4.2 summarizes the equilibrium values for the steady growth paths. Cases W and O indicate the values with and without life insurance, respectively.

First, using the parameter values obtained in the previous section, we simulate cases with and without life insurance to obtain equilibrium values in the steady growth path. First, we normalize the initial level of human capital, h_t^1, to one to make it easy to calculate and compare the values. Then, the capital stocks per effective labor unit in the steady growth path, k^*, become 8.175 and 7.913 with and without life insurance, respectively.[14] This indicates that life insurance has a positive effect

[13] The pension age has been recently raised to 65.

[14] By normalizing the initial level of human capital to unity, the initial level of capital stock per person becomes the same as that of per effective labor unit.

Table 4.2 Effect of insurance on the steady growth paths

	Case W	Case O
k^*: Capital stock per effective labor unit (million yen/year)	8.175	7.913
a^1: Assets per effective labor unit in age 1 (million yen/year)	12.443	13.065
a^2: Assets per effective labor unit in age 2 (million yen/year)	9.075	9.134
e: Length of education per person in age 1 (year)	0.082	0.074
$1 + \xi e(k^*)^{\psi}$: Human capital accumulation or economic growth rate (%/year)	3.500	3.333
b: Government bonds (million yen/year)	1.908	2.208

on the accumulation of physical capital by 0.262 million yen per year during the stable economic growth period.

Based on the values of capital stocks, the levels of assets, length of education, human capital growth rate, and government bonds are simultaneously obtained. Both assets in ages 1 and 2 are *less* with life insurance than without it. As we can see in Eq. (4.4), if individuals spend more time on education, there is less labor supply; consequently, wage income and, thus, assets decline in ages 1 and 2.

However, the physical capital per effective labor unit accumulates more with life insurance than without it, because the length of education is 0.008 years longer with life insurance than without it. This indicates that individuals with life insurance can invest more in education under the certainty of their lifespan. As seen in Sect. 4.1, average years of schooling were increasing during the steady economic period; thus, our findings are consistent with this observation.[15] Accordingly, the level of physical capital per capita continues to be even higher with life insurance than without it.

As seen in Eq. (4.1), an increase in the length of education accelerates the accumulation of human capital, which is a source of economic growth. Notably, the human capital growth rate with life insurance is 0.167 percentage points per year higher than that without life insurance.

Furthermore, the value of government bonds also clearly differs. The effect of the insurance market is considerably important not only for economic growth but also for government debt reduction, as shown in Eq. (4.17).

Note that previous studies have only emphasized the risk reduction of individual income or welfare with life insurance using a partial equilibrium model. Besides this feature of life insurance, our analysis validates another feature by constructing an endogenous growth framework with human capital accumulation: the acceleration of economic growth due to human capital accumulation.

These results provide supporting evidence that the prevalence of life insurance ownership in Japan was crucial for economic development from 1975 to 1994. This implies that one of the reasons for the current prolonged economic stagnation in Japan may be the recent unpopularity of life insurance and lesser educational

[15] Using a simulation for the lost decades in Japan, Yanagihara et al. (2012) show the similar results.

investment. As we are aware of the importance of life insurance, especially with the uncertainty in the COVID-19 era, we should not neglect the use of life insurance.

4.5 Conclusion

From our numerical analysis, we find that life insurance reduces the risk of investing in education under uncertainty. Because education decisions are made according to the individual will, some individuals may hesitate to invest more in education if life insurance is unavailable. When life insurance is available, it reduces this risk and provides an incentive to study longer.

Second, our analysis reveals an important feature of human capital accumulation: with life insurance, the economy uses more resources for human capital than for physical capital; consequently, it grows faster under certainty. This reflects the fact that individuals who purchase life insurance spend more time on education, and consequently, the level of human capital is higher in the case with than without life insurance.

Importantly, our findings provide useful implications for insurance policy. Specifically, promoting life insurance in other developing countries with underdeveloped social security systems can be meaningful in terms of its effect on economic growth.

Finally, this study has some limitations.[16] First, we devalue individual moral hazards. Moral hazard is a common practice when we deal with the issue of life insurance. Hence, further research should consider introducing heterogeneous individuals and government regulations based on contract theory. Second, we assume a perfectly competitive insurance market. Thus, future studies can use models that incorporate the monopolistic nature of insurance companies.

Acknowledgements I appreciate the advice and comments from Professor Emeritus Shuetsu Takahashi, and the editors and authors of this book. All errors and imprecisions are my own.

References

Barro Lee Data Set. http://barrolee.com/. Accessed 30 Mar 2022

Beck T, Webb I (2003) Economic, demographic, and institutional determinants for life insurance consumption across countries. World Bank Econ Rev 17(4):51–88

Bouzahzah M, De la Croix D, Docquier F (2002) Policy reform and growth in computable OLG economies. J Econ Dyn Control 26(12):2093–2113

[16] In addition, we should include the analysis during the transition period to examine the effect of introducing life insurance in the short run. This analysis will be useful for other countries that are considering the introduction of the insurance system.

Cabinet Office, Government of Japan (1957–2021) 'SNA'
Chuma H, Asano S (1993) Bequest motives and demand for life insurance. Econ Rev 44(2):137–148
Fukuchi Y (2014) Kojin hoken no juyo youin bunseki: Sengo no waga kuni niokeru seiho shijo no jukyu kouzou. J Econ Sci 11:77–91
Horioka CY (2002) Are the Japanese selfish, altruistic, or dynastic? Jpn Econ Rev 53(1):26–54
Japan Institute of Life Insurance (1965–2021) 'Seimei hoken ni kansuru zenkoku jittai chousa'
Kikkawa T (2002) Kiken shisan ni taisuru nihon no kakei no kinyuu shisan sentaku koudou. Seijo Univ Econ Pap 163:73–87
Lewis F (1989) Dependents and the demand for life insurance. Am Econ Rev 79(3):452–467
Li D, Moshirian F, Nguyen P, Wee T (2007) The demand for life insurance in OECD countries. J Risk Insur 74(3):637–652
Lucas R (1988) On the mechanics of economic development. J Monet Econ 22(1):3–42
Ministry of Education, Culture, Sports, Science, and Technology (1976–1995) 'Monbu kagaku toukei youran'
Ministry of Finance. https://www.mof.go.jp/policy/budget/reference/statistics/data.htm. Accessed 30 Mar 2022
Ministry of Health, Labour, and Welfare (1976–1995) 'Basic Survey on Wage Structure'
Ministry of Health, Labour, and Welfare (2008) 'Kousei nenkin hoken jukyuusha no heikin nenkin tsuki gaku no suii'
Ministry of Health, Labour, and Welfare (2021a) 'Reiwa 2 nen kani seimei hyo no gaiyo'
Ministry of Health, Labour, and Welfare (2021b) 'Jinko dotai toukei nenpo'
Shindo Y (2010a) The effects of education subsidies on human capital accumulation: a numerical analysis of macroeconomy in China. Australas J Reg Stud 16(1):71–83
Shindo Y (2010b) The effect of education subsidies on regional economic growth and disparities in China. Econ Model 27(5):1061–1068
Yaari ME (1965) Uncertain lifetime, life insurance, and the theory of the consumer. Rev Econ Stud 32(2):137–150
Yanagihara M, Shindo Y, Lu C (2012) Seimei hoken ga jinteki shihon keizai seichou ni hatasu yakuwari. Seimei hoken ni kansuru chousa kenkyu houkoku:1–30

Chapter 5
The Effects of Patience in a Growth Model with Infrastructure and a Related Externality

Kei Hosoya

Abstract This chapter introduces an endogenous time preference function into the model of economic growth and discusses how the different functional form of time preference affects the status of long-term steady state and equilibrium dynamics. We assume that the rate of time preference is determined by the ratio of total consumption to infrastructure levels. Then, we consider two cases in which an increase in the ratio either increases or decreases the agent's time preference. The former case corresponds to increasing marginal impatience: people become less patient as this ratio that changes their rate of time preference increases (i.e., degree of patience decreases with increases in this ratio). By contrast, the latter case corresponds to decreasing marginal impatience: people become more patient as this ratio increases (i.e., degree of patience increases with increases in this ratio). Accounting for the different functional form of endogenous time preference reveals that it makes a substantial difference in the dynamics of the model. After presenting the dynamic system of the model, the effect on the steady-state equilibrium is assessed specifically by numerical analysis. Then, for a clearer understanding, an investigation based on phase diagrams is developed.

Keywords Economic growth · Endogenous time preference · Indeterminacy · Infrastructure · Patience

JEL Classification C61; H54; O40

K. Hosoya (✉)
Faculty of Economics, Kokugakuin University, Shibuya-ku, Tokyo, Japan
e-mail: khosoya@kokugakuin.ac.jp

S. Takahashi et al. (eds.), *Modern Macroeconomics with Historical Perspectives*,
New Frontiers in Regional Science: Asian Perspectives 67,
https://doi.org/10.1007/978-981-99-1067-0_5

5.1 Introduction

It is known that the preference status of agents plays an important role in trying to describe the dynamic aspects of the macroeconomy. As well as being analytically important, consideration of preference status is indispensable in practice in situations in which long-term issues must be tackled, such as global environmental issues and the infrastructure investment problem, among others. Preference parameters that are given such importance include the rate of time preference and intertemporal elasticity of substitution (Ogaki and Atkeson 1997).[1] This chapter focuses on the rate of time preference.

Uzawa (1968) conducted an important study that focused on the importance of time preference under the dynamic framework and incorporated it into the model as an endogenous variable. In a model with endogenous time preference, unlike the case of standard exogenous and constant time preference, the rate of time preference is expressed as a function of one or more economic variables (endogenous variables) and is determined endogenously. Uzawa (1968) was followed by Epstein (1987) and Obstfeld (1990), who formed benchmark models in the field.[2]

The endogenous time preference function used by Uzawa (1968), Epstein (1987), and Obstfeld (1990) appears to implement two important features. First, the rate of time preference is determined by individual and internal variables such as individual consumption levels. There are many variations on the specification. For instance, Nishimura and Shimomura (2002), Das (2003), and Sarkar (2007) assumed that individual consumption affects time preference. Dai (2007) considered the impact of individual wealth stocks coupled with individual consumption.[3] Second, as the employed variable (e.g., individual consumption level) increases, so does the rate of time preference. A person with a higher rate of time preference would discount the future more strongly, and therefore, we can consider such a person as an agent with a stronger preference for present rather than future economic status. So, regarding patience, it can be assumed that an agent with strong time preference is relatively impatient. At this point, some studies including that by Uzawa (1968) are classified as having the property of *increasing marginal impatience*. Let us take a closer look at these two features, which are crucial in determining the characteristics of the model.

---

[1] Hirose and Ikeda (2015) also note that "time preference formation could be thought of as one of the most important elements that affect wealth distribution and capital accumulation."

[2] In addition, Becker and Mulligan (1997) established a basis for modern research in the field and shed light on the multifaceted nature of time preference. In particular, the rate of time preference was specified by a *future pleasures factor S*. Studies directly linked to this include those by Gong (2006), Nakamoto (2009), Kawagishi (2012, 2014), and Kawagishi and Mino (2012), among others.

[3] Instead of individual consumption levels, individual capital and wealth levels or wealth accumulation rates have also been considered in the literature (e.g., Kam and Missios 2003; Kam 2005; Cui et al. 2008; Strulik 2012; Bouché 2017).

In the aforementioned benchmark models including that by Uzawa (1968), it is assumed implicitly that an agent knows its own status on time discount, and we deny neither this nor other possibilities. More specifically, there may be cases in which an agent does not know its own preferences well. We can also think of a general situation in which time preference is affected by factors beyond an agent's control; this is seen clearly in the relationship between global environmental problems and people's economic behavior. Chu et al. (2016), who developed a dynamic analysis focused on the impact of environmental factors on time preference, suggested the following influence routes.

> For example, if environmentalists declare that the problem of global warming will become very severe in the near future, one would expect that consumption will increase and that saving will fall, because saving (for future consumption) now becomes more uncertain. This means that fears of an environmental disaster may alter people's time preferences so that they will prefer current consumption. (Chu et al. 2016, p. 1653)

As pointed out above, when individuals make decisions, it is often possible in reality that their time horizon is affected by social factors. The study by Meng (2006) is a notable one that focused on the rate of time preference determined by social situation and gave important results in a dynamic sense; that is, it showed that the endogeneity of time preference is a source of local and global indeterminacy of long-term equilibrium. This result does not come as a surprise because when the time preference function is characterized by exogenous factors such as the social average or total amount of a variable, such a function acts as a type of externality. Externality and indeterminacy are closely related, so the model by Meng (2006) is classified as showing a new research direction, and studies of this type are introduced herein.

Palivos et al. (1997) examined the differences in growth rates among countries while accounting for the ratio of individual consumption and average capital level in the economy. Drugeon (1998) introduced a unique specification for the time preference function that considers both individual and average consumption levels and showed the emergence of an endogenous business cycle. Bian and Meng (2004) focused on the effect of average consumption. In the study by Agénor (2008, 2010), publicly provided health services affected an agent's time preference, along with individual capital and income level. Dioikitopoulos and Kalyvitis (2010, 2015), whose specification of the time preference function ours is based on, considered both consumption and public and human capital stock at the macroscopic level.[4] Time preference (time discounting) is related particularly closely to environmental issues. The studies by Yanase (2011), Vella et al. (2015), and Chu et al. (2016) are recent contributions that have introduced endogenous time preference into the growth framework with some type of environmental factor. Yanase (2011) specified a model in which both individual consumption and environmental quality determine an agent's time preference. In contrast, Vella et al. (2015) used aggregate consumption rather than individual consumption, but their model is the same as that of Yanase (2011) in that it incorporates environmental quality. As mentioned earlier,

[4] The macroeconomic variables are measured in terms of aggregate or average.

the model by Chu et al. (2016) is similar but assumes that the rate of time preference depends only on environmental quality. As a more recent contribution, Tamai (2019) introduced an external time preference function that is affected by social variables such as average consumption and average income, and the effect of fiscal policy in a small open economy setting was investigated.

Next, we describe a problem related to the property of the time preference function pointed out above. The question is whether people become more patient or impatient as they become richer. A detailed discussion is given in Sect. 5.2, so here we give only an overview of research trends. The earlier models including that by Uzawa (1968) assumed an increasing marginal impatience that wealth makes people more impatient. In addition to Epstein (1987) and Obstfeld (1990), Epstein and Hynes (1983) and Lucas and Stokey (1984) also used a time preference function based on the assumption of increasing marginal impatience. However, several empirical studies questioned the relevance of this assumption. In the literature, it has been confirmed that the marginal rate of time preference decreases, and therefore, people become more patient as their income and wealth increase. We summarize below the related and prevailing empirical studies.

Using the Panel Study of Income Dynamics (PSID) in the United States, Lawrance (1991) showed that rich households are likely to have relatively low rates of time preference. Based on field experiments in Denmark, Harrison et al. (2002) confirmed that higher-income people have significantly lower discount rates. Also based on field experiments but this time in Vietnam, Tanaka et al. (2010) reported that household income is correlated with patience. In a more recent study by Hardardottir (2017), the relationship between macroeconomic variables and the rate of time preference was examined using a Dutch household panel survey; it was found that in general, people seem to become more patient when the rate of economic growth increases and income inequality decreases. Moreover, Falk et al. (2018) investigated the global variation in economic preferences based on a survey data set collected from 80,000 people in 76 countries; in specifications both with and without geographic controls, that comprehensive study found that people's patience is strongly correlated with per capita income.[5]

Given the suspicion regarding the relevance of increasing marginal impatience and the growing number of empirical studies that disprove it, the theoretical research trend for endogenous time preference is inevitably moving toward *decreasing marginal impatience*. More specifically, as described above, many empirical studies support the view that "more wealth makes people more patient," and papers based on this assumption have begun to appear in recent years. The contributions by Das (2003) and Hirose and Ikeda (2008) may be mentioned as basic ones belonging to this class. As shown by several empirical results, as long as consumption and

[5] Using household-level panel data collected in India, Ogaki and Atkeson (1997) confirmed that the rate of time preference does *not* vary with the level of wealth; this may be because the standard dynamic general equilibrium models assume a constant rate of time preference. In addition, Gourinchas and Parker (2002) and Cagetti (2003) found no clear evidence for a relationship between living standards and patience.

wealth levels are the determinants of individual time preference, the concept of decreasing marginal impatience is considered to be highly relevant. However, there is no doubt that various factors are involved in shaping people's preferences, so it is natural to think that what influences time preference the most depends on not only individuals but also countries and regions. For instance, for those in danger of losing land because of rising sea levels stemming from global warming, this environmental factor should be particularly important regardless of the property of impatience with respect to consumption. Therefore, it is safe to assume that the property of the time preference function differs depending on the analytical target.

In this chapter, our growth model considers provision of publicly provided infrastructure and an endogenously determined time preference.[6] Infrastructure provision is assumed to be via public investment financed by income tax, with the further assumption that external factors characterized by the ratio of private capital to existing infrastructure value also affect the process of infrastructure development. We call this type of externality a *capital-deepening externality*.[7] Based on the two viewpoints described so far, the present model is characterized as follows:

(i) The rate of time preference is characterized by the two macroeconomic (i.e., external) variables.
(ii) For the composite index defined by the two variables, we analyze the cases of both increasing and decreasing marginal impatience.

This chapter introduces not only consumption level but also the stock of public infrastructure as an additional determinant variable for time preference. Our analysis comprehensively examines the cases of increasing and decreasing marginal impatience. Considering both cases, a dynamically interesting contrast is observed. Summarizing the results, several different dynamics are indicated because of the different property of the time preference function and the different levels of intertemporal elasticity of substitution. Herein, we analyze these situations from a global perspective by means of phase diagrams.

The rest of this chapter is as follows. In Sect. 5.2, we present our model and explain our specification of the time preference function in detail. In Sect. 5.3, we use numerical analysis to characterize the long-term equilibrium of the model, and we discuss the validity of the model from a numerical perspective. In Sect. 5.4, we introduce possible equilibrium dynamics arising from this model. Finally, we make concluding remarks in Sect. 5.5.

[6] A companion article using a similar model to this chapter and examining different topics was accepted for publication in *Portuguese Economic Journal* in November 2022 (Hosoya 2022, forthcoming).

[7] See Hosoya (2017).

5.2 The Model

We focus herein on the case of a *decentralized* economy. The basic structure of the present model is identical to that of the model by Hosoya (2016) except for the specification of the endogenously determined time preference function.

Many identical immortal agents derive their utility from the consumption of a private good, $u(c)$. The total labor force, L, is assumed to be constant with no population growth, so L is normalized to unity.[8] Unlike in the standard dynamic general equilibrium model, the rate of time preference, ρ, depends on aggregate consumption, C, and economy-wide public infrastructure level, H. Each household maximizes the following intertemporal utility function:

$$\max_{c} \int_0^{\infty} u(c) \exp\left[- \int_0^t \rho(C(s), H(s)) \mathrm{d}s \right] \mathrm{d}t, \tag{5.1}$$

where the instantaneous utility function is assumed to be

$$u(c) = \frac{c^{1-\theta} - 1}{1 - \theta}, \quad \theta > 0,\ \theta \neq 1.$$

In the time preference part $\rho(\cdot)$ of (5.1), both C and H are factors external to the agent, and so each household maximizes its own utility while taking these macroscopic factors as given. The specification of $\rho(\cdot)$ basically follows that by Dioikitopoulos and Kalyvitis (2015), but other theoretical possibilities are also considered in the present chapter.

5.2.1 *The Case of Increasing Marginal Impatience*

The study by Uzawa (1968) was an early one in which the variability of time preference is introduced into a dynamic optimization model. Uzawa's formulation of an increase in consumption level increasing an agent's time preference is known to capture increasing marginal impatience (referred to hereinafter as IMI).[9] We now extend Uzawa's specification for our time preference function given the view of Dioikitopoulos and Kalyvitis (2015), where the time preference is socially determined and *positively* (resp., *negatively*) associated with aggregate consumption (resp., aggregate human capital level). Following them, we begin by assuming that the rate of time preference is positive and bounded below by $\tilde{\rho}$.[10] Therefore, ρ depends in a basic way on C/H and could be written as $\rho(C/H)$. The relationship

[8] Note that $\int_0^1 l_i \mathrm{d}i = L = 1$, where l denotes an individual agent's (household's) labor supply.

[9] Nishimura and Shimomura (2002) referred to this as the *Uzawa assumption*.

[10] As Strulik (2012) noted, this bound seems to correspond to a "natural lower bound."

with C represents an effect similar to the so-called *keeping up with the Joneses effect* in the literature focusing on status preference. Herein, we assume that the accumulation of infrastructure inherently makes people more patient. One can assume that a general improvement in the level of infrastructure would provide relief to residents and promote taking a long-term perspective on matters. To reflect this, we assume $\rho'(\cdot) > 0$ and $\rho''(\cdot) < 0$.

5.2.2 The Case of Decreasing Marginal Impatience

In introducing endogenous time preference into the dynamic general equilibrium model, it can be said that Uzawa's assumption of IMI has served as a *convenient* assumption, regardless of its practical relevance. In other words, there are many cases in which dynamic stability of equilibrium is secured by assuming IMI, and this is the reason for its convenience. However, regarding its practical relevance, assuming that improving living standards makes agents more impatient is rather questionable.

Herein, we consider the case of decreasing marginal impatience (referred to hereinafter as DMI) in addition to the case of IMI within the present framework. According to Nishimura and Shimomura (2002), the origin of DMI can probably be traced back to Fisher (1907). More specifically, the assumption suggests that the rate of time preference decreases as the consumption level increases. Applying this initial idea to our framework, an improvement in living standards (e.g., consumption levels) will make people more patient, while development in infrastructure will make people more impatient.[11] Therefore, we assume $\rho'(\cdot) < 0$ and $\rho''(\cdot) > 0$.

Each individual agent provides one unit of labor and receives capital income, rk, and wage income, w. Here, r is the interest rate and k is the per capita physical capital. Total (pre-tax) income, y, is divided between consumption, c, investment, $\dot{k}$, and tax. The government imposes a flat tax, $\tau \cdot y$, on total income to finance investment in public infrastructure. Ignoring capital depreciation, each household's budget constraint is

$$\dot{k} = (1 - \tau)(rk + w) - c. \tag{5.2}$$

The output of individual firms is produced according to the following production function:

$$y = f(k, l, H) = k^{\alpha}(Hl)^{1-\alpha} = k^{\alpha}H^{1-\alpha}, \tag{5.3}$$

[11] While this latter effect requires further investigation, such as through empirical studies, this is beyond the scope of the present study.

where $0 < \alpha < 1$ is the share of physical capital in goods production and $l = 1$ is assumed. Because we assume that infrastructure level boosts labor productivity, the *effective* labor is defined as the product of the labor input and the infrastructure, H.[12] From (5.3), a competitive firm's profit maximization yields $r = \alpha(y/k) = \alpha(k/H)^{\alpha-1}$.

The specification for the accumulation of public infrastructure follows that by Hosoya (2017, 2019). Government expenditure for infrastructure, G, is financed by an income tax imposed on each household (i.e., $G = \tau Y$).[13] In addition, there exists a capital-deepening externality, S, that governs the efficiency of infrastructure expenditure. This externality is characterized by the ratio of private capital to public infrastructure, which can capture overall living standards in a general context.[14] Therefore, we define $S \equiv (K/H)^{\epsilon}$. From the above arguments, the equation governing public infrastructure is given by

$$\dot{H} = \delta G S = \delta G \left(\frac{K}{H}\right)^{\epsilon}, \quad \delta > 0, \ \epsilon \in (0, 1-\alpha), \tag{5.4}$$

where δ represents an efficiency related to the technology of public infrastructure accumulation and ϵ denotes the degree of the capital-deepening externality. Both parameters are positive constants.

Because the process of infrastructure accumulation, (5.4), is given exogenously for an agent, maximizing (5.1) optimally with respect to (5.2) leads to

$$\frac{\dot{c}}{c} = \frac{1}{\theta}[(1-\tau)r - \rho(\cdot)] = \frac{1}{\theta}\left[\alpha(1-\tau)\left(\frac{k}{H}\right)^{\alpha-1} - \rho(\cdot)\right], \tag{5.5}$$

where we apply $r = \alpha(k/H)^{\alpha-1}$.[15] The corresponding transversality condition is given by

$$\lim_{t\to\infty} \lambda(t)k(t)\exp\left[-\int_0^t \rho\left(\frac{C(s)}{H(s)}\right) \mathrm{d}s\right] = 0.$$

Under the aggregation conditions of homogeneity and symmetricity for the agents, $c = C$ and $k = K$ hold at equilibrium. The growth rates of aggregate consumption, C, aggregate physical capital, K, and economy-wide infrastructure,

12 This type of specification is often found in studies on labor augmentation of human capital and public input (e.g., Lucas 1988; Raurich 2003).

13 Note that $\int_0^1 y_i \mathrm{d}i = Y$, $\int_0^1 k_i \mathrm{d}i = K$, and $\int_0^1 c_i \mathrm{d}i = C$.

14 The "capital deepening" in this case is assumed to be measured by the total amount of private capital per unit of public infrastructure.

15 For the optimization problem, the detailed calculation results are available from the author upon request.

H, are written as (from (5.2)–(5.5))

$$\frac{\dot{C}}{C} = \frac{1}{\theta}\left[\alpha(1-\tau)\left(\frac{K}{H}\right)^{\alpha-1} - \rho\left(\frac{C}{H}\right)\right], \tag{5.6}$$

$$\frac{\dot{K}}{K} = (1-\tau)\left(\frac{K}{H}\right)^{\alpha-1} - \frac{C}{K}, \tag{5.7}$$

$$\frac{\dot{H}}{H} = \delta\tau\left(\frac{K}{H}\right)^{\alpha+\epsilon}, \tag{5.8}$$

which establish the dynamics of the model. Along the balanced growth path, the equilibrium relations of $g \equiv g_Y = g_C = g_K = g_H$ are satisfied. By introducing the new variables $x \equiv C/K$ (i.e., a control-like variable) and $z \equiv K/H$ (i.e., a state-like variable), we can reduce the original three-dimensional system on C, K, and H to a two-dimensional system on x and z. From (5.6)–(5.8), the following hold:

$$\frac{\dot{x}}{x} = \frac{1}{\theta}[\alpha(1-\tau)z^{\alpha-1} - \rho(x\cdot z)] - (1-\tau)z^{\alpha-1} + x, \tag{5.9}$$

$$\frac{\dot{z}}{z} = (1-\tau)z^{\alpha-1} - x - \delta\tau z^{\alpha+\epsilon}. \tag{5.10}$$

5.3 Unique Equilibrium Situation

5.3.1 *The Benchmark Case*

First, the growth rate of the economy along the balanced growth path is derived directly from (5.8) as $g = \delta\tau\bar{z}^{\alpha+\epsilon}$, where $\bar{z} > 0$ denotes the steady-state value. If $\bar{z} > 0$, then g is certainly positive. To ensure the positivity of $\bar{x}$, using (5.10), the domain for $\bar{z}$ should be restricted to $0 < \bar{z} < \left(\frac{1-\tau}{\delta\tau}\right)^{1/(1+\epsilon)}$.[16] Applying the steady-state condition $\dot{x}/x = 0$ and $\bar{x}$ (see footnote 16) to (5.9) and rearranging it, we obtain

$$\Phi(\bar{z}) = \underbrace{\frac{\alpha}{\theta}(1-\tau)\bar{z}^{\alpha-1} - \delta\tau\bar{z}^{\alpha+\epsilon}}_{\Gamma} - \underbrace{\frac{1}{\theta}\rho(\bar{x}(\bar{z})\cdot\bar{z})}_{\Psi} = 0. \tag{5.11}$$

The value of $\bar{z}$ that satisfies $\Phi(\bar{z}) = 0$ is the long-term equilibrium value. As shown in (5.11), following conventional practice, Φ is divided into two functions Γ

[16] Note that $\bar{x} = (1-\tau)\bar{z}^{\alpha-1} - \delta\tau\bar{z}^{\alpha+\epsilon} > 0$.

and Ψ.[17] Thus,

$$\Gamma(z) = \frac{\alpha}{\theta}(1-\tau)z^{\alpha-1} - \delta\tau z^{\alpha+\epsilon}. \tag{5.12}$$

Then, according to the sign of the first derivative of the endogenous time preference function, the function Ψ is one of the following two cases:

$$\begin{cases} \Psi(z) = \frac{1}{\theta} \cdot \rho(x(z) \cdot z) = \frac{1}{\theta}(a \times [x \cdot z] + \tilde{\rho}), & \text{for } \rho'(\cdot) > 0, \quad (5.13) \\ \Psi(z) = \frac{1}{\theta} \cdot \rho(x(z) \cdot z) = \frac{1}{\theta}\left(\frac{a}{[x \cdot z]} + \tilde{\rho}\right), & \text{for } \rho'(\cdot) < 0, \quad (5.14) \end{cases}$$

where a is a positive constant and $\tilde{\rho}$ is a lower (or upper) bound on the time preference. The specified functional form of (5.13) is the same as that used by Dioikitopoulos and Kalyvitis (2015) except for our H, which stands for public infrastructure; the feature whereby an increase in $C/H = x \cdot z$ increases ρ corresponds to the case of IMI. In contrast, (5.14) is derived from (5.13) and describes the case of DMI.

The number of intersections of these functions (Γ and Ψ) in the relevant space will determine the number of steady-state equilibria. Theoretically, multiple equilibria are possible, but we know beforehand that such solutions are unlikely to be economically meaningful. Therefore, herein we investigate the case in which the long-term steady-state equilibrium is determined uniquely.

Here, we show typical situations of single-equilibrium cases in Fig. 5.1 under the specification of (5.13) and Fig. 5.2 under the specification of (5.14).[18] The underlying exogenous parameter set is given in the upper part of Table 5.1. These values seem reasonable given those in the literature. For instance, as noted in Sect. 5.1, θ is one of the most fundamental parameters for dynamic general equilibrium models, and we set $\theta = 1.2$ on the basis of Benhabib et al. (1994), Barro et al. (1995), Ortigueira and Santos (1997), and others; also, $\alpha = 0.3$ is a standard value in the literature (Barro and Sala-i-Martin 2003; Jones 2020). However, after these two parameters, the others have no reliable standard values, so instead we set them while observing the actual condition of the steady-state equilibrium. In the lower part of Table 5.1, the values of the two endogenous variables $\bar{x}$ and $\bar{z}$, the rate of endogenously determined time preference ρ, and the growth rate of income g are presented for each case.

---

[17] In the following, because our study develops essentially given a steady-state situation, $\bar{x}$ and $\bar{z}$ are written as x and z, respectively, for simplicity.

[18] From Fig. 5.1, we find that Γ is a strictly decreasing and convex function in the (z, Γ) plane and that Ψ has a maximum value and an inverse U shape in the (z, Ψ) plane. From Fig. 5.2, we also find that Ψ has a minimum value and a U shape in the (z, Ψ) plane (Γ is the same as in Fig. 5.1).

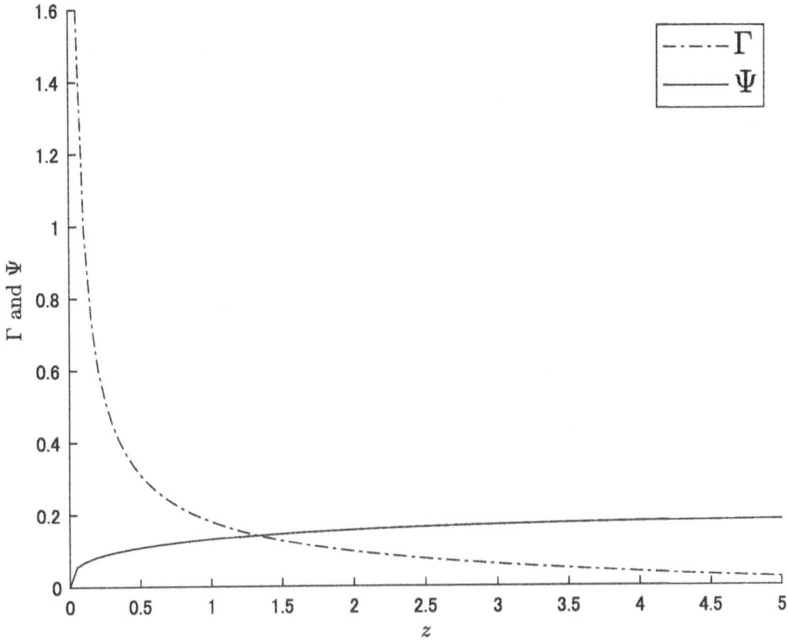

Fig. 5.1 Single-equilibrium case under (5.13) (IMI)

Table 5.1 Exogenous parameters and endogenous variables in the typical cases

α	θ	τ	δ	ϵ	a	$\tilde{\rho}$
0.3	1.2	0.2	0.1	0.15	0.2	0.001
IMI						
$\bar{x}$	$\bar{z}$	ρ	g			
0.6324	1.3303	0.1693	0.0227			
DMI						
$\bar{x}$	$\bar{z}$	ρ	g			
0.9914	0.7182	0.2819	0.0172			

For the case of IMI (Fig. 5.1), the equilibrium growth rate in the long-term steady state is a favorable value of around 2.3%; also, the values of the endogenous variables and the rate of time preference are not particularly problematic. For the case of DMI (Fig. 5.2), the performance of the unique equilibrium is also favorable in economically meaningful situations.

Based on the basic model under the alternative specifications of IMI and DMI, the equilibrium dynamics are examined closely in Sect. 5.4.

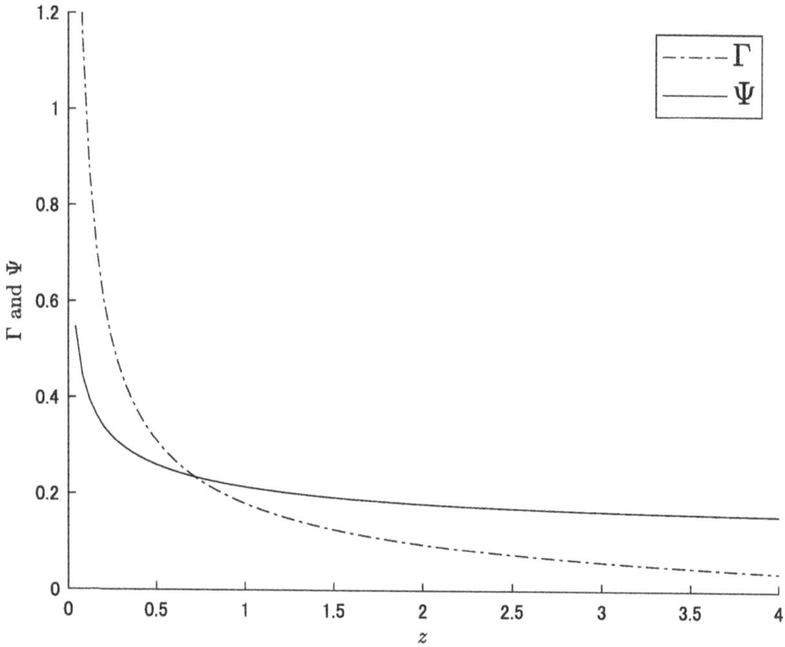

Fig. 5.2 Single-equilibrium case under (5.14) (DMI)

5.3.2 *Verification of Numerical Results*

Although the results obtained above show good numerical performance, they are contrary to expectations in an important aspect, i.e., the long-term growth rate is lower in the DMI case. Numerical analysis can occasionally yield such paradoxical results because of various influencing factors, but it is not wasteful to examine the causes.

In a situation in which agents make decisions in a dynamic environment, patient consumers should endure their current consumption while increasing their savings in the hope of more fruit in the future. Therefore, income growth rate is expected to be higher under DMI (which embodies that situation) than under IMI. One way to obtain results that are consistent with this expectation is to adjust and improve the exogenous parameters in the time preference function. Dioikitopoulos and Kalyvitis (2015) used a larger value of the positive constant (i.e., a) than ours.[19] Until now, this parameter has not been explained specifically, but along with $\tilde{\rho}$, it should reflect differences in individual, regional, and national attributions on preference. Demonstrating our current understanding of this issue is far beyond the present

[19] Parameter a herein is denoted as b by Dioikitopoulos and Kalyvitis (2015), and the benchmark value that they use is 0.5.

Table 5.2 Another numerical example

α	θ	τ	δ	ϵ	a	$\tilde{\rho}$
0.3	1.2	0.2	0.1	0.15	0.07	0.001
IMI						
$\bar{x}$	$\bar{z}$	ρ	g			
0.3382	2.9975	0.0720	0.0328			
DMI						
$\bar{x}$	$\bar{z}$	ρ	g			
0.3319	3.0682	0.0697	0.0331			

scope, but it seems very important; therefore, we consider it as an issue that should be addressed in the near future, taking into account the results of empirical studies based on equivalent field experiments.[20] For now, let us set a small value for a by changing its value from 0.2 to 0.07; the other parameters are the same as before. Table 5.2 summarizes the results.

With the present parameter set, the long-term growth rate is indeed higher under DMI than under IMI, and the low rate of endogenous time preference contributes to this result. As noted before, the situation in Table 5.2 is achieved by patient agents exhibiting less-myopic-saving behavior. Therefore, this case can be regarded as an accurate description of dynamic optimizing behavior under endogenous time preference.

5.4 Equilibrium Dynamics

To examine the global dynamics and stability of the equilibrium, we perform a phase-diagram analysis in which we use a converted two-dimensional system. From (5.9) and (5.10), the loci $\dot{x} = 0$ and $\dot{z} = 0$ can be derived (Figs. 5.5 and 5.6 in Appendix show the shapes and positional relation of the two loci). From (5.9), we obtain

$$\frac{\partial(\dot{x}/x)}{\partial x} = 1 - \frac{\rho'(\cdot)}{\theta} z. \tag{5.15}$$

We find that the sign of $\rho'(\cdot)$ is important in (5.15). Although the motion of x is not determined at this point, the following can be stated. If $\partial(\dot{x}/x)/\partial x > 0$, then x increases above the $\dot{x} = 0$ locus ($\dot{x} > 0$) and decreases below it ($\dot{x} < 0$). Oppositely, if $\partial(\dot{x}/x)/\partial x < 0$, then x decreases above the $\dot{x} = 0$ locus ($\dot{x} < 0$) and increases below it ($\dot{x} > 0$). As will be shown later, depending on the status of (5.15), different dynamic patterns can occur in this model.

[20] For existing empirical studies, see Dioikitopoulos and Kalyvitis (2015) and Sect. 5.1 of the present chapter, for instance.

Now, it is quite interesting that the dynamics of the model are characterized by the vital variable (z) and the prime parameters (ρ and θ) for the converted model. As with standard dynamic general equilibrium models, the importance of the intertemporal elasticity of substitution and the rate of time preference cannot be overemphasized.

Next, from (5.10), we have

$$\frac{\partial(\dot{z}/z)}{\partial z} = \underbrace{(\alpha - 1)(1-\tau)z^{\alpha-2}}_{-} - \underbrace{\delta\tau(\alpha+\epsilon)z^{\alpha+\epsilon-1}}_{+} < 0. \tag{5.16}$$

From the result indicated by (5.16), we can confirm that z decreases above the $\dot{z} = 0$ locus ($\dot{z} < 0$) and increases below it ($\dot{z} > 0$). This is always true in our model.

From the above considerations, the following four cases (Propositions 5.1–5.4) can occur depending on the property of (5.15).

Proposition 5.1 *If $\rho'(\cdot) = 0$, then $\partial(\dot{x}/x)/\partial x = 1 > 0$ is obtained. This implies that the model exhibits saddle-path stability.*

This corresponds to the case of exogenously given time preference, which is used frequently in standard dynamic general equilibrium models (e.g., Cass 1965; Barro et al. 1995). The typical situation is shown in Fig. 5.3, which shows the global dynamics corresponding to the situation in Proposition 5.1. The uniquely determined common long-term steady-state equilibrium exhibits saddle-point stability. For example, an economy starting from $z(0) = K(0)/H(0)$ heads for the equilibrium while steadily increasing z and steadily decreasing x. This is considered to be typical for the process of economic development brought about with capital accumulation.

Proposition 5.2 *If $\rho'(\cdot) < 0$, then $\partial(\dot{x}/x)/\partial x > 0$ is obtained. This implies that the model exhibits saddle-path stability.*

Fig. 5.3 Saddle-path stability

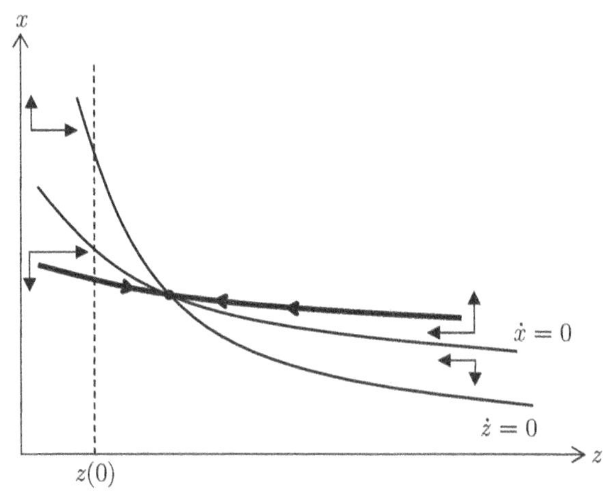

If the agents' time preference is characterized by DMI, then the long-term equilibrium of the model is a saddle point. The typical situation is also shown in Fig. 5.3. For example, a well-known model whose long-term equilibrium is a saddle point under DMI is that by Das (2003).

Of particular interest are the following two cases.

Proposition 5.3 *If* $\rho'(\cdot) > 0$ *and* $\rho'(\cdot)z/\theta < 1$, *then* $\partial(\dot{x}/x)/\partial x > 0$ *is obtained. This implies that the model exhibits saddle-path stability.*

If the agents' time preference is characterized by IMI and the intertemporal elasticity of substitution is relatively small, then the model exhibits saddle-path stability. Even if the agents are impatient, provided that they tend to dislike fluctuations in consumption over time, the long-term equilibrium is determined uniquely. In view of the literature, this seems to be a reasonable case. For example, Obstfeld (1990) showed the stability of equilibrium under the *Uzawa assumption*. The typical situation is also shown in Fig. 5.3.

Proposition 5.4 *If* $\rho'(\cdot) > 0$ *and* $\rho'(\cdot)z/\theta > 1$, *then* $\partial(\dot{x}/x)/\partial x < 0$ *is obtained. This implies that the equilibrium path toward the steady-state equilibrium is indeterminate.*

This result is in contrast to that obtained in Proposition 5.3; if the agents' time preference is characterized by IMI and the intertemporal elasticity of substitution is relatively large, then the equilibrium trajectory is indeterminate (i.e., a sink).[21] Nishimura and Shimomura (2002) obtained a similar result through local stability analysis. Roughly speaking, if there are many agents who are impatient and willing to accept great fluctuations in their economic status, then there are various possibilities until the economy reaches long-term equilibrium. This is consistent with the situation in previous studies in which indeterminacy occurs. The typical situation is shown in Fig. 5.4. Even if the economy starts from the same level of z (i.e., $z(0)$), different consumption levels (i.e., different x) can be selected, and the economy then reaches a common long-term steady-state equilibrium through various growth paths. In this process, the business cycle happens endogenously without relying on exogenous shocks.

The above considerations confirm clearly that the global dynamics of the model depend on the properties of the introduced endogenous time preference function. At the same time, it was found that another preference parameter, i.e., the magnitude of intertemporal elasticity of substitution, is also important, albeit less so. Table 5.3 summarizes the obtained results.

The results in Table 5.3 seem to be interesting. A major drawback in assuming DMI is that it is considered to be unfavorable in terms of dynamic stability, and IMI is arguably often assumed despite doubts from intuitive grounds and empirical results (Das 2003). A drawback often pointed out about DMI is that it destabilizes

[21] That is, there exists a continuum of equilibrium paths converging to a common steady state.

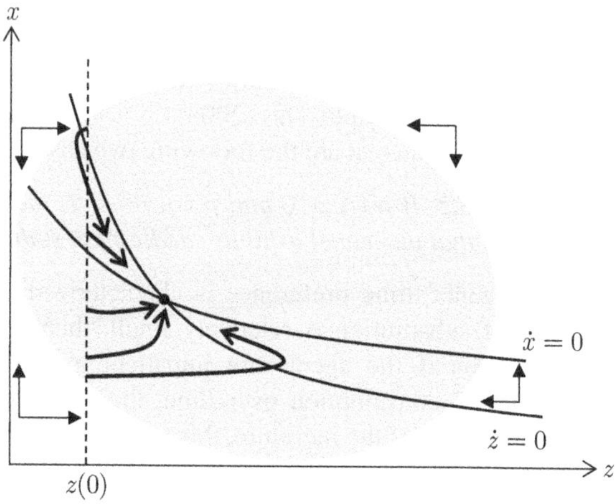

Fig. 5.4 Indeterminacy of equilibrium paths

Table 5.3 Four results for equilibrium dynamics

Time preference	Condition	Property of equilibrium dynamics
Exogenous	$\rho'(\cdot)=0$	Saddle path
DMI	$\rho'(\cdot)<0$	Saddle path
IMI	$\frac{\rho'(\cdot)}{\theta}z<1$	Saddle path
IMI	$\frac{\rho'(\cdot)}{\theta}z>1$	Indeterminate (Sink)

the dynamic system of the model; in other words, richer consumers are patient and more willing to save and invest in the future, which makes them even richer.

In this model, however, the long-term equilibrium exhibits saddle-path stability under DMI, and instead a dynamically interesting phenomenon (i.e., indeterminacy) arises under IMI. The fact that impatient consumers cause various processes of economic development is, in a sense, reasonable and an issue to be explored further.

5.5 Concluding Remarks

Herein, we constructed a growth model that includes public infrastructure and related external effects, and we introduced into it an endogenous time preference function that depends on socially determined factors. We then clarified the dynamic properties of the model both analytically and numerically. Two notable results can be pointed out. First, the steady-state equilibrium exhibits saddle-path stability when marginal impatience declines with increasing C/H; this is preferable both intuitively and from empirical results and is deemed reasonable. Second, when marginal impatience rises with increasing C/H, the equilibrium path toward the uniquely determined steady-state equilibrium may be indeterminate, depending on the preference-related parameters. In an economy composed of agents who make relatively myopic decisions, we find that the equilibrium dynamics of the economy *may* fluctuate, which is a very interesting result.

When an endogenous time preference function is introduced into a dynamic model, how it relates to interesting phenomena such as indeterminacy and multiple equilibria is often discussed. However, many unknowns remain, including the specification of functional form. Consequently, the role of preference formation in macroeconomic dynamics is an important issue that needs to be explored in detail in future research.

Acknowledgments The author thanks Professor Emeritus Shuetsu Takahashi and Dr. Mitsuyoshi Yanagihara, Dr. Tsuyoshi Shinozaki, Dr. Hiroaki Masuhara, and seminar participants at several online meetings on *Modern Macroeconomics with Historical Perspectives* for helpful comments and suggestions. The author also gratefully acknowledges the Japan Society for the Promotion of Science (JSPS KAKENHI Grant Numbers JP15K03448 and JP21K01507) and the Japan Center for Economic Research for financial support. Any errors are the responsibility of the author.

Appendix

Supplementary Figures

Figures 5.5 and 5.6 show the $\dot{x} = 0$ and $\dot{z} = 0$ loci under the specification of (5.13) and (5.14), respectively. In both cases, we use the same parameter set of $(\alpha, \theta, \tau, \delta, \epsilon, a, \tilde{\rho}) = (0.3, 1.2, 0.2, 0.1, 0.15, 0.2, 0.001)$.

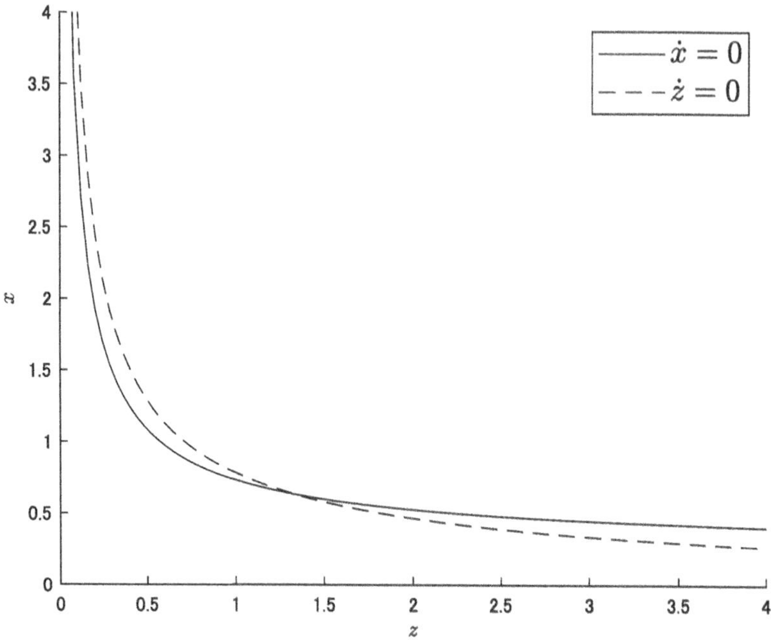

Fig. 5.5 Numerical example of positional relation of $\dot{x} = 0$ and $\dot{z} = 0$ loci under (5.13)

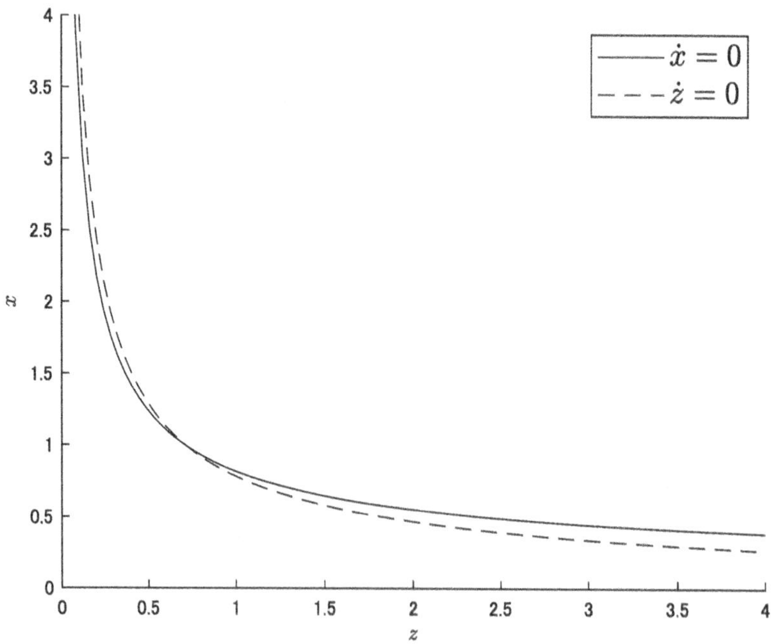

Fig. 5.6 Numerical example of positional relation of $\dot{x} = 0$ and $\dot{z} = 0$ loci under (5.14)

References

Agénor PR (2008) Health and infrastructure in a model of endogenous growth. J Macroecon 30(4):1407–1422
Agénor PR (2010) A theory of infrastructure-led development. J Econ Dyn Control 34(5):932–950
Barro RJ, Mankiw NG, Sala-i-Martin X (1995) Capital mobility in neoclassical models of growth. Amer Econ Rev 85(1):103–115
Barro RJ, Sala-i-Martin X (2003) Economic growth, 2nd edn. MIT Press, Cambridge
Becker G, Mulligan C (1997) The endogenous determination of time preference. Quarterly J Econ 112(3):729–758
Benhabib J, Perli R, Xie D (1994) Monopolistic competition, indeterminacy and growth. Ricerche Econ 48(4):279–298
Bian Y, Meng Q (2004) Preferences, endogenous discount rate, and indeterminacy in a small open economy model. Econ Lett 84(3):315–322
Bouché S (2017) Learning by doing, endogenous discounting and economic development. J Mathemat Econ 73:34–43
Cagetti M (2003) Wealth accumulation over the life cycle and precautionary savings. J Business Econ Statist 21(3):339–353
Cass D (1965) Optimum growth in an aggregative model of capital accumulation. Rev Econ Stud 32(3):233–240
Chu H, Lai CC, Liao CH (2016) A note on environment-dependent time preferences. Macroecon Dyn 20(6):1652–1667
Cui X, Gong L, Yang J, Zou HF (2008) Marshallian time preferences and monetary non-neutrality. Econ Modell 25(6):1196–1205
Dai M (2007) Endogenous wealth-depending time preference and fiscal policy in open economy. Econ Bull 8(7):1–7
Das M (2003) Optimal growth with decreasing marginal impatience. J Econ Dyn Control 27(10):1881–1898
Dioikitopoulos E, Kalyvitis S, (2010) Endogenous time preference and public policy: growth and fiscal implication. Macroecon Dyn 14(S2):243–257
Dioikitopoulos E, Kalyvitis S, (2015) Optimal fiscal policy with endogenous time preference. J Public Econ Theory 17(6):848–873
Drugeon JP (1998) A model with endogenously determined cycles, discounting and growth. Econ Theory 12(2):349–369
Epstein LG (1987) A simple dynamic general equilibrium model. J Econ Theory 41(1):68–95
Epstein LG, Hynes JA (1983) The rate of time preference and dynamic economic analysis. J Political Econ 91(4):611–635
Falk A, Becker A, Dohmen T, Enke B, Huffman D, Sunde U (2018) Global evidence on economic preferences. Q J Econ 133(4):1645–1692
Fisher I (1907) The rate of interest. MacMillan, London
Gong L (2006) Endogenous time preference, inflation, and capital accumulation. J Econ 87(3):241–255
Gourinchas PO, Parker JA (2002) Consumption over the life cycle. Econometrica 70(1):47–89
Hardardottir H (2017) Long term stability of time preferences and the role of the macroeconomic situation. J Econ Psychol 60:21–36
Harrison GW, Lau MI, Williams MB (2002) Estimating individual discount rates in Denmark: a field experiment. Amer Econ Rev 92(5):1606–1617
Hirose K, Ikeda S (2008) On decreasing marginal impatience. Jpn Econ Rev 59(3):259–274
Hirose K, Ikeda S (2015) Decreasing marginal impatience destabilizes multi-country economies. Econ Modell 50:237–244
Hosoya K (2016) Recovery from natural disaster: a numerical investigation based on the convergence approach. Econ Modell 55:410–420

Hosoya K (2017) Accounting for growth disparity: Lucas's framework revisited. Rev Develop Econ 21(3):874–887
Hosoya K (2019) Importance of a victim-oriented recovery policy after major disasters. Econ Modell 78:1–10
Hosoya K (2022) Endogenous time preference and infrastructure-led growth with an unexpected numerical example. Port Econ J forthcoming
Jones CI (2020) Macroeconomics, 5th edn. W.W. Norton, New York
Kam E (2005) A note on time preference and the Tobin effect. Econ Lett 89(1):127–132
Kam E, Missios P (2003) Wealth effects in a cash-in-advance economy. Econ Bull 5(2):1–7
Kawagishi T (2012) Endofenous time preference, investment externalities, and equilibrium indeterminacy. Math Soc Sci 64(3):234–241
Kawagishi T (2014) Investment for patience in an endogenous growth model. Econ Modell 42:508–515
Kawagishi T, Mino K (2012) Time preference and long-run growth: the role of patience capital. Econ Bull 32(4):3243–3249
Lawrance EC (1991) Poverty and the rate of time preference: evidence from panel data. J Polit. Econ 99(1):54–77
Lucas RE Jr (1988) On the mechanics of economic development. J Monetary Econ 22(1):3–42
Lucas RE Jr, Stokey N (1984) Optimal growth with many consumers. J Econ Theory 32(1):139–171
Meng Q (2006) Impatience and equilibrium indeterminacy. J Econ Dyn Control 30(12):2671–2692
Nakamoto Y (2009) Consumption externalities with endogenous time preference. J Econ 96(1):41–62
Nishimura K, Shimomura K (2002) Indeterminacy in a dynamic small open economy. J Econ Dyn Control 27(2):271–281
Obstfeld M (1990) Intertemporal dependence, impatience, and dynamics. J Monet Econ 26(1):45–75
Ogaki M, Atkeson A (1997) Rate of time preference, intertemporal elasticity of substitution, and level of wealth. Rev Econ Stat 79(4):564–572
Ortigueira S, Santos MS (1997) On the speed of convergence in endogenous growth models. Amer Econ Rev 87(3):383–399
Palivos T, Wang P, Zhang J (1997) On the existence of balanced growth equilibrium. Int Econ Rev 38(1):205–224
Raurich X (2003) Government spending, local indeterminacy and tax structure. Economica 70(280):639–653
Sarkar J (2007) Growth dynamics in a model of endogenous time preference. Int Rev Econ Financ 16(4):528–542
Strulik H (2012) Patience and prosperity. J Econ Theory 147(1):336–352
Tamai T (2019) A note on fiscal policy, indeterminacy, and endogenous time preference. Econ Bull 39(1):615–625
Tanaka T, Camerer CF, Nguyen Q (2010) Risk and time preferences: linking experimental and household survey data from Vietnam. Amer Econ Rev 100(1):557–571
Uzawa H (1968) Time preference, the consumption function, and optimum asset holdings. In: Wolfe JN (ed) Value, capital and growth: papers in honour of Sir John Hicks. Edinburgh University Press, Edinburgh, pp 485–504
Vella E, Dioikitopoulos EV, Kalyvitis S (2015) Green spending reforms, growth, and welfare with endogenous subjective discounting. Macroecon Dyn 19(6):1240–1260
Yanase A (2011) Impatience, pollution, and indeterminacy. J Econ Dyn Control 35(10):1789–1799

Chapter 6
Intergenerational Inequalities and Policy Options for Achieving Generational Balance in Japan

Yasuhito Sato

Abstract Using the methodology of generational accounting, this chapter estimates intergenerational inequality (generational imbalance) in Japan and compares policy options for restoring generational balance. We use the latest dataset to develop generational accounting for the base year of 2019 in Japan and discuss the policy options needed to restore generational balance. The results showed that the generational imbalance in Japan remains large, but has been decreasing over the last decade, and that restoring generational balance is possible but will require considerable additional net tax burdens. We also found a conflict of interest between younger and future generations and elderly generations regarding preferable policy measures.

Keywords Generational accounting · Intergenerational inequality · Generational balance · Generational conflicts of interest

JEL Classification: E62, H60

6.1 Introduction

This chapter aims to estimate intergenerational inequality (generational imbalance) in Japan by using generational accounting methods. It then compares policy options for restoring generational balance.

Auerbach et al. (1991) developed the method of generational accounting as an alternative to annual cash flow accounting, which fails to reflect the intertemporal stance of fiscal policy. Generational accounting evaluates fiscal policy from a

Y. Sato (✉)
Faculty of Economics, Tohoku Gakuin University, Sendai, Miyagi, Japan
e-mail: yasuhito@mail.tohoku-gakuin.ac.jp

S. Takahashi et al. (eds.), *Modern Macroeconomics with Historical Perspectives*, New Frontiers in Regional Science: Asian Perspectives 67,
https://doi.org/10.1007/978-981-99-1067-0_6

medium- to long-term perspective, and views the impact of demographics on government debt as a matter of generational imbalance.[1]

Generational accounting is a useful tool for quantitatively assessing the imbalance of benefits and burdens between generations. There are many previous studies, including those by Auerbach et al. (1991, 1992a, b, 1994, 1995); Cutler (1993); Kotlikoff (1993, 2003); Boll et al. (1994); Haveman (1994); Diamond (1996); Auerbach et al. (1999); Bonin (2001); and Gokhale and Smetters (2003), among others.[2] In addition, in some countries such as the Netherlands and Norway, governments have used generational accounting estimates as a basis for fiscal management, and estimates were also made in the United Kingdom and the United States for a while (Anderson and Sheppard, 2009).

Several such studies have been conducted in Japan. Previous studies on generational accounting have shown that generational imbalances in Japan are very large. For instance, Auerbach et al. (1999) conducted generational accounting for 17 countries using data from 1995 as the base year, and found that Japan had the largest generational imbalance. Yoshida (2006) also estimated generational accounting for the year 2000 and showed that Japan's generational imbalance was even larger. Although recent studies (Miyazato 2015; Mizutani 2016; Sato 2013; Shimasawa et al. 2014) have been conducted since then, they cannot be directly compared owing to different estimation assumptions and other factors, studies indicate that Japan's generational imbalance remains very large.

In this chapter, we use data from the Cabinet Office's Annual Report on National Accounts for 2019 to estimate generational accounts and compare policy options for achieving generational balance.

The remainder of this paper is organized as follows. Section 6.2 explains generational accounting methodology and describes the data used in this study. Section 6.3 presents the estimation results. Section 6.3 then compares the estimated results with historical estimates to confirm the extent of the generational imbalance in Japan today. Section 6.4 compares the policy measures to eliminate generational imbalances and restore generational balances. Section 6.5 summarizes the conclusions of this study and presents the remaining issues.

[1] Generational imbalance refers to the difference in net tax burden—taxes (burden) paid minus transfers (benefit) received—between the current and future generations.

[2] Cutler (1993), Haveman (1994), and Diamond (1996) are the critical surveys on the underlying theoretical and empirical issues. Auerbach et al. (1994) and Kotlikoff (1997) are replies to these studies.

6.2 The Methodology of Generational Accounting

6.2.1 *The Model*

This study uses generational accounting, developed by Auerbach et al. (1991). Generational accounting is based on government's intertemporal budget constraints, under which current or future generations bear current net government debt and future government spending.

The government's intertemporal budget constraint is shown in (6.1):

$$\sum_{s=0}^{D} N_{t,t-s} + \sum_{s=1}^{\infty} N_{t,t+s} = \sum_{s=t}^{\infty} G_s(1+r)^{(t-s)} - W_t. \tag{6.1}$$

Equation (6.1) shows that current and future generations' future net tax payments must be sufficient, in present value, to cover the present value of future government consumption, and initial government debt.

The first term on the left-hand side of (6.1) is the present value of the remaining lifetime net tax payments. $N_{t,\, t-s}$ is the generational account of the generation born in year $t - s$. *where* D denotes the maximum life expectancy. The second term on the left-hand side represents the generational account of future generation. In other words, it is the generational account for the generation born after year t, the base year of the estimation. The first term on the right-hand side is the sum of the discounted present value of future government consumption G. r is the discount rate (interest rate). The second term on the right-hand side is the government's net wealth (assets minus liabilities) as base year t of the estimation.

Generational account $N_{t,\, k}$ is then defined by (6.2):

$$N_{t,k} = \sum_{s=\max(t,k)}^{k+D} T_{s,k} P_{s,k} (1+r)^{(t-s)}. \tag{6.2}$$

In (6.2), $T_{s,\, k}$ is the average net tax payment to the government in year s by the generation born in year k. $P_{s,\, k}$ is the number of survivors in year s of the generation cohort born in year k.

Net tax payments $T_{s,\, k}$ are defined as the difference between each individual's tax and social insurance contributions to the government, $\tau_{s,\, k}$, and the benefits from government transfer payments, such as social security benefits, $b_{s,\, k}$, that is, $T_{t,\, k} = \tau_{s,\, k} - b_{s,\, k}$. Generational accounts are forward-looking because past net taxes are not included.

6.2.1.1 The Fiscal Burden Facing Future Generation

The generational accounts for future generations, that is, the fiscal burden to be borne by future generations, are calculated as a residual from the government's intertemporal budget constraint.

First, the base year's individual benefits and burdens for each age group are estimated. Based on this, individual benefits and burdens for each age group in the future were determined and discounted to the base year value to estimate the net future burden for each age group on the current generation. Furthermore, the net tax burden on future generations is determined to satisfy the government's intertemporal budget constraints.

For the value of future government consumption G, we assume that it changes at the same rate as the taxes and transfers included in net tax payments, that is, G grows at the rate of productivity given by g in the future. Thus, since the net wealth of the government is known, we can determine the sum of the generational accounts of the current generation and the present value of government consumption, and use it as a residual to determine the sum of the generational accounts of future generations.

6.2.1.2 Indicator of Generational Imbalance

The difference between the lifetime net tax burden of the current (newborn) generation and the lifetime net tax burden of future generations, as described above, is the generational imbalance in generational accounting. Expressing the lifetime net tax burden per person as $n_{t,\,k}(=N_{t,\,k}/P_{t,\,k})$, generational imbalance (GI) is expressed by Eq. (6.3):

$$\mathrm{GI} = \left(n_{t,t+1} - n_{t,t}\right) / n_{t,t}. \tag{6.3}$$

A positive generational imbalance (GI > 0) indicates that sufficient future government revenue (burden) is insufficient to finance future government expenditures (benefits). This implies that current policies are not sustainable.

6.2.2 *Assumptions Underlying Generational Accounting Calculations*

This section describes the assumptions underlying generational accounting calculations. To estimate generational accounts for each age group, future taxes, transfers, government spending, and population projections are needed. We also need data on the government's initial net wealth—its assets minus its explicit debt—in year t and assumptions about the discount rate.

6.2.2.1 Fiscal Data

This study used data from the Cabinet Office's Annual Report on National Accounts for 2019 (Benchmark Year Revision of 2015). This study considers government revenues as individual contributions and government expenditures as individual benefits based on income and outlay accounts and capital and financial accounts of national accounts for 2019.

Table 6.1 shows the government revenues and expenditures for 2019. In this study, data from the National Survey of Family Income and Expenditure and other sources, such as the Population Census and Estimates of National Medical Care Expenditure, were used to distribute the items shown in Table 6.1, for each age group.[3]

The structure of the benefits and burdens by age group in 2019 is shown in Fig. 6.1. Figure 6.1 shows that the burden for each age group increased rapidly after the 20s, with peaks in the 40s and 50s, while the benefits were concentrated mainly in the age group of 60 and older.

6.2.2.2 Growth and Discount Rates

The economic growth rate is set in this study based on the Cabinet Office's Economic and Fiscal Projections for Medium-to-Long-Term Analyses. This projection assumes that a real economic growth rate of 2.0% will be achieved in the medium to long term in the economic growth achieved case, and 1.0% in the baseline case. In this study, the economic growth rate was assumed to be 1.5%, adopting an intermediate between the two cases of the Cabinet Office's economic and fiscal projections. We conducted a sensitivity analysis in three ways, 1.0%, 1.5%, and 2.0%.

The interest rate is used as the discount rate. In the long run, we set the interest rate as the growth rate plus the gap between the interest rate and the growth rate. The gap between the interest rate and growth rate is assumed to be 1.5% in the study by Masujima et al. (2009). We also conducted a sensitivity analysis in three ways, 1.0%, 1.5%, and 2.0%, with 1.5% as the center.

6.2.2.3 Population

As generational accounts are the net tax burden per capita converted to the present value, their value is affected by the size and age of each generation's population.

[3] The data obtained from the National Survey of Family Income and Expenditure are for households, not for individuals. It would be preferable to use individual-level data for estimation. However, individual-level data is not well developed in Japan. In addition, data on income and consumption expenditures by age group are only used to determine the relative distribution among generations. Therefore, household-level data are used in this study.

Table 6.1 Income and outlay of the general government in 2019

		(Billion yen)
	Outlay	Income
Income and outlay accounts		
Allocation of primary income account		
Property income, payable	8593.6	
Taxes on production and imports, receivable		46, 693.8
(less) Subsidies, payable	3005.3	
Property income, receivable		8140.3
Secondary distribution of income account		
Social benefits other than social transfers in kind, payable	68, 551.5	
Other current transfers, payable	73, 877.7	
Current taxes on income, wealth, etc., receivable		56, 594.2
Net social contributions, receivable		74, 054.9
Other current transfers, receivable		67, 879.3
Redistribution of income in kind account		
Social transfers in kind, payable	68, 357.4	
Use of income account		
Actual final consumption (actual collective consumption)	42, 910.7	
Capital and financial accounts		
Gross fixed capital formation	21, 737.7	
(less) consumption of fixed capital	18, 975.2	
Changes in inventories	−72.7	
Purchases of land, net	1609.6	
Capital transfers, receivable		3831.8
(less) Capital transfers, payable	3832.8	
	273, 428.4	257, 194.3

Source: Annual Report on National Accounts for 2019 (Benchmark Year revision of 2015), The Cabinet Office, Government of Japan

Population size is relevant for calculating the net tax amount needed to finance government spending and service debt. In Japan, the population of the future generations is expected to decline. Fewer people bear the total net taxes needed to finance government spending and service their debt. In addition, most taxes and transfers are age-specific or closely related to age. Thus, the population's age structure (population structure) has a decisive impact on the absolute net tax amount.

For population trends, this study, like many previous studies, used medium estimates (medium fertility assumptions with medium mortality) of the National Institute of Population and Social Security Research's "Population Projections for Japan (2017)." As these projections began with the 2015 Population Census and continued until 2115, we assumed that the population would be in a steady (constant) state after 2115.

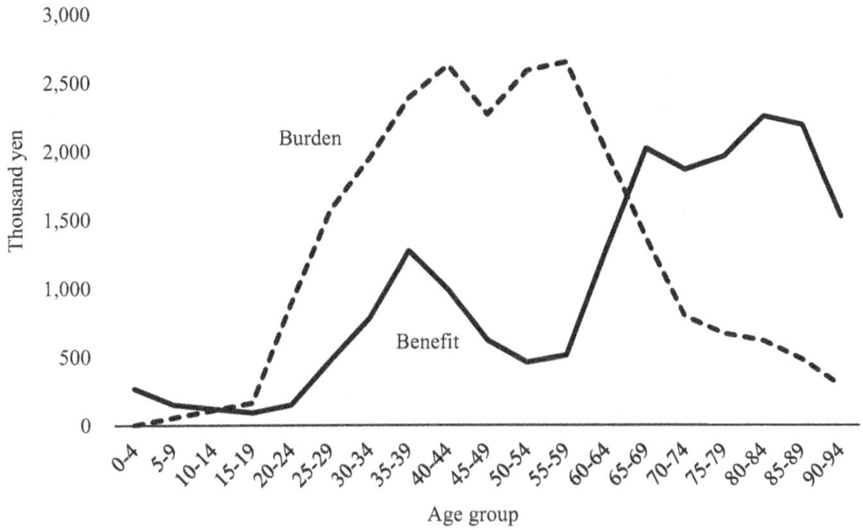

Fig. 6.1 Benefit/burden structure of 2019. (Source: Author's calculations)

6.2.2.4 Reflect the Impact of Changes in the System on Generational Accounting

In the generational accounting method, institutional and policy changes that have already been legally determined and are certain to be implemented are reflected in the estimates. In this study, macroeconomic indexing, introduced in the 2004 revision of the public pension system, and the impact of the consumption tax rate increase are reflected in the estimates.

The Revision of 2004 Public Pension System

Japan's public pension system experienced several major reforms in 2004. This reform introduced an insurance premium-level fixation method. In addition, a benefit-level adjustment mechanism called macroeconomic indexation is introduced. Macroeconomic indexation is a mechanism for automatically adjusting benefit levels within the limits of financial resources to ensure long-term balance between pension benefits and contributions. The objectives of macroeconomic indexation are to (1) prevent excessive premium burdens on the working-age population and (2) ensure future benefit levels.

Under macroeconomic indexing, during the period in which it is applied (benefit-level adjustment period), the benefit level of pensions reflects a decrease in the number of insured persons and an increase in average life expectancy. That is, the benefit level is reduced by this amount. After macroeconomic indexing, the revision rate returns to its original value.

According to the 2019 Actuarial Valuation by the Ministry of Health, Labour and Welfare, the income replacement rate, an indicator of the level of public pension benefits, will decline by approximately 20% in the standard case (Case III) owing to benefit-level adjustments caused by macroeconomic indexing.

In this study, we refer to Yoshida (2006) and reflect in our estimates the assumption that future pension benefit levels will be suppressed in Case III of the 2019 Actuarial Valuation.

Increase in the Consumption Tax Rate

Japan's consumption tax, a type of VAT, was introduced in 1989 at a rate of 3%. The tax rate subsequently increased to 5% in 1997 and 8% in 2014. Subsequently, it increased to 10% in October 2019.

In this study, the 8% tax rate was applied until September 2019, and the estimates reflect an increase in the 10% tax rate from October 2019 onward.[4]

6.3 Findings: Basic Results and Comparisons

6.3.1 Generational Accounting for 2019

This section presents generational accounting for the base year 2019, estimated based on the above preparations. The estimation results are presented in Fig. 6.2.

Figure 6.2 shows the generational accounts—the (remaining) lifetime net tax burden—by age group as of 2019. FG indicates future generations not born in the base year. Generational accounts are typically negative for the elderly generation and positive for the younger generation.[5] This is because the elderly can expect to receive, on average, more transfers over their remaining lifetime than they pay taxes. In contrast, young people's net tax-paying years are directly ahead of them, and their net transfer-receiving years are many years in the future.

[4] The reduced tax rate system was introduced at the same time as when the consumption tax rate was raised to 10%. According to the newspaper at the time of the introduction of the reduced tax rate, the introduction of the reduced tax rate would reduce tax revenues by approximately 1 trillion yen annually. If the decrease in tax revenues increases the annual budget deficit, it is expected to cause an increase in future government debt and increase the burden on future generations. This, however, was not considered in this study.

[5] Note that the generational accounts for different living cohorts are not comparable. Only the generational accounts for future generations and newborn generation can be compared because in these cases the generational accounts are computed over full life cycles.

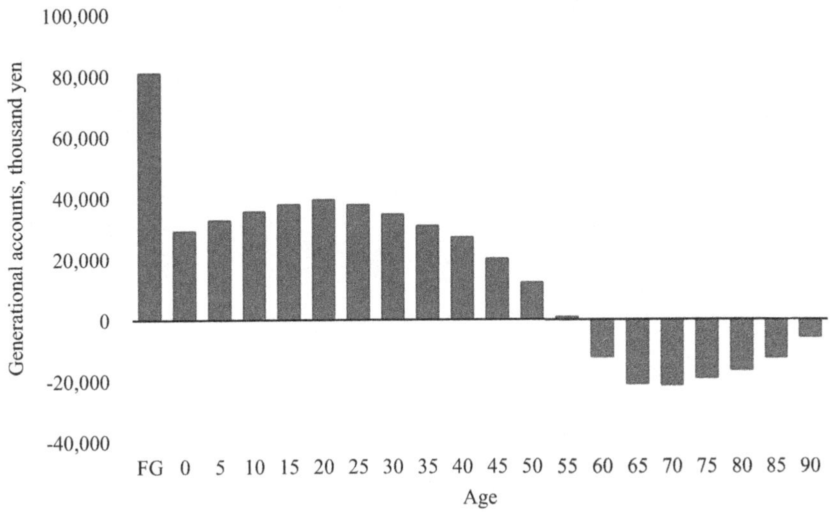

Fig. 6.2 Generational accounting for 2019. Note: The growth rate is assumed to be 1.5%, and the gap between the interest rate and growth rate is 1.5%. FG stands for "future generations". (Source: Author's calculations)

As a result, the lifetime net tax burden of the generation born in 2019 (the zero-year-old generation; newborn generation) was approximately 29.05 million yen, and the lifetime net tax burden of the generation born in the future (the future generation) was approximately 80.96 million yen. This means that future generations will face a lifetime net tax burden about 2.8 times that of current generations. Thus, the generational imbalance is 178.7%, and the absolute generational imbalance is 51.91 million yen.

6.3.1.1 Sensitivity Analysis

As mentioned, this study estimated generational accounting, assuming an economic growth rate of 1.5% and an interest rate growth rate differential of 1.5%. Because the estimation results of generational accounting depend on these assumptions, their validity is problematic. Therefore, a sensitivity analysis is conducted using multiple economic growth and discount rates (interest rates).

Table 6.2 shows the estimated results of generational accounting when the economic and interest rate growth rate gaps are 1.0% and 2.0%, respectively, based on an economic growth rate of 1.5% and an interest rate growth rate gap of 1.5%.

According to the sensitivity analysis results, the value of generational imbalance is affected by the economic growth rate and gap between the interest rate and growth rate settings. When interest rates are held constant, higher economic growth rates increase the net tax burden on each generation. This is because a higher rate of

Table 6.2 Sensitivity analysis

Growth rate	1.0%			1.5%			2.0%		
The gap between the interest rate and growth rate	1.0%	1.5%	2.0%	1.0%	1.5%	2.0%	1.0%	1.5%	2.0%
(Interest rate)	(2.0%)	(2.5%)	(3.0%)	(2.5%)	(3.0%)	(3.5%)	(3.0%)	(3.5%)	(4.0%)
Net tax burden (thousand yen)									
Current generation (age zero)	33,370.0	28,553.8	24,244.8	34,017.6	29,045.8	24,627.2	34,058.3	29,107.5	24,703.0
Future generation	87,026.4	81,631.2	78,804.9	86,566.8	80,957.4	78,023.3	86,582.4	81,010.1	78,083.6
Generational imbalance									
Percentage	160.8%	185.9%	225.0%	154.5%	178.7%	216.8%	154.2%	178.3%	216.1%
Thousand yen	53,656.5	53,077.3	54,560.1	52,549.3	51,911.6	53,396.1	52,524.1	51,902.6	53,380.7

Source: Author's calculations

economic growth increases the tax burden and pension benefits, but pension benefits are discounted more than the tax burden because they occur later; thus, the net tax burden is higher. In addition, when the economic growth rate is held constant, higher interest rates (a larger gap between the interest rate and growth rate) reduce the net tax burden on each generation. This is because future values will be more discounted; thus, the net tax burden in the discounted present value will be smaller.

We note that when the gap between the interest rate and the growth rate is held constant, the net tax burden in terms of monetary value is different, but the percentage imbalances between the current (newborn) and future generations are close to each other and stable.

6.3.2 Comparison with Generational Accounts for 2010 and 2015

In this section, we develop net tax profiles for 2010 and 2015, estimate generational accounts, and compare them with the 2019 generational accounts.

Generational accounts for 2010 and 2015 were estimated independently under the following assumptions. The same data were used for the 2019 generational accounts for the allocation basis for proportionally distributing government revenues and expenditures by age group and for future population projections. For macroeconomic indexing, it was assumed that benefit-level adjustments would be made through FY2038 for the 2010 generational accounts and through FY2043 for the 2015 generational accounts, based on the actuarial valuation results at that time. The consumption tax rate was assumed to be 5% from March 2014, 8% from April 2014 to September 2019, and 10% after October 2019.

The estimated results for 2010 and 2015 generational accounts are listed in Table 6.3.

Estimates show that Japan's generational imbalance has considerably decreased over the past decade. The generational imbalance decreased from 403.3% in 2010 to 227.8% in 2015, and 178.7% in 2019.

The reduction in generational imbalance between 2010 and 2015 was significant. The reason for this can be seen by decomposition of the net tax burden change during this period into benefits and burden. The increase in the net tax burden on those in their 20s–50s between 2010 and 2015 is significant. Comparing the burdens and benefits separately, the burdens on younger generations increased significantly during this period, while the increase in benefits was small or even decreased for those in their 40s and above. The increased burden on the younger generations during this period was due to the income tax reforms implemented in the 2010s

Table 6.3 Comparison with generational accounts for 2010, 2015 and 2019

									(Thousand yen)
	2010			2015			2019		
	Burden	Benefit	Net tax burden	Burden	Benefit	Net tax burden	Burden	Benefit	Net tax burden
0	49, 616.2	30, 504.9	19, 111.4	57, 020.4	32,047.2	24, 973.2	62, 740.4	33, 694.6	29, 045.8
5	53, 116.8	31, 627.2	21, 489.6	61, 182.2	33,148.2	28, 034.0	67, 399.7	34, 759.5	32, 640.3
10	57, 182.6	33, 640.0	23, 542.6	65, 158.3	34,778.8	30, 379.5	71, 921.8	36, 484.0	35, 437.8
15	58, 547.7	34, 538.2	24, 009.6	68, 848.4	36,532.4	32, 315.9	76, 019.1	38, 232.4	37, 786.8
20	61, 250.4	36, 413.9	24, 836.5	71, 824.5	38,299.3	33, 525.3	79, 162.4	39, 788.1	39, 374.3
25	61, 784.2	38, 457.2	23, 326.9	71, 692.5	39,938.3	31, 754.2	79, 280.7	41, 537.1	37, 743.6
30	60, 545.4	39, 474.7	21, 070.6	69, 625.7	40,683.3	28, 942.3	76, 632.3	42, 082.5	34, 549.9
35	57, 973.8	39, 282.5	18, 691.3	66, 058.4	40,217.1	25, 841.2	71, 945.5	41, 162.9	30, 782.6
40	54, 201.3	38, 179.7	16, 021.6	60, 406.6	37,473.6	22, 932.9	64, 522.6	37, 468.0	27, 054.6
45	46, 938.2	37, 219.5	9718.7	53, 594.8	36,560.8	17, 034.0	55, 237.6	35, 247.9	19, 989.6
50	38, 561.3	38, 028.2	533.0	45, 288.4	36,722.3	8566.1	47, 524.9	35, 403.4	12, 121.5
55	29, 142.7	39, 967.0	−10, 824.2	35, 394.4	38,793.2	−3398.7	37, 641.8	36, 840.3	801.5
60	21, 638.7	42, 611.9	−20, 973.2	24, 941.0	40,912.8	−15, 971.8	26, 725.4	39, 007.1	−12, 281.6
65	17, 397.8	43, 731.4	−26, 333.6	18, 059.5	41,354.9	−23, 295.4	18, 054.1	39, 179.1	−21, 124.9
70	12, 779.0	39, 223.7	−26, 444.7	13, 287.8	37,154.5	−23, 866.6	12, 003.4	33, 472.4	−21, 469.0
75	9835.2	33, 796.8	−23, 961.6	10, 123.4	31,847.8	−21, 724.4	8957.1	28, 170.1	−19, 213.0
80	7432.0	28, 983.6	−21, 551.7	7256.8	26,208.2	−18, 951.4	6467.7	23, 063.6	−16, 595.9
85	4957.9	22, 175.2	−17, 217.4	5022.3	20,859.2	−15, 836.9	4078.1	16, 718.6	−12, 640.5
90	2936.6	14, 973.6	−12, 037.0	2617.4	12,115.4	−9498.1	1642.4	7586.6	−5944.2
Future generations			96, 192.0			81, 706.1			80, 957.4
Generational imbalance (percentage)			403.3%			227.2%			178.7%
Generational imbalance (thousand yen)			77, 080.6			56, 732.9			51, 911.6

Note: The growth rate is assumed to be 1.5%, and the gap between the interest rate and growth rate is 1.5%
Source: Author's calculations

and an increase in the consumption tax rate.[6] It can be seen that this has increased the net tax burden. The increase in the net tax burden of the younger generation leads to a decrease in potential net government debt, which, in turn, decreases the burden on future generations.

6.4 Policy Options for Restoring Generational Balance

6.4.1 Alternative Policy Measures for Restoring Generational Balance

This section considers alternative policy measures to eliminate generational imbalance and restore generational balance.

A positive generational imbalance indicates that there will not be sufficient future government revenue (burden) to finance future government expenditures (benefits). Therefore, there are two ways to eliminate this imbalance and restore generational balance—equalizing the lifetime net tax payments of the 2019 newborn and future generations. The first is to increase the burden on current generation. The second approach involves reducing government transfer spending (benefits). Moreover, these policies could be combined.

Kotlikoff and Burns (2004) referred to immediate and permanent policy options for achieving such a generational balance as a "menu of pain." Table 6.4 shows the menu items for pain. It provides immediate and permanent policy options for achieving generational balance. The four options discussed here are (a) increasing all burdens, including taxes and social insurance contributions; (b) increasing the income tax burden; (c) increasing consumption tax; and (d) reducing all benefits, such as social security.

(a) **Increase in All Taxes.**

Immediate and permanent increases in all burdens, including various tax burdens and social insurance contributions.

Restoring generational balance by increasing taxes would require increasing all burdens to approximately 1.33 times the current level.

(b) **Increase in Income Tax.**

This is intended to restore generational balance by immediately and permanently raising the income tax burden.

Restoring generational balance through an increase in income tax would require an increase in the income tax burden by about 2.49 times the current level.

---

[6] In Japan, the income tax system was reformed almost every year in the 2010s. These included a reduction in the payroll tax deduction, an increase in the income tax rate on gains from stock transfers and dividends, and an increase in the maximum income tax rate.

Table 6.4 Policy options for restoring generational balance: the menu of pain

Policy	Percentage change	Percentage change if policy delayed 5 years	Percentage change if policy delayed 10 years
Increase in all taxes	32.8	38.7	46.4
Increase in income tax	149.4	177.7	214.1
Increase in consumption tax	152.1	178.8	212.7
Cut in transfer payments	41.2	47.7	55.8

Note: All taxes include local tax, and social insurance contributions (the Japanese counterpart of the social security tax) are included in taxes
Source: Author's calculations

(c) **Increase in Consumption Tax.**

This is intended to restore the generational balance by immediately and permanently increasing the consumption tax burden.

Restoring generational balance through an increase in consumption tax would require an increase in the consumption tax burden by about 2.52 times the current level.[7] This is equivalent to a consumption tax rate of approximately 20%.

(d) **Cut in Transfer Payments**

Immediate and permanent reduction of all benefits, such as pensions, medical care, and welfare.

Restoring the generational balance through cut-in-transfer payments requires a 41.2% reduction in all benefit levels. This means reducing all benefits, including pensions, medical care, and welfare, to the current level of 58.8.

6.4.2 Achieving Generational Balance: Policy Simulation

The net tax burden of each generation changes as generational balance is restored, but the amount of change depends on the means (policy measures) used to achieve generational balance.

The amount of tax and social insurance contributions (burdens) and benefits, such as pensions and medical care, differ by age. Therefore, the change in the net tax burden for each generation will differ depending on the policy measures used to restore the generational balance.

[7] We assume an immediate and permanent increase in the consumption tax rate in 2019.

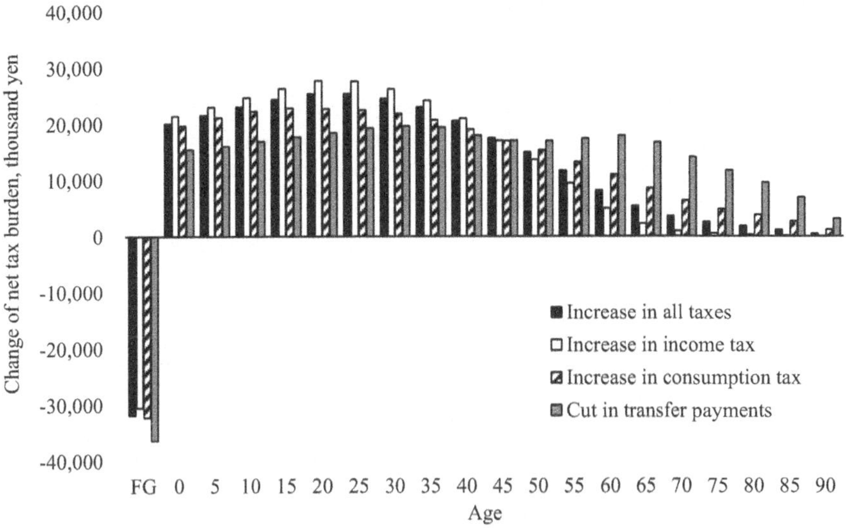

Fig. 6.3 Changes of net tax burden by age group. Note: The growth rate is assumed to be 1.5%, and the gap between the interest rate and growth rate is 1.5%. FG stands for "future generations". (Source: Author's calculations)

Figure 6.3 shows the changes in the net tax burden from the basic result of generational accounting for the base year of 2019 (the base case), if generational balance is achieved.

6.4.2.1 Achieving Generational Balance Through Increased Burden and Decreased Benefits

Comparing the change in net tax burdens for each generation by different means of achieving generational balance, the net tax burden increase is smaller for generations under the age of 45 when generational balance is achieved by reducing benefits than when it is achieved by increasing burdens. On the contrary, the increase in net tax burdens for those aged 50 years and older is smaller when generational balance is achieved by increasing burdens rather than reducing benefits. In particular, the net tax burden increases significantly for generations aged 60 years and older because of the reduction in benefits. This is because the generation under age 45 will bear a large burden of taxes and social insurance premiums at the present time (or in the near future), while those aged 60 and older, especially those aged 65 and older, have already paid (most of) the burden of taxes and social insurance premiums.

6.4.2.2 Achieving Generational Balance Through Increased Income Tax Burden

The change in the net tax burden for each generation due to an increase in the income tax burden is similar to the increase in any burden. Compared to achieving generational balance through reductions in benefits, the net burden on the generation under age 45 is larger, and that amount is larger than in the case of an increase in any burden. The increase in the net tax burden in the 20–25 age group was particularly large.

6.4.2.3 Achieving Generational Balance Through Increased Consumption Tax Burden

The increase in the net tax burden for each generation due to an increase in the consumption tax is characterized by a smaller bias between age groups in the increase in the net tax burden compared to the increase in all taxes, the increase in the income tax, or the cut in transfer payments. Of course, because the consumption tax burden depends on income levels (consumption), the higher the income level (larger consumption), the greater the burden. A burden bias exists toward the working-age population, which, on average, has higher incomes. However, compared to the income tax burden increase, the additional burden on the elderly generation aged 60 years and older is relatively large.

6.4.2.4 Net Tax Burden of Future Generations When Generational Balance Achieved

Any policy measure substantially reduces the net tax burden on future generations when generational balance is achieved. In terms of differences by measures of achieving generational balance, the net tax burden on future generations is smallest when generational balance is achieved by reducing benefits and largest when generational balance is achieved by increasing income tax burdens.

6.4.3 *The Menu of Delayed Pain*

Achieving generational balance requires additional increases in the burden. However, policy decisions involving additional burden increases are expected to be difficult in the policymaking process. In addition, achieving generational balance has an incentive to be delayed. The reason for this is the conflict of interest between the current and future generations. By delaying the achievement of generational balance, the current generation, especially the elderly, will be exempt from an additional increase in burden. Therefore, the possibility of delaying the achievement of generational balance cannot be denied.

Delaying it for a few years before implementing policies to achieve generational balance is costly (Gokhale and Kotlikoff 1999). Table 6.4 shows that the required tax hikes or transfer cuts will have to be larger if we delay them for 5 or 10 years before implementing them. For example, the burden increase delays for 5 years means having to raise them by 38.7% rather than 32.8%. Similarly, an increased burden associated with delays was shown for other policy measures. The reason for the cost (and increased burden) of this delay is that a delay in achieving generational balance results in additional new debt.

Delays also increase the lifetime net tax burden for each generation, including the future generations. This suggests that policy changes to achieve balance must be introduced sooner, rather than later.

6.4.4 Policy Mixes for Restoring Generational Balance

In the past, the Japanese government (Ministry of Finance) set as one of its policy goals to maintain the potential national burden ratio, including the budget deficit, below a certain level—specifically, below 50%. It is also possible to achieve a generational balance through a combination of alternative policy measures. This section considers a scenario in which taxes and social insurance contributions are limited to 50% of national income.

As discussed earlier, restoring generational balance through an increase in all taxes would require increasing all tax (including social insurance contribution) burdens to about 1.33 times the current levels. According to data from the Ministry of Finance, the share of tax and social insurance contributions in 2019 was 44.4%. Therefore, if the tax and social insurance burden in 2019 were simply multiplied by 1.33, it would increase the tax and social insurance burden to 58.9%.

Therefore, in this section, we consider the possibility of reducing the burden rate of taxes and social insurance contributions to 50%, eliminating the remaining generational imbalance by reducing benefits, and discuss the impact on the generational accounts of each generation in this case.

To maintain the tax and social insurance contribution rate at the 50% level, the level of increase in all taxes would have to be reduced to approximately 1.13 times the current level. Figure 6.4 shows the generational accounts for each generation in the case of such a policy mix. In this case, the generational imbalance was 86.9%. A 25.4% cut in transfer payments should be implemented in addition to the 12.6% increase in all taxes to eliminate the remaining imbalance and achieve a generational balance.

As shown in Fig. 6.4, except for some generations, the increase in the net tax burden in achieving generational balance for most generations, including future generations, is smaller than either the increase in all taxes or the reduction in transfer payments.

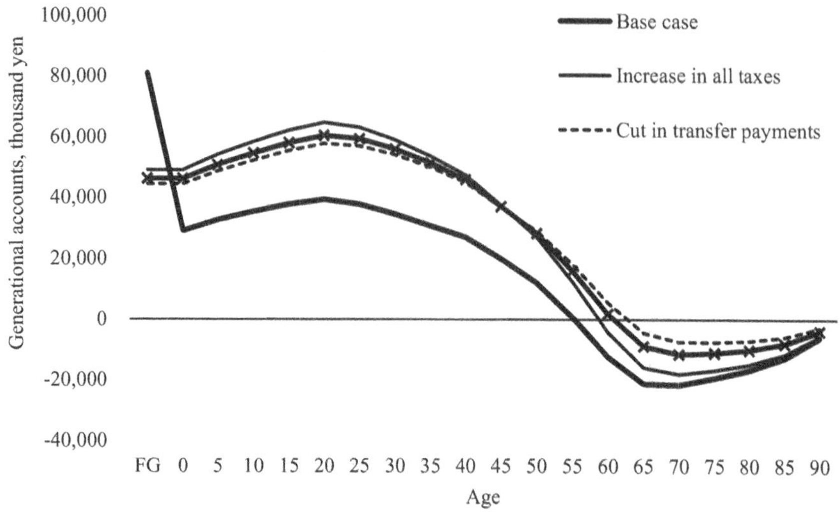

Fig. 6.4 Generational accounts when generational balance achieved: policy mix. Note: The growth rate is assumed to be 1.5%, and the gap between the interest rate and growth rate is 1.5%. FG stands for "future generations". (Source: Author's calculations)

6.4.5 Preferable Policy Measures for Achieving Generational Balance

In this section, we first consider the criterion for a preferable policy measure to achieve generational balance. Perhaps, a preferable policy measure for all generations is not to increase anyone's burden. However, this is not feasible. The government's intertemporal budget constraint formula illustrates the zero-sum nature of the fiscal policy: no free lunches. In other words, generational balance always requires an increase in someone's burden.

Therefore, this study considers the following two criteria for preferable policy measures (Sato 2011).

Criterion A The smaller the increase in net tax burden, the better

This is based on the idea that, even though the net tax burden will inevitably increase as generational balance is restored, the increase should be as small as possible.

Under this criterion, among the measures to achieve generational balance, the "preferable" policy measure results in the smallest increase in the net tax burden after the achievement of generational balance compared to the base case.

Criterion B The smaller the net tax burden of future generation, the better

This is based on the idea that the smaller the net tax burden on future generations, the better.

Under this criterion, among the measures to achieve generational balance, the "preferable" policy measure is that which will result in the smallest net tax burden on future generations after generational balance is achieved.

6.4.5.1 Generational Conflicts of Interest

In this section, we describe the conflicts of interest among generations for "preferable" policy measures of generational balance. As noted earlier, this study set two criteria for preferable policy measures. Under either criterion, it is clear that intergenerational conflicts of interest arise regarding the preferred policy measures.

Based on Criterion A, the preferred policy measures for each generation are those that result in a smallest increase in net tax burdens after the generational balance is restored compared to before it is restored. Comparing the increase in net tax burdens associated with achieving generational balance across the different policy measures to be used, the increase in net tax burdens associated with restoring generational balance is smaller for generations under age 45 in the order of reductions in all benefits, increases in the consumption tax burden, increases in all burdens, and increases in income tax burdens. Thus, for the relatively young generation under age 45, a reduction in all benefits, an increase in the consumption tax burden, an increase in all burdens, and an increase in the income tax burden are preferable in that order. However, for those aged 50 and older (especially the elderly generation aged 60 and older), the increase in the net tax burden is smaller in the following order: an increase in the income tax burden, an increase in all burdens, an increase in the consumption tax burden, and a reduction in all benefits. Thus, preferable policy measures differ across generations, with the relatively young generation preferring a reduction in benefits, whereas the elderly prefer an increase in burdens.

In addition, under Criterion B, the preferable policy measures are those that result in smaller net tax burdens on future generations after the restoration of the generational balance. Thus, based on Criterion B, the order of preference is the reduction of all benefits, increase in the consumption tax burden, increase in all burdens, and increase in the income tax burden. This is the same as the order of preferable policy measures for the relatively young generation, as seen in Criterion A. This means that the young and future generations are coincident in their interests, and there is a conflict of interest between the elderly and younger and future generations.

Compared to restoring generational balance through the policy mix, it is preferable for both the young and elderly generations to restore generational balance through either benefits or burdens alone. In other words, restoring generational balance through a policy mix is a means that is relatively easy for both the young and elderly generations to accept.

However, it should be noted that there is a potential conflict of interest between the current and future generations in restoring generational balance. In other words, by postponing the achievement of generational balance, the current generation, especially the elderly, will be exempted from an additional increase in the burden.

6.5 Conclusion

This chapter estimates generational accounting for the base year of 2019 in Japan and compares policy options to achieve generational balance. The results show, first, that the generational imbalance in Japan remains large at 178.7% but has been decreasing over the last decade. Second, we considered policy options to eliminate generational imbalance and restore generational balance and found that restoring generational balance is possible, but would require considerable additional net tax burdens to achieve it. Furthermore, in doing so, the analysis in this chapter also showed that there is a conflict of interest between the young/future generations and the elderly generations regarding the preferred policy options.

Regarding the considerations in this chapter, some issues must be studied further. First, it is necessary to examine in more detail the factors that contributed to the decreasing generational imbalance over the last decade, including institutional and policy changes, and changes in the economic environment during this period. Second, although this chapter has shown the existence of generational conflicts of interest for preferable policy measures, it is necessary to examine the possibility of intergenerational adjustment of interests. In addition, the criteria for "preferable" need to be examined.

Acknowledgements We thank Professor Emeritus Shuetsu Takahashi and Professor Kei Hosoya for their valuable comments and suggestions. All remaining errors are my own. This study was supported in part by the JSPS Grant-in-Aid for Scientific Research (C) No. 19K01692.

References

Anderson B, Sheppard J (2009) Fiscal futures, institutional budget reforms, and their effects: what can be learned? OECD J Budg 3:7–117

Auerbach AJ, Gokhale J, Kotlikoff LJ (1991) Generational accounts: a meaningful alternative to deficit accounting. Tax Policy Econ 5:55–110

Auerbach AJ, Gokhale J, Kotlikoff LJ (1992a) Social security and medicare policy from the perspective of generational accounting. Tax Policy Econ 6:129–145

Auerbach AJ, Gokhale J, Kotlikoff LJ (1992b) Generational accounting: a new approach to understanding the effects of fiscal policy on saving. Scand J Econ 94(2):303–318

Auerbach AJ, Gokhale J, Kotlikoff LJ (1994) Generational accounting: a meaningful way to evaluate fiscal policy. J Econ Perspect 8(1):73–94

Auerbach AJ, Gokhale J, Kotlikoff LJ (1995) Restoring generational balance in US fiscal policy: what will it take? Econ Rev 31(1):2–12

Auerbach AJ, Kotlikoff LJ, Leibfritz W (eds) (1999) Generational accounting around the world. The University of Chicago Press, Chicago

Boll S, Raffelhüschen B, Walliser J (1994) Social security and intergenerational redistribution: a generational accounting perspective. Public Choice 81(1):79–100

Bonin H (2001) Generational accounting: theory and application. Springer Science & Business Media, New York

Cutler DM (1993) Book review: generational accounting: knowing who pays, and when, for what we spend. Natl Tax J 46(1):61–67

Diamond P (1996) Generational accounts and generational balance: an assessment. Natl Tax J 49(4):597–607

Gokhale J, Kotlikoff LJ (1999) Generational justice and generational accounting. In: Williamson J, Watts-Roy DM, Kingson ER (eds) The generational equity debate. Columbia University Press, New York, pp 75–86

Gokhale J, Smetters KA (2003) Fiscal and generational imbalances: new budget measures for new budget priorities. American Enterprise Institute, Washington, DC

Haveman R (1994) Should generational accounts replace public budgets and deficits? J Econ Perspect 8(1):95–111

Kotlikoff LJ (1993) Generational accounting: knowing who pays, and when, for what we spend. Free Press, New York

Kotlikoff LJ (1997) Reply to Diamond's and Cutler's reviews of generational accounting. Natl Tax J 50(2):303–314

Kotlikoff LJ (2003) Generational policy. MIT Press, Cambridge

Kotlikoff LJ, Burns S (2004) The coming generational storm: what you need to know about America's economic future. MIT Press, Cambridge

Masujima M, Shimasawa M, Murakami T (2009) Study on generational accounting model with the social security system (in Japanese), ESRI discussion paper, 217, Economic and Social Research Institute, Cabinet Office, Government of Japan

Miyazato N (2015) Intergenerational redistribution policies of the 1990s and 2000s in Japan: an analysis using generational accounting. Jpn World Econ 34:1–16

Mizutani T, (2016) Current status of intergenerational imbalance in Japan: Generational accounting for FY2013 (in Japanese), The Hikone Ronso, 407, Shiga University, 56–71

Sato Y (2011) Restoring generational balance and intergenerational conflicts (in Japanese). J Econ Policy Stud 8(2):87–90

Sato Y (2013) A comparison of 2010 and 2005 intergenerational inequalities in Japan (in Japanese). Econ Rev 181:43–61

Shimasawa M, Oguro K, Masujima M (2014) Population aging, policy reforms, and lifetime net tax rate in Japan: a generational accounting approach, PRI discussion paper series, 14A-04, policy research institute, the Ministry of Finance, Japan

Yoshida H (2006) Intergenerational imbalance and fiscal reform in Japan: approach with generational accounting—revised—(in Japanese), PIE discussion paper, 287, Project on Intergenerational Equity, Institute of Economic Research, Hitotsubashi University

Chapter 7
Social Security Finance in Japan: Trends, Issues, and Some Measures for Stabilization

Masahito Abe

Abstract In Japan, stabilizing the financial system for social security is one of the most critical policy issues. Social insurance, such as pension and medical care, is the core of social security, and these benefits are increasing with the aging population. In system operation and management, the burden of social insurance premiums and taxes has been raised, and the increase in benefits has been restrained. The shortage of financial resources depends on the revenue from the issuance of public bonds, while the debt balance and its ratio to GDP are increasing. In contrast, as the main bearer of financial resources, the number of younger workers is decreasing with the declining birthrate, and the number of older workers with some health risks tends to increase. The following measures are being considered and implemented to address these issues: secure financial resources by increasing the consumption tax and maintain the labor force and social security bearers by promoting preventive health care. The latter has an important meaning as a new measure to deal with the financial problems of social security.

Keywords Social security · Aging population · Consumption tax · Health risks · Preventive health care

JEL Classification: H51, H55, I12, I18, J11

M. Abe (✉)
School of Social Welfare, Hokusei Gakuen University, Sapporo, Hokkaidō, Japan
e-mail: abe919@hokusei.ac.jp

S. Takahashi et al. (eds.), *Modern Macroeconomics with Historical Perspectives*, New Frontiers in Regional Science: Asian Perspectives 67,
https://doi.org/10.1007/978-981-99-1067-0_7

7.1 Introduction

This chapter presents an overview of the trends in benefits and financial resources of social security in Japan and considers some measures for stabilizing the system, based on pension and medical care. As is widely known, the population in Japan is aging rapidly, and the benefits are increasing accordingly. Social insurance premiums and public funds (burden of central and local governments) are the basis of financial resources. However, part of the public funds is covered by the issuance of public bonds owing to economic growth stagnation and prolonged fiscal deficit, and the debt balance has increased. Consequently, national burdens such as social insurance premiums and taxes have been increased, whereas benefit increases have been restrained (including the increase in co-payment).

In addition to the economic and financial trends, discussions based on population trends and changes in disease structure have become more important. Regarding population trends, with the birthrate declining and the population aging, the total population is decreasing. Additionally, the number of workers as the main bearer, especially younger workers, is decreasing, whereas the number of older workers with health risks is increasing. In general, health risks begin increasing around the late 30s, and the incidence of lifestyle-related diseases increases gradually with aging. Changes in disease structure refer to the increase in such diseases.

As these issues are being raised, some measures have been considered and implemented based on the financial problems. This chapter focuses on two factors. The first is "comprehensive reform of social security and tax," and the second is "promotion of preventive health care."

The former aims to secure financial resources by increasing consumption tax (raising the tax rate) and to allocate them to social security benefits. The latter aims to maintain the quality of life (QOL) for each person over the long term by controlling health risks and incidence/aggravation of diseases. As a concrete method, health maintenance and promotion based on primary and secondary prevention are emphasized. Although not directly related to the discussion of financial resources, they have significant implications as a measure for maintaining labor productivity, securing social security bearers, and restraining the increase in medical care expenditure.

This chapter is organized as follows. Section 7.2 overviews the fiscal trend in social security. Section 7.3 summarizes some problems related to financial resources. Section 7.4 considers the methods and issues of the two abovementioned factors, and Sect. 7.5 looks at the future directions.[1]

---

[1] The term "employee" used in this chapter is a person who receives salaries from an employer and engages in work. "Worker" refers to a self-employed person (including farmers, etc.) in addition to an employee and is also the main bearer of social security. "The insured" is the eligible person for social insurance benefits.

7.2 Benefits and Financial Resources of Social Security

7.2.1 Outline of Social Security System and Trends of the Benefits

7.2.1.1 Outline of the System

Social security benefits can be viewed in terms of "category of department" and "category of function." In Japan, social insurance, such as a pension, medical care, and long-term care, account for most benefits; the former classification is useful for confirming these.[2] Before considering these trends, we will summarize the outline of each system (2019) based on pension, medical care, and other welfare (including long-term care).

The first is pension. This is centered on national pension (generally, basic pension) and employees' pension that are publicly operated and managed on the universal pension insurance system. The national pension is for people 20 years old and over (including self-employed persons, nonworkers such as dependent spouses, and students). The employees' pension is for employees of companies (including public servants, teachers, and staff of private schools). Pension benefits refer to the basic pension common to all insured on insurance premiums at a fixed amount and the supplemented pension to the employee according to the burden of insurance premiums.[3]

The age of receiving pension is 65 years old in principle.[4] The breakdown of financial resources for the national pension is 50% of insurance premiums and 50% of public funds (the central government's burden), and employees' pension benefits are 100% of insurance premiums. Regarding insurance premiums, the national pension is borne by each insured, and the employees' pension is borne by the employee and the employer at about 50% each.

The second is medical care. This is centered on national health insurance, employees' health insurance, and the medical care system for the latter-stage elderly.[5] These are publicly operated and managed on the universal medical care insurance system. The national health insurance is for the self-employed persons and nonworkers (some employees such as part-time workers are also included).

---

[2] The category of function is divided into (1) elderly, (2) health care, (3) family, (4) bereaved family, (5) disability, (6) livelihood protection and others, (7) unemployment, (8) occupational accident, and (9) housing. Among these, the amounts for (1) and (2) are large; since the mid-1990s, these two items have accounted for 75–80% of the total benefits.

[3] Self-employed persons can supplement their basic pension by contributing. This is the national pension fund system.

[4] This age has been gradually raised due to the revision of the system. In Japan, a pay-as-you-go system is a basis for the benefits and burdens of the pension.

[5] People aged 75 and over are the latter-stage elderly, and those aged 65–74 are the early-stage elderly. These population trends will be confirmed in Sect. 7.3.2.

The employees' health insurance is primarily intended for employees (and their dependents). These employees will enroll in the national health insurance after retirement and become eligible for the medical care system for the latter-stage elderly at the age of 75.

The breakdown of financial resources in the national health insurance is 50% of insurance premiums and 50% of public funds (in principle, 41% by the central government and 9% by local governments). Those of the employees' health insurance are based on insurance premiums, while public funds (burden of the central government) are partially allocated for medical care benefits of the insured of small- and medium-sized companies. In the medical care system for the latter-stage elderly, insurance premium is 50% (10% of the latter-stage elderly and 40% of contributions from the employees' health insurance), and public funds are 50% (33.3% by the central government and 16.7% by local governments). Regarding insurance premiums, the national health insurance and the medical care system for the latter-stage elderly are borne by each insured. The employees' health insurance is borne by the employee and the employer at about 50% each. In principle, the co-payment rate for treatment is 30% of those under 70 years old (infants under 6 years old is 20%), 20% of 70–74 years old, and 10% of 75 years old and over.

The third is other welfare. This refers to long-term care insurance, child welfare, welfare for the disabled, and public assistance. Long-term care was operated and managed on public funds until 1999, and it shifted to the public insurance system from 2000. This insurance covers people in need of long-term care, among those 65 years old and over or 40–64 years old with specified diseases caused by aging.[6] The breakdown of financial resources is 50% of public funds (25% by the central government and 25% by local governments), and the remaining 50% is insurance premium (23% for 65 years old and over and 27% for 40–64 years old). The co-payment rate when receiving services is 10% in principle.

There are various benefits for child welfare and welfare for the disabled, which are generally covered by public funds except for some co-payment. Public assistance refers to cash and medical benefits for people who have difficulty in living, and public funds cover the financial resources. Additionally, as workers' accident compensation insurance, there are compensation benefits related to pension, medical care, and living expenses, which the central government bears in principle.

7.2.1.2 Trends of the Benefits

Table 7.1 provides an overview of the trends in total benefits A, national income B, and the ratio of total benefits to national income A/B from 1970 to 2019, respectively. A does not include co-payment in medical care and long-term care.

[6] Specified diseases related to this mainly refer to terminal cancer, osteoporosis, presenile dementia, and cerebrovascular disease.

Table 7.1 Trends in social security benefits and national income

	1970	1980	1990	2000	2010	2015	2019
Total benefits A	3,523.9 (100%)	24,929.0 (100%)	47,423.8 (100%)	78,406.2 (100%)	105,364.7 (100%)	116,813.3 (100%)	123,924.1 (100%)
Pension	856.2 (24.3%)	10,333.0 (41.4%)	23,777.2 (50.1%)	40,536.7 (51.7%)	52,228.6 (49.6%)	54,092.9 (46.3%)	55,452.0 (44.7%)
Medical care	2,075.8 (58.9%)	10,759.8 (43.2%)	18,625.4 (39.3%)	26,604.9 (33.9%)	33,644.0 (31.9%)	38,564.0 (33.0%)	40,722.6 (32.9%)
Other welfare	592.0 (16.8%)	3,836.2 (15.4%)	5,021.2 (10.6%)	11,264.6 (14.4%)	19,492.1 (18.5%)	24,156.4 (20.7%)	27,749.4 (22.4%)
Long-term care (included in other welfare)	—	—	—	3,280.6 (4.2%)	7,508.2 (7.1%)	9,510.6 (8.1%)	10,736.1 (8.7%)
National income B	61,029.7	203,878.7	346,892.9	390,163.8	364,688.2	392,629.3	401,287.0
A/B	5.77%	12.2%	13.7%	20.1%	28.9%	29.8%	30.9%

Note 1: The unit is a billion yen. The bracket is the percentage of total benefits
Note 2: Long-term care was included in other welfare until 1999, but it has been displayed separately since 2000
Source: National Institute of Population and Social Security Research (2021)

In Japan, the universal pension and medical care insurance system was introduced in 1961, and some revisions were made to expand the system throughout the 1970s. The main examples were an increase in pension benefits on the index-linked system and an increase in the benefit rate of medical care insurance. Additionally, the construction of medical institutions (primarily hospitals) and social welfare facilities was promoted in each region.

Since then, total benefits A have increased centered on pension and medical care and were 78,406.2 billion yen in 2000. After exceeding 100 trillion yen in 2009, this amounted to 123,924.1 billion yen in 2019. A reason why pension and medical care benefits are large is primarily the progress of aging and the abovementioned institutional and policy factors. Regarding the proportion of benefits, long-term care has increased since 2000. This increased by 4.5 percentage points from 4.2% in 2000 to 8.7% in 2019. By contrast, pension decreased by 7 percentage points from 51.7 to 44.7% during the same period, and medical care decreased by 1 percentage point from 33.9 to 32.9%.

National income B was 61,029.7 billion yen in 1970 and 390,163.8 billion yen in 2000. This did not increase significantly during the 1990s, largely owing to the effects of the "collapse of the economic bubble."[7] This decreased to 364,688.2 billion yen in 2010 due to the recession in 2001 and 2008, and then increased to 401,287 billion yen in 2019. The main cause of the recession in 2001 was the "collapse of the IT bubble," and in 2008, the "bankruptcy of the Lehman Brothers."[8]

[7] The collapse of the economic bubble in the early 1990s refers to a phenomenon in which the value of assets such as stocks and land had fallen sharply. Along with this, the economy stagnated for a long time.

[8] The collapse of the IT bubble refers to the reactionary fall of stock prices in the United States, which had risen due to overinvestment in IT-related companies. The bankruptcy of Lehman Brothers refers to the failure of Lehman Brothers, which caused the global financial crisis and

Table 7.2 Trends in financial resources for social security

	1970	1980	1990	2000	2010	2015	2019
Total financial resources	5,468.1 (100%)	33,555.4 (100%)	65,308.6 (100%)	89,141.1 (100%)	109,678.7 (100%)	125,357.7 (100%)	132,374.6 (100%)
Social insurance premiums	3,260.1 (59.6%)	18,623.8 (55.5%)	39,515.4 (60.5%)	54,963.7 (61.7%)	58,482.2 (53.3%)	66,932.2 (53.4%)	74,008.2 (55.9%)
Insured contribution	1,555.8 (28.5%)	8,884.4 (26.5%)	18,496.6 (28.3%)	26,656.0 (29.9%)	30,329.1 (27.7%)	35,372.7 (28.2%)	38,966.5 (29.4%)
Employer contribution	1,704.3 (31.2%)	9,739.4 (29.0%)	21,018.8 (32.2%)	28,307.7 (31.8%)	28,153.0 (25.7%)	31,559.6 (25.2%)	35,041.7 (26.5%)
Public funds	1,642.0 (30.0%)	11,070.5 (33.0%)	16,190.8 (24.8%)	25,164.4 (28.2%)	40,798.3 (37.2%)	48,255.2 (38.5%)	51,913.7 (39.2%)
Central government	1,442.5 (26.4%)	9,823.2 (29.3%)	13,493.6 (20.7%)	19,800.6 (22.2%)	29,528.7 (26.9%)	32,552.8 (26.0%)	34,406.7 (26.0%)
Local governments	199.5 (3.6%)	1,247.3 (3.7%)	2,697.2 (4.1%)	5,363.8 (6.0%)	11,269.7 (10.3%)	15,702.4 (12.5%)	17,507.0 (13.2%)
Other revenues	566.0 (10.4%)	3,861.1 (11.5%)	9,602.3 (14.7%)	9,013.1 (10.1%)	10,398.2 (9.5%)	10,170.3 (8.1%)	6,452.6 (4.9%)
Asset income	479.6 (8.8%)	3,268.2 (9.7%)	8,358.0 (12.8%)	6,497.6 (7.3%)	838.8 (0.8%)	2,057.1 (1.6%)	1,594.4 (1.2%)
Others	86.4 (1.6%)	592.9 (1.8%)	1,244.3 (1.9%)	2,515.5 (2.8%)	9,559.4 (8.7%)	8,113.2 (6.5%)	4,858.2 (3.7%)

Note: The unit is a billion yen. The bracket is the percentage of total financial resources. The difference between the total benefits (Table 7.1) and the total financial resources (Table 7.2) for each year is carried over to the next year
Source: National Institute of Population and Social Security Research (2021)

In general, the growth rate of national income has remained at a low level since the late 1990s until 2019.

When comparing trends in total benefits A and national income B over 50 years from 1970 to 2019, the former increased 35.17 times, whereas the latter increased 6.58 times. Along with this, the ratio of A/B rose from 5.77% in 1970 to 20.1% in 2000 and 30.9% in 2019.

7.2.2 *Financial Resources for Social Security*

Social security benefits are covered by social insurance premiums, public funds, and other revenues. Table 7.2 shows these contents and trends from 1970 to 2019.

As social security benefits increase over the long term (Table 7.1), their related financial resources also increase. The total amounts in 1970 were 5468.1 billion yen, which increased significantly to 89,141.1 billion yen in 2000 and 132,374.6 billion yen in 2019. Social insurance premiums are covered by the insured and employer contributions. Considering the 74,008.2 billion yen in 2019, the former was 38,966.5 billion yen (29.4%), and the latter was 35,041.7 billion yen (26.5%).

Public funds refer to the burdens of central and local governments, and the latter has been increasing as a long-term trend since 1970. In 2019, the central government

subsequent stock market stagnation. The recession caused by these factors has also had an impact on the Japanese economy.

burden was 34,406.7 billion yen (26%), and that of the local governments was 17,507 billion yen (13.2%). From 2000 to 2019, the proportion of social insurance premiums decreased from 61.7 to 55.9%, whereas the proportion of public funds increased from 28.2 to 39.2%.

One of the reasons why public funds are used as part of social security benefits is to restrain increasing social insurance premiums. The other is to control the disparity in insurance premiums or the ability to pay among medical care insurers (mainly the national health insurance and the employees' health insurance). Public funds are also essential financial resources for benefits (such as child welfare, welfare for the disabled, etc.) other than social insurance.

Other revenues are the total of asset income and others. The former is primarily the performance of public pension funds' investments (interest and dividend income), while the latter is acceptance from pension reserves. These amounts and proportions have fluctuated over the long term. As seen in 2019, other revenues were 6452.6 billion yen (4.9%); among this, asset income was 1594.4 billion yen (1.2%), and others were 4858.2 billion yen (3.7%).

7.3 Basic Issues Related to Social Security Finance

7.3.1 National Burden Ratio and Latent National Burden Ratio

It is useful to look at the national and latent national burden ratios as indicators for considering financial problems. Table 7.3 gives an overview of these trends from 1970 to 2019.

Each burden ratio in Table 7.3 is defined as a proportion in relation to national income. The national burden ratio A, which is the sum of the social security burden ratio and the tax burden ratio, has increased over the long term, except for temporary fluctuations. This was 24.3% in 1970 and 35.6% in 2000, exceeding 40% in recent years and reaching 44.4% in 2019.

Table 7.3 Trends in national burden ratio and latent national burden ratio

	1970	1980	1990	2000	2010	2015	2019
National burden ratio A	24.3%	30.5%	38.4%	35.6%	37.2%	42.3%	44.4%
Social security burden ratio	5.4%	8.8%	10.6%	13.0%	15.8%	17.1%	18.6%
Tax burden ratio	18.9%	21.7%	27.7%	22.6%	21.4%	25.2%	25.8%
National tax	12.7%	13.9%	18.1%	13.5%	12.0%	15.3%	15.5%
Local taxes	6.1%	7.8%	9.6%	9.1%	9.4%	10.0%	10.3%
Latent national burden ratio B	24.9%	38.7%	38.5%	45.1%	48.1%	48.4%	49.7%
Fiscal deficit ratio B − A	0.6%	8.2%	0.1%	9.5%	10.9%	6.1%	5.3%

Source: Ministry of Finance (2021a)

Among them, the social security burden ratio increased by 13.2 percentage points, from 5.4% in 1970 to 18.6% in 2019. As seen in the previous section, the burden of long-term care insurance has been included since 2000. The tax burden ratio increased by 6.9 percentage points, from 18.9% in 1970 to 25.8% in 2019. Personal income, corporate income, and consumption tax are the main components of a national tax. Local taxes include resident and enterprise taxes in prefectures and municipalities.

In Japan, the fiscal deficit has been prolonged, and the revenue from the issuance of public bonds covers the resulting shortage of financial resources. The latent national burden ratio B is a concept that includes the fiscal deficit, and the difference in B-A will lead to an increase in the burden on future generations. Public bonds refer to national and local bonds, and the issuance amount of the former is increasing as a long-term trend. One of the reasons is that the central government has an essential role in the operation and management of social security.

Fiscal consolidation through spending restraint has been promoted as part of administrative and fiscal reforms since 2000. Furthermore, since around 2010, a certain amount of tax revenue has been secured, the difference in B-A has gradually narrowed to 6.1% in 2015 and 5.3% in 2019 (see Sect. 6.3.2 in the previous chapter).[9] However, the amount of new issuance of public bonds continues to exceed the expenditure for debt redemption and interest payments, and the debt balance has increased accordingly.[10]

The debt balance (its ratio to GDP) was about seven trillion yen (10%) in 1970, 266 trillion yen (59%) in 1990, and 646 trillion yen (122%) in 2000. This exceeded 1000 trillion yen (188%) in 2014 and reached approximately 1106 trillion yen (198%) in 2019.[11] The breakdown of the debt balance in 2019 was 914 trillion yen of national bonds and 192 trillion yen of local bonds.

Although the revenue from issuing public bonds is essential as part of public funds in social security, the increase in debt balance is also a factor that restricts the stabilization of the system. One of the fundamental issues of social security

[9] In 1999, after the collapse of the bubble economy, B-A was 11.9%. B was 47.4%, and A was 35.5%. In 2009, immediately after the bankruptcy of Lehman Brothers, B-A was 14.5%. B was 51.7%, and A was 37.2%. These main factors were the decrease in corporate and personal income tax. The trend of tax revenue will be confirmed in Sect. 7.4.1.

[10] Using the 2019 general account as a reference, the outline is as follows. The total expenditure was 101,366.5 billion yen. The largest item was the social security-related expenditure of 33,500.7 billion yen (the proportion was 33%). The second was national bond expenditure of 22,285.7 billion yen (22%). The breakdown was 14,658.1 billion yen for debt redemption (14.5%) and 7627.6 billion yen for interest payments (7.5%). In contrast, the total revenue amounted to 109,162.4 billion yen (including carryover to the next year). The largest item was the tax and stamp revenue, which totaled 60,180 billion yen (55.1%). The second was revenue from the issuance of national bonds of 36,581.8 billion yen (33.5%). When national bond expenditure and issuance revenue are compared, the latter is greater, which is one factor leading to fiscal rigidity.

[11] For comparison, the ratio of debt balance to GDP in other countries (2019) was 108.2% in the United States, 98.1% in France, 85.2% in the United Kingdom, and 59.6% in Germany. Ministry of Finance (2021b, c).

is to secure stable financial resources for the benefits while promoting fiscal consolidation.

7.3.2 Changes in Population and Disease Structure

The main beneficiaries of social security are the elderly, and the main bearers are the workers. Changes in population structure are an important indicator for confirming these trends. We will summarize the basic issues related to these factors, considering several health risks associated with aging.

Table 7.4 shows trends in the total population, elderly population, working-age population A, and young population. B shown as references is the number of workers.

The total population increased over the long term after exceeding 100 million in 1967 and was 126.93 million in 2000. It peaked at 128.08 million in 2008 and decreased to 125.77 million in 2019. Subsequent estimates show a decrease to 122.54 million in 2025 and 110.92 million in 2040.

Table 7.4 Changes in population structure

	1970	1980	1990	2000	2010	2019	2025	2040
Total population	10,467 (100%)	11,706 (100%)	12,361 (100%)	12,693 (100%)	12,806 (100%)	12,577 (100%)	12,254 (100%)	11,092 (100%)
Elderly population	740 (7.1%)	1,065 (9.1%)	1,489 (12.0%)	2,201 (17.3%)	2,924 (22.8%)	3,592 (28.6%)	3,677 (30.0%)	3,920 (35.3%)
65-74 years old (the early-stage elderly)	516 (4.9%)	699 (6.0%)	892 (7.2%)	1,301 (10.2%)	1,517 (11.8%)	1,740 (13.8%)	1,497 (12.2%)	1,681 (15.2%)
75 years old and over (the latter-stage elderly)	224 (2.1%)	366 (3.1%)	597 (4.8%)	900 (7.1%)	1,407 (11.0%)	1,852 (14.7%)	2,180 (17.8%)	2,239 (20.2%)
Working-age population A 15-64 years old	7,212 (68.9%)	7,883 (67.3%)	8,590 (69.5%)	8,622 (67.9%)	8,103 (63.3%)	7,462 (59.3%)	7,170 (58.5%)	5,978 (53.9%)
Number of working-age population per elderly population	9.8	7.4	5.8	3.9	2.8	2.1	1.9	1.5
References Number of workers B	5,153 (49.2%)	5,650 (48.3%)	6,384 (51.6%)	6,766 (55.3%)	6,632 (51.8%)	6,724 (53.5%)	6,350 (51.8%)	5,650 (50.9%)
Number of workers per elderly population	6.9	5.3	4.3	3.1	2.3	1.9	1.7	1.4
Young population 0-14 years old	2,515 (24.0%)	2,751 (23.5%)	2,249 (18.2%)	1,847 (14.6%)	1,680 (13.1%)	1,524 (12.0%)	1,407 (11.5%)	1,194 (10.8%)
Age unknown	0 (0%)	7 (0.1%)	33 (0.27%)	23 (0.18%)	98 (0.77%)	0 (0%)	0 (0%)	0 (0%)

Note: The unit is 10,000 people (excludes number of working-age population per elderly population and number of workers per elderly population). The bracket is the percentage of the total population. It may not be 100% because it is rounded off to the nearest whole number. These numbers are actual until 2019 and estimated after this year. 2025 is the time when the so-called "baby boomer generation" will become the latter-stage elderly. 2040 is the time when the "baby boomer junior generation" will become the early-stage elderly. Number of workers B refers to those engaged in work and does not include the unemployed. Estimates for 2025 and 2040 in B are expected to increase if the employment rate of older people rises

Sources: Cabinet Office (2021), Mizuho Research Institute (2017), National Institute of Population and Social Security Research (2022)

The elderly population is increasing regardless of the increase or decrease in the total population, and its proportion to the total population (the aging rate) is rising accordingly. It increased by 21.5 percentage points over 50 years, from 7.1% in 1970 to 28.6% in 2019,[12] and it is expected to reach 30% in 2025 and 35.3% in 2040. In terms of these trends, the number of the latter-stage elderly is growing more than the number of the early-stage elderly.

The working-age population A has increased from 72.12 million (68.9%) in 1970, peaking at 87.16 million (69.4%) in 1995 and decreasing to 74.62 million (59.3%) in 2019. This is estimated to be 71.7 million (58.5%) in 2025 and 59.78 million (53.9%) in 2040. The main reason is the declining birthrate.[13] The young population has decreased by nearly ten million (12% points) over 50 years, from 25.15 million (24%) in 1970 to 15.24 million (12%) in 2019 and is expected to continue declining in the long term. The number of working-age populations per elderly population was 9.8 in 1970, 3.9 in 2000, and 2.1 in 2019. It is predicted to be 1.9 in 2025 and 1.5 or less after 2040.

The number of workers B, including workers over 65 years old, was 51.53 million (49.2%) in 1970 and in the range of 66.32–67.66 million (51.8–55.3%) from 2000 to 2019. This is estimated to decrease to 63.5 million (51.8%) in 2025 and 56.5 million (50.9%) in 2040. The number of workers per elderly population has decreased from 6.9 in 1970 to 3.1 in 2000 and 1.9 in 2019. It is predicted to be 1.7 in 2025 and 1.4 or less after 2040. Furthermore, while the number of workers aged 25–44 has been decreasing, the number of workers aged 45–64 is increasing in recent years.[14] Along with this, the average age of workers is gradually rising, and it is thought that this trend will not change over the long term.

As one of the methods in maintaining a certain workforce, it is necessary to deal with health risks and lifestyle-related diseases. The main examples of health risks are blood pressure, blood glucose, obesity, smoking and drinking habits, lack of exercise and sleep, and stress (in a broad sense, including pre-existing illnesses). These are considered a factor of lifestyle-related diseases, although there are individual differences depending on age, gender, and diathesis. Such diseases refer to malignant neoplasm, heart disease, cerebrovascular disease, diabetes mellitus, and hypertensive disease. With changes in the disease structure, the proportion of these diseases and the number of patients has increased, respectively.

There are two issues related to these, the first is declining labor productivity, and the second is decreasing number of workers. The first is due to presenteeism and absenteeism, as will be discussed in Sect. 7.4.2. Presenteeism refers to "working in poor physical and mental health," and absenteeism refers to "absence due to

[12] For comparison, the aging rates in other countries (2019) were 21.6% in Germany, 20.4% in France, 18.5% in the United Kingdom, and 16.2% in the United States. Ministry of Internal Affairs and Communications (2021a).

[13] The birthrate was 2.13 in 1970, and after falling below 1.5 in 1992, it was 1.36 in 2019.

[14] Ministry of Internal Affairs and Communications (2021b). The number of workers aged 60 and over or 65 and over (including part-time workers) also tends to increase.

treatment or hospitalization of illnesses and injuries."[15] The second issue arises when the number of relatively young workers decreases and long-term work by older workers (generally workers over 60 years old) becomes difficult due to health reasons. The decrease in workers will also make it more difficult to secure social security bearers.

In addition, it has been reported that more than half of the causes of death and one-third of medical care expenditure are due to lifestyle-related diseases (Fig. 7.1). The primary reason is the aggravation of these diseases.

Governments, companies, and medical care insurers advocate the importance of health promotion and disease prevention. These will benefit the workers and employers (companies), and everyone.

Next, Sect. 7.4 considers the methods and issues of the following two measures. The first is securing the financial resources for social security and fiscal consolidation, and the second is controlling health risks and lifestyle-related diseases (including a restraining increase in medical care expenditure).

7.4 Some Measures for Stabilization of the Social Security System

7.4.1 Comprehensive Reform of Social Security and Tax

Social insurance, such as pension and medical care, is the core of social security. When these benefits increase, the financial resources are, in principle, covered by raising social insurance premiums. However, since around 2000, the proportion of public funds has been increasing, as seen in Sect. 7.2. The following four are pointed out as the main reasons.

First, as the number of workers decrease, it is becoming more difficult to increase employee contributions. Second, there is not enough consensus on increasing employer contributions due to the prolonged slow economic growth. Third, a certain percentage of employee and employer medical insurance premiums are used for elderly medical care, increasing these burdens. Fourth, because pension benefits have not been substantially increased, raising insurance premiums for the elderly is becoming difficult.

Among the public funds covered from the revenues of central and local governments, consumption tax revenue has increased since the 1990s. This tax system was introduced by abolishing excise tax in 1989 (excluding the transfer of land and securities, interest on savings and loans, medical and long-term care services). While the consumption tax rates were 3% in 1989 and 5% in 1997, the tax revenue

[15] Stress is regarded as the leading cause of mental health-related illnesses among health risks. When it becomes severe, it necessitates long-term hospitalization. The number of such workers has grown in recent years.

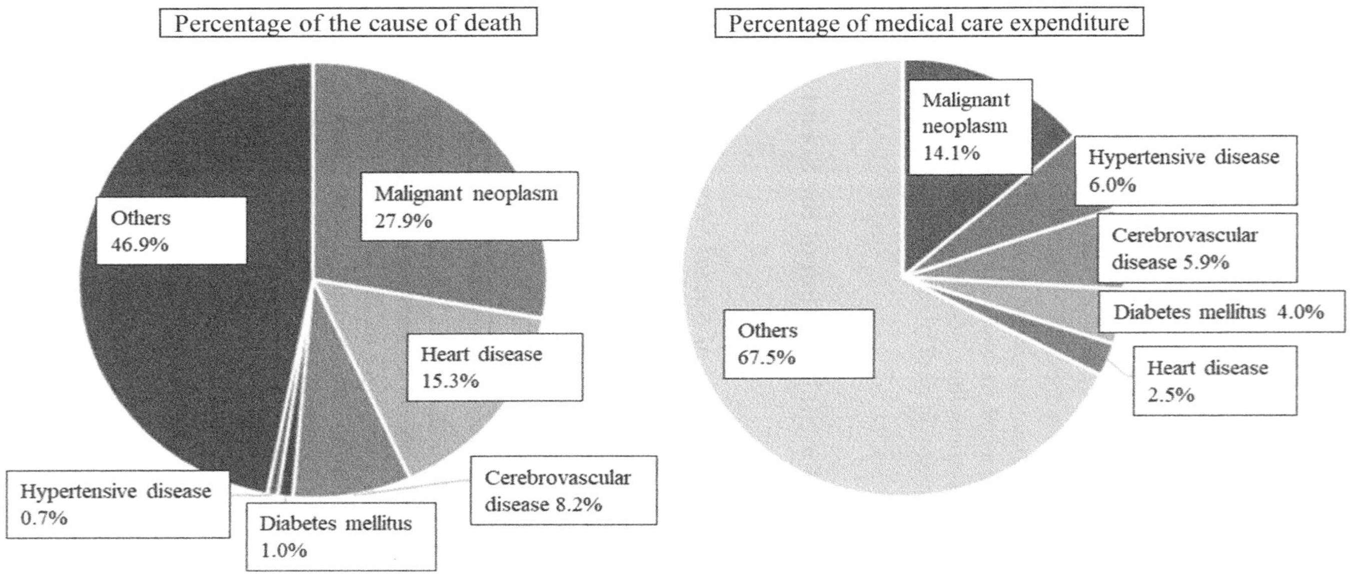

Fig. 7.1 Percentage of lifestyle-related diseases in the cause of death and medical care expenditure. [Source: Japan Preventive Association of Life-style related Disease (2019)]

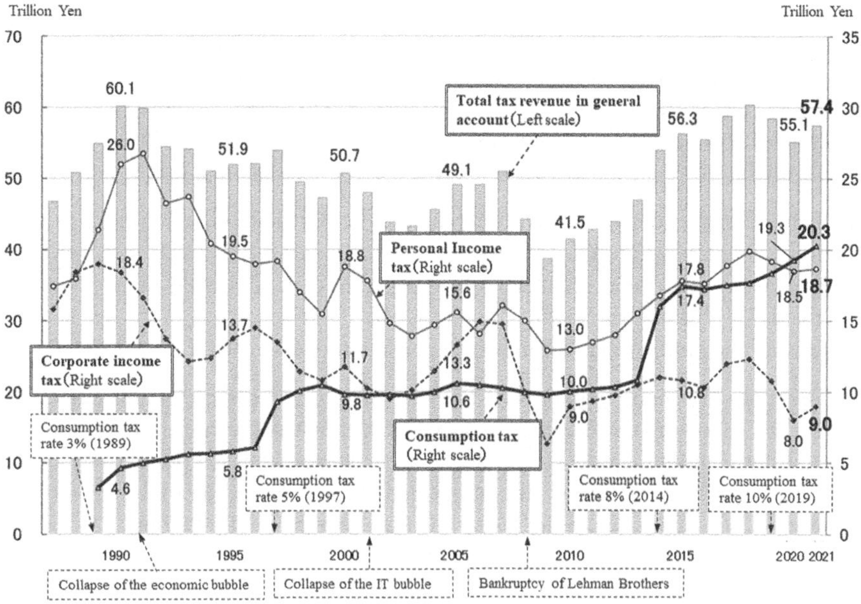

Fig. 7.2 Trends in the tax revenues in general account. Note: 2020 is the revised amount. 2021 is the budget amount. [Source: Ministry of Finance (2021d)]

from this was insufficient as a financial resource for social security. It also did not contribute to restraining the fiscal deficit.

The comprehensive reform of social security and tax (CRSST) was proposed in 2012 as one of the measures to address these issues and was approved by the Cabinet in 2014.[16] Although the tax rate of 10% was assumed in the original plan, considering the impact on economic activity, this was set at 8% in 2014 and then raised to 10% in 2019 (the breakdown is 7.8% for national consumption tax and 2.2% for local consumption tax).

There are two reasons why the consumption tax is desirable to secure financial resources. First, consumption expenditure is less affected by economic trends than personal and corporate income, so stable tax revenues are expected. Second, since consumption expenditure is tax based, it is possible to secure the revenue in a way that does not bias the burden on workers. About the first, Fig. 7.2 outlines the trends in tax revenues of personal income tax, corporate income tax, and consumption tax in the general account.

Personal and corporate income tax revenues tended to decrease, following the collapse of the economic bubble, the collapse of the IT bubble, and the bankruptcy of Lehman Brothers (except for the impact on tax revenue due to tax reform). These had little effect on consumption tax revenue, which remained relatively stable even

[16] For detailed content, Iwamoto (2008), Nakamura (2021), and Tajika (2021) are useful.

when the tax rate was raised in 1997 and 2014. This tax revenue is expected to exceed personal and corporate income tax revenues after 2020.

Approximately 14 trillion yen is supposed to be a financial resource on CRSST. This is the tax revenue secured by the difference between the tax rate of 5% in 2013 and that of 10% in 2019 (tax revenue per 1% is approximately 2.8 trillion yen). The following three are the uses of such tax revenue (budget amount, proportion):

1. Stabilizing the social security system and reducing the burden on future generations (about 7.3 trillion yen, 52.1%)
2. Expansion of pension, medical care, long-term care, and child-rearing support (about 3.5 trillion yen, 25%)
3. Raising the public funds for the basic pension (about 3.2 trillion yen, 22.9%)

These are the concrete plans of CRSST, which are, in principle, measures until 2025. The following two are the main issues, the first is the consumption tax rate in the future, and the second is the problem associated with the regressivity of the burden. Regarding the former, the abovementioned tax revenue of 14 trillion yen is only 11.29% compared to the social security benefits in 2019 (about 124 trillion yen). Therefore, the timing and method of raising the tax rate will be considered an important issue.[17]

One of the factors that would affect the consumption tax rate is the trend of social security benefits. These are estimated to be at least 140.2 trillion yen in 2025 (nominally 1.13 times that of 2019) and 188.2 trillion yen in 2040 (1.52 times that of 2019). Among them, the increase in medical care expenditure is large, which was about 40.7 trillion yen in 2019, while it is estimated to be 47.8 trillion yen in 2025 (1.17 times that of 2019) and 66.7 trillion yen in 2040 (1.64 times that of 2019).[18]

In order to suppress the increase in the consumption tax rate that would be necessary along with this, it is required to take some measures. The main methods are as follows: (1) promotion of the family doctor system in outpatient care, (2) correcting long-term hospitalization and expanding home medical care, (3) appropriate medication (prescription) and review of the drug pricing system, (4) promotion of preventive health care, (5) strengthening the functions of medical care insurers, and (6) introduction of telemedicine (online health care). These are emphasized in the health-care system reform or the Ministry of Health, Labour and Welfare measure. The basic directions are improving the efficiency of the medical care provision system and controlling the rate of increase in medical fees.[19]

A certain amount of financial resources is necessary to maintain universal health insurance while reducing the fiscal deficit. By contrast, to minimize the impact on consumption and production activities, it would be required to suppress the

[17] This is also an issue related to "Social security for all generations," which is being proposed as the next measure for CRSST (an outline will be summarized in Sect. 7.5).

[18] Ministry of Finance (2020)

[19] In recent years, medical fees have gradually shifted from a fee-for-service payment system to a flat (fixed) payment system centered on inpatient medical care.

excessive burdens such as consumption tax and insurance premiums for medical care. Among the above methods, (4)–(6) are also new themes related to this, and the purpose and outline will be considered in Sect. 7.4.2.

When the direction of increasing the consumption tax is selected, it is important to deal with the regressivity of the burden as the second issue. Except for the reduced tax rate on certain goods and services, a measure is not always implemented in CRSST. Some of the basic policies for this issue are to increase benefits and lower insurance premiums for low-income earners. Furthermore, the upper limits of insurance premium rates for high-income earners would need to be raised.

In addition, discussions on the long-term perspective are becoming necessary when considering the allocation of the tax burden. The relationship among income (including salary, interest and dividend, pension), consumption (expenditure), and inheritance in each person's life will generally be as follows:

$$[1] \text{ Received inheritance} + [2] \text{ Income} \fallingdotseq [3] \text{ Consumption} + [4] \text{ Remaining inheritance}$$

In the constraint on the left side ([1] + [2]), [3] on the right side is the consumption tax base, and the rest other than it will be [4]. It would be one of the options to raise the inheritance tax (including the gift tax) as a progressive tax on [4], if the consumption tax is emphasized as a basic financial resource.

In general, the expansion of social security benefits has been positively evaluated, and the increase in the burden of taxes and insurance premiums has been viewed critically. However, increasing these burdens is a critical issue for the long-term stability of the system, and several proposals have been made since the latter half of the 1990s. While CRSST is more useful as one of them, it may be required to address the above two issues.

7.4.2 *Promotion of Preventive Health Care*

In Japan, health promotion and disease prevention are advocated as a theme related to health care and the economy (including social security finance). The following three measures have been considered and implemented since around 2010. The first is Health and Productivity Management,[20] the second is Health Japan 21,[21] and the

[20] ACOEM guidance statement (2009), Berger et al. (2003), Hull (2008), Loeppke (2008), Ministry of Economy, Trade, and Industry (2017), Ogata (2018), Parkinson (2013). The origin of Health and Productivity Management is in the United States, called *KenkoKeiei* in Japan. *Kenkokeiei* is a registered trademark of the NPO Health Management Study Group.

[21] Ministry of Health, Labour and Welfare (2012, 2016)

third is Data Health Plan.[22] Although there are differences in the backgrounds and methods, these are important measures that are interrelated. We will consider mainly the first and second and look at the future direction.

The first Health and Productivity Management aims to simultaneously manage workers' health and productivity and minimize some costs caused by presenteeism and absenteeism (especially the former). According to an example of the fact-finding survey, the costs would vary depending on the number and condition of health risks (see Sect. 7.3.2 about health risks). These costs are estimated to be about 900,000 yen as annual cost per worker at maximum; the breakdown (proportion to total cost) is pointed out as follows. Productivity loss due to presenteeism is 78%, medical care expenditure is 15.7%, and productivity loss due to absenteeism is 4.4% (others, sickness and injury allowance is 1%; occupational accident compensation cost is 0.9%).[23]

Health and Productivity Management is supposed to deal with these issues based on the collaboration between companies and medical care insurers. The method is primary prevention, which generally refers to encouraging periodic health checkups, specific health checkups and specific health guidance,[24] and stress checks. Additionally, a wellness program that is an effort of health promotion in each workplace is recommended, and it includes the practice of "work-life balance."

Secondary prevention is also needed to prevent the prolonged declines in QOL and productivity of workers associated with illness or injury. This is intended to reduce aggravation and long-term hospitalization, and early detection and treatment are required. Early detection is based on detailed examinations such as computed tomography (CT) and magnetic resonance imaging (MRI). Early treatment refers to treatment at an early stage on these examination results.

These have significant implications for each worker and company, as well as for the economy and social security finance more broadly. Concretely, when many workers' physical and mental health is maintained, and employment opportunities for workers with long-term motivation to work are secured, a substantive discussion about pension finance stabilization would be possible.[25] These measures are also

[22] Ministry of Health, Labour and Welfare (2017). Some examples of each medical care insurer can be viewed on the website.

[23] Ministry of Economy, Trade and Industry (2016), Todai Policy Alternatives Research Institute (University of Tokyo) (2016). These risks and costs vary by industry, occupation, age, and gender. Such research and analysis are important issues for the future.

[24] Specific health checkups for people aged 40–74 years focus on metabolic syndrome. Specific health guidance refers to advice provided by specialized personnel such as health nurses and registered dietitians and is intended for people who are at high risk of developing lifestyle-related diseases. In this case, the method is based on the results of specific health checkups. These two goals are to prevent lifestyle-related diseases, which account for nearly 60% of causes of death, and one-third of medical care expenditure (see Fig. 7.1).

[25] As an example, in addition to raising the age of receiving pension, the "Act on Stabilization of Employment of Elderly Persons" will be promoted. The purposes of this act are the following two: (1) to make the retirement age of 65 years old mandatory (transitional period until March 2025)

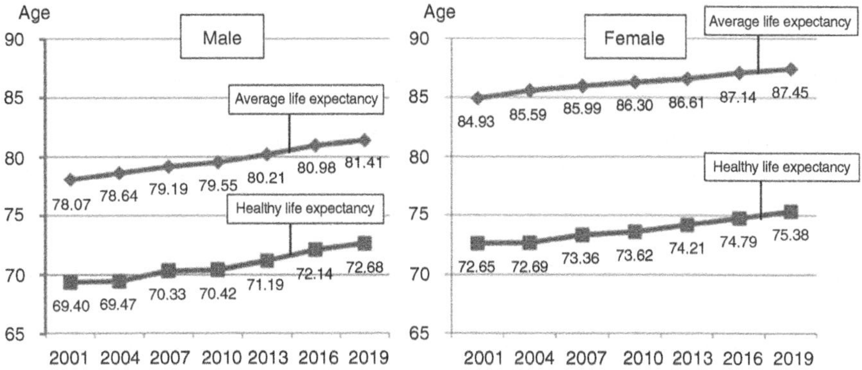

Fig. 7.3 Trends in average life expectancy and healthy life expectancy. [Source: Ministry of Health, Labour and Welfare (2021)]

thought to be effective in controlling medical care expenditure and containing increases in insurance premiums.

The second Health Japan 21 aims to maintain the QOL of each person over the long term and extend healthy life expectancy. This expectancy is a concept advocated by the WHO (World Health Organization) in 2000 and generally refers to the period in which health reasons do not restrict daily life, and a self-reliant life is possible. Figure 7.3 shows changes in Japan's average life expectancy and healthy life expectancy.

The difference between average and healthy life expectancy is approximately 9 years for males and 12.5 years for females. In Health Japan 21, it is a critical issue to reduce the gap while extending healthy life expectancy by about 3 years. As one of the methods, health promotion after around the late 30s, when health risks begin to rise, is considered effective. There are various types of health risks, and each person needs to respond appropriately, so medical care insurers and IT-related companies provide support, such as providing information.

Health Japan 21 has become an important measure for workers' families (mainly spouses and the elderly) in relation to the first Health and Productivity Management. In this regard, when someone in the family (including a family living far away) needs treatment or home care, the worker may be absent from work to accompany or care for the family. Preventive health care for families is emphasized in minimizing the decline in productivity associated with these reasons.

As a role of medical care insurers in the above two measures, evidence-based health services are advocated. The third Data Health Plan is a measure based on this, and long-term health and medical data utilization are premised. This is based on the following three premises: (1) collection of information such as results of

and (2) to create an environment where people who are willing to work regardless of age can be employed up to 70 years old (in the future, 75 years old).

periodic and specific health checkups and health insurance claims, (2) analysis of health risk types and incidence risks, and (3) utilization of information for health management, health guidance, and early treatment. These are also the requirements for preventive health care throughout each person's life and would be a significant effort toward Japan approaching the society of "100-years of life."

The first, second, and third measures have been practically implemented since around 2015 and are being investigated and researched for further promotion and improved outcomes. The following three are the main issues in the future, and among them, [3] is a new theme related to using ICT (information and communication technology).[26]

1. **Strengthening from primary prevention to secondary prevention**
   While the above three measures are based on primary prevention, the seamless practice with secondary prevention is considered effective for suppressing aggravation and long-term hospitalization. As a concrete measure, it is needed to strengthen the cooperation between medical care insurers and medical institutions and establish a system in which the information on primary prevention can be utilized for early detection and treatment as secondary prevention.
2. **Expansion of self-care (including self-medication)**
   Central and local governments, companies (employers), and medical care insurers advocate for preventive health care. The requirement to promote this and improve the outcomes is the voluntary participation of each person/patient, and self-care is one of the essential opportunities. In this case, it is necessary to provide and utilize the information that raises their awareness of participation in prevention. This is also related to the next issue.
3. **Introduction and utilization of Personal Health Record (PHR)**
   PHR is an individual record that contains digitized information such as vital data, examination results, treatment, and medication history. In a narrow sense, it is shared by patients and their doctors. The opportunities for utilization are not only office visits (face-to-face medical care) and video visits (telemedicine) but also self-care, health management, and home care. PHR is the basic information for each person/patient to participate in these in the long run, and as one of the ICT, some tests for introduction and utilization are currently underway.[27]

[26] Ministry of Health, Labour and Welfare (2020), Ministry of Internal Affairs and Communications (2017)

[27] Although PHR is useful information, it is considered difficult to widely use it under the current system. The main reason is that the Japan's health-care system emphasizes "face-to-face medical care with free access," and medical fees are set and revised accordingly. The term "free access" means that, in principle, patients are free to choose a clinic or hospital when receiving medical care. Reviewing such systems, particularly the outpatient care system (including the medical fee) is a premise for introducing and utilizing PHR. In this case, it would be necessary to consider expanding the family doctor system and telemedicine (online medical care) while protecting personal privacy.

7.5 Summary and Future Directions

The fundamental issue of social security in Japan is increasing and stabilizing the financial resources, in addition to reviewing the scope and method of benefits. Comprehensive reform of social security and tax aims to secure financial resources by raising the consumption tax, and is considered one of the basic policies for the stabilization of the system.

Such a measure is also a premise for promoting "Social security for all generations" in anticipation of 2040 when the number of workers will further decrease as the benefits increase with the progress of aging.[28] This is intended to reduce the excessive burden on workers and stabilize the benefits throughout each person's life. The main issues in the future are the methods of raising the consumption tax rate and allocating financial resources to each system.

In addition to these measures directly related to the financial resources and benefits, the measures based on the population trends and the changes in disease structure are becoming more important. The background is that the number of young workers is decreasing while the number of older workers with some health risks is increasing. Preventive health care aims to reduce these risks and lifestyle-related diseases and maintain each person's QOL in the long term. Health and Productivity Management, Health Japan 21, and Data Health Plan are concrete methods that are being phased in.

These are considered effective for maintaining labor productivity and the labor force, securing the bearers in pension, and reducing the increase in medical care expenditure. The main issues in the future are the strengthening from primary prevention to secondary prevention and the utilization of ICT (especially PHR) that encourages the voluntary participation of each person. These efforts would be beneficial in modern society, where the awareness of health (or healthy life expectancy) is increasing, and the technologies of examination and treatment are advancing.

The comprehensive reform of social security and tax (including the subsequent social security for all generations) and the promotion of preventive health care are mutually related measures. The latter is not originally aimed at securing financial resources. However, it has an important meaning as one of the new measures for stabilizing financial systems such as pension and medical care.

Acknowledgements I would like to thank Professor Emeritus Shuetsu Takahashi and Professor Kei Hosoya for some valuable suggestions. I also would like to thank seminar participants at several meetings on *modern macroeconomics with historical perspectives*. Furthermore, I have received significant comments from Dr. Takeshi Yamamoto (Sapporo Medical University) regarding his medical expertise. All errors and imprecisions are my responsibility.

[28] See footnote 17 in Sect. 7.4.1.

References

ACOEM Guidance Statement (2009) Healthy workforce/healthy economy: the role of health, productivity, and disability management in addressing the nation's health care crisis. J Occup Environ Med 51(1):114–119

Berger M, Howell R, Nicholson S, Sharda C (2003) Investing in healthy human capital. J Occup Environ Med 45(12):1213–1225

Cabinet Office (2021) Annual report on the ageing society. https://www8.cao.go.jp/kourei/english/annualreport/2021/pdf/. Accessed 19 Sept 2021

Hull S (2008) A larger role for preventive medicine, American Medical Association. J Ethics 10(11):724–729

Iwamoto Y (2008) Taxes and insurance premiums as social security resources. Research Institute of Economy, Trade and Industry, Tokyo, pp 1–25

Japan Preventive Association of Life-Style Related Disease (2019.) What is a lifestyle-related disease? https://www.seikatsusyukanbyo.com/prevention/about.php. Accessed 23 Jan 2021

Loeppke R (2008) The value of health and the power of prevention. Int J Workplace Health Manag 1(2):95–108

Ministry of Economy, Trade and Industry (2016) The 9th health investment WG secretariat explanatory materials. https://www.meti.go.jp/committee/kenkyukai/shoujo/jisedai_healthcare/kenkou_toushi_wg/pdf/009_02_00.pdf. Accessed 19 Sept 2020

Ministry of Economy, Trade and Industry (2017) Promotion of health management and health investment. http://www.kk-kaigi.com/pdf/2017material_nishikawa.pdf. Accessed 19 Sept 2020

Ministry of Finance (2020) About social security: reference material. https://www.mof.go.jp/about_mof/councils/fiscal_system_council/sub-of_fiscal_system/proceedings/material/zaiseia20201008/02.pdf. Accessed 3 Jan 2022

Ministry of Finance (2021a) Trends in national burden ratio. https://www.mof.go.jp/policy/budget/topics/futanritsu/sy202102a.pdf. Accessed 19 Sept 2021

Ministry of Finance (2021b) Materials related to public finance in Japan. https://www.mof.go.jp/policy/budget/fiscalcondition/related_data/202110_00.pdf. Accessed 14 Dec 2021

Ministry of Finance (2021c) International comparison of national burden ratio 2019. https://www.mof.go.jp/policy/budget/topics/futanritsu/sy202102b.pdf. Accessed 23 Jan 2021

Ministry of Finance (2021d) Trends of tax revenue in general account. https://www.mof.go.jp/tax_policy/summary/condition/010.pdf. Accessed 15 Mar 2021

Ministry of Health, Labour and Welfare (2012) Reference materials for promoting Health Japan, p 21. https://www.mhlw.go.jp/bunya/kenkou/dl/kenkounippon21_02.pdf. Accessed 3 Jan 2020

Ministry of Health, Labour and Welfare (2016) Annual health, labor and welfare report 2016-thinking about a social model that overcomes the aging population. Nikkei Printing, Tokyo

Ministry of Health, Labour and Welfare (2017) Data health planning guide: revised edition. https://www.mhlw.go/jp/file/06-Seisakujouhou-12400000-Hokenkyoku/0000201969.pdf. Accessed 23 Sept 2020

Ministry of Health, Labour and Welfare (2020) A system that allows the person to electronically check and utilize medical examination/examination information. https://www.mhlw.go.jp/content/12600000/000639832.pdf. Accessed 27 Feb 2021

Ministry of Health, Labour and Welfare (2021) Trends in average life expectancy and healthy life expectancy. https://www.mhlw.go.jp/content/10904750/000872952.pdf. Accessed 23 Jan 2022

Ministry of Internal Affairs and Communications (2017) Medical ICT policy promoted by the Ministry of Internal Affairs and Communications. https://www.soumu.go.jp/main_content/000518773.pdf. Accessed 9 Dec 2020

Ministry of Internal Affairs and Communications (2021a) Population of the elderly. https://www.stat.go.jp/data/topics/topi1211.html. Accessed 3 Jan 2022

Ministry of Internal Affairs and Communications (2021b) Labor force survey. https://www.stat.go.jp/data/roudou/sokuhou/nen/ft/pdf/index1.pdf. Accessed 11 Sept 2021

Mizuho Research Institute (2017) 40% decrease in working population due to declining birthrate and aging population, https://www.mizuho-rt.co.jp/publication/mhri/research/pdf/insight/pl170531.pdf, Accessed 17 Feb 2023

Nakamura S (2021) What is the comprehensive reform of social security and tax? A necessary step to protect, evolve and maintain Japan's social security system. J Soc Secur Res 5(4):9

National Institute of Population and Social Security Research (2019) Population projections for Japan: 2016–2065. http://www.ipss.go.jp/ss-cost/j/fsss-h30/H30.pdf. Accessed 8 Nov 2021

National Institute of Population and Social Security Research (2021) Financial statistics of social security in Japan: 2019. http://www.ipss.go.jp/ss-cost/j/fsss-R01/R01.pdf. Accessed 19 Sept 2021

National Institute of Population and Social Security Research (2022) Population statistics collection, https://www.ipss.go.jp/syoushika/tohkei/Popular/Popular2022.asp?chap=8, Accessed 17 Feb 2023

Ogata H (2018) Current status and issues of health management in Japan (in Japanese), Meiji Yasuda Research Institute, Inc. https://www.myri.co.jp/publication/myilw/pdf/myilw_no95_feature_2.pdf. Accessed 19 Sept 2021

Parkinson M (2013) Employer health and productivity roadmap™ strategy. J Occup Environ Med 55(12):46–51

Tajika E (2021) Synchronized reform of social welfare and tax: why did it fail to achieve the fiscal balance of Japan? J Soc Secur Res 5(4):449–459

Todai Policy Alternatives Research Institute (University of Tokyo) (2016) Visualization of health issues through the framework of health management. http://square.umin.ac.jp/hpm/hpmintro.html. Accessed 28 Sept 2020

Chapter 8
The Effect of Political Uncertainty and Political Lobbying

Eriko Aihara and Tsuyoshi Shinozaki

Abstract This chapter aims to show that a desirable level of public investment is not achieved under political uncertainty. First, we theoretically analyze whether public investment increases with the degree of special interest politics and decreases with degree of political uncertainty. Second, using 2007–2017 Japanese data, we empirically investigate whether our theoretical hypothesis is justified. Our results show that (1) public consumption increases as the number of local councilors increases and (2) public investment and consumption increases in prefectures with more construction workers (i.e., more special interest groups). Hence, coexistence of the opposite effects of public uncertainty and lobbying pressure from interest groups may lead to policies in the desired direction.

Keywords Political uncertainty · Political lobbying · Public investment · Two-period model

JEL Classification: E62, H30, H72

8.1 Introduction

This chapter aims to show that a desirable public investment policy is not implemented under political uncertainty and political lobbying. It has been shown both theoretically and empirically that a desirable level of public investment is not achieved during periods when political regime changes occur frequently. One of

E. Aihara (✉)
Toyota Tsusho Systems USA, Plano, TX, USA

T. Shinozaki
Faculty of Economics, Tohoku-Gakuin University, Sendai, Miyagi, Japan
e-mail: shinozaki@mail.tohoku-gakuin.ac.jp

S. Takahashi et al. (eds.), *Modern Macroeconomics with Historical Perspectives*, New Frontiers in Regional Science: Asian Perspectives 67,
https://doi.org/10.1007/978-981-99-1067-0_8

the pioneering works, Besley and Coate (1998), demonstrated that, under political uncertainty, governments may forego public investments, which is "political failure," even if it will benefit them in the future. Moreover, it has recently become evident that political failures occur because of various reasons. Recent studies have shown that this is caused by the reelection motive under a two-party system and special interest politics.

Regarding the former, two types of studies exist: one based on a (two-period) static model and the other based on an economic growth model. Using a static framework, Bohn (2007) recently presented a two-period static model incorporating political uncertainty and polarization and analyzed the optimal composition of government spending. He found that the greater the degree of political uncertainty and polarization, the more inefficient the ruling party increases public consumption to increase its chances of being elected. The same model can also explain under-investment in the pension problem (Elder and Wagner 2015) and accumulation of public debt (Bohn 2019). However, Darby et al. (2004) analyzed it using an endogenous growth model. They analyzed how political uncertainty affects the optimal composition of government spending and demonstrated that reduced public investment and increased public consumption to obtain votes from current voters would result in a negative impact on economic growth. Moreover, they conclude that the steady-state equilibrium is inefficient and does not maximize social welfare.

Regarding the latter, several related studies have demonstrated that the politics of interest groups influence government spending composition. Persson (1998) and Persson and Tabellini (1999) demonstrate that regions with interest groups benefiting from public goods are more influenced by their political pressure than the socially optimal level. Local governments with politicians interested in political contributions misallocate local public investment and consumption goods.

These theoretical studies indicate that (1) political uncertainty causes a shift to public consumption, increasing current utility of voters instead of public investment, which increases the utility for future voters. (2) The political activity of interest groups has the effect of increasing government spending associated with those interest groups.

From the perspective of empirical analysis, the focus is on the impact of political uncertainty on the behavior of political interest groups. Regarding political uncertainty, numerous analyses about political uncertainty index have been made using various countries' data. In situations of high political uncertainty, the uncertainty of economic policies chosen by politicians increases, such as the economic policy uncertainty (EPU) index based on the number of newspaper articles describing political uncertainty by Baker et al. (2016). Saxegaard et al. (2022) recently applied this index to Japan to index policy uncertainty. Before 2005, because the Liberal Democratic Party was a long-ruling party, EPU was low around 2005. However, this index increased in the following periods: (1) in 2009, because the ruling party shifted from the long-ruling Liberal Democratic Party to the Democratic Party of Japan; (2) in 2010, because the Democratic Party of Japan's Prime Minister Hatoyama resigned; and (3) in 2011, because the US debt rating was downgraded, European debt crisis worsened, and Prime Minister Kan resigned.

Based on this background, we analyze the effect of political uncertainty and lobbying in Japan by conducting a panel data analysis using data from Japan's 47 prefectures from 2007 to 2017. We used 2007–2017 data because, in 2007–2011, the ruling party shifted from the Liberal Democratic Party to the Democratic Party of Japan (in fact EPU increased). Moreover, in the period 2012–2017, the opposition parties repeated dissolutions and mergers.

First, from the theoretical analysis, we explain that public investment increases with special interest groups and decreases with political uncertainty. Second, from an empirical analysis, we demonstrate that (1) an increase in the number of local Democratic Party legislators increases public consumption and (2) an increase in the number of construction workers increases public investment and consumption.

The remainder of this chapter is organized as follows. Section 8.2 presents our theoretical model. Section 8.3 discusses the testable implications of the model using empirical evidence. Finally, Sect. 8.4 discusses the policy implications and explores possibilities for future research.

8.2 Model

We extend the model constructed by Bohn (2007) to describe the situation of political uncertainty between the two major parties to add political lobbying of private firms constituting special interest groups.

8.2.1 *Basic Setting*

The model comprised two periods. There are two sectors: the government (current and opposing parties) and private sectors. Preferences of the current government, $j(=f, g)$, over periods 1 and 2, are the sum of the utility from private sectors $V_i(\cdot)$ $(i = 1, 2)$, and the sum of the utility in government j's provision of the amounts of two public consumption goods, $H_i^j(\cdot, \cdot)$, in both periods and the amount of campaign contribution, $Z^j(I)$ as follows:

$$W^f = V_1(C_1) + H_1^f\left(F_1^f, G_1^f\right) + Z^f(I) + E\left\{\rho\left(V_2(C_2) + H_2^f\left(G_2^f, F_2^f\right)\right)\right\}, \tag{8.1}$$

where C_j and I represent the private sector consumption and the public investments, respectively, and also G_j^i and F_j^irepresent the amount of two types of public goods provided government $i(=f, g)$ in periods $j(=1, 2)$, respectively. F_j^i is beneficial only to one group in society and G_j^i exclusively to the other. E is the expectation operator, and $\rho(<1)$ is the government's discount factor. Both subutility functions $V_i(C_i)$ and $Z^j(I)$ are strictly concave.

The incumbent government has utility in the provision of public consumption goods. F provides a benefit only to one (interest) group and G exclusively to the other (opposing interest group supported by another party).

Political uncertainty and polarization exist. We define P as the exogenous (fixed) probability from the viewpoint of period 1 that the current government loses, and $1 - P$ as the probability that it wins. The two types of government (f and g) each provide two types of public consumption goods, but to different degrees. Preferences for H_i^f and H_i^g are expressed by their respective public consumption goods as follows:

$$
\begin{aligned}
H^f\left(F^f, G^f\right) &= \min\left[\frac{F^f}{\alpha^f}, \frac{G^f}{1-\alpha^f}\right], 1 > \alpha^f \geq \tfrac{1}{2}, \\
H^g\left(F^g, G^g\right) &= \min\left[\frac{F^g}{1-\alpha^g}, \frac{G^g}{\alpha^g}\right], 1 > \alpha^g \geq \tfrac{1}{2}.
\end{aligned} \tag{8.2}
$$

Exogenous parameter α^j captures the relative weight that government j places on the provision of F rather than G. Following Bohn (2007), we assume that the discrepancy between the two governments in the provision of public goods is symmetrically parameterized; that is, $\alpha^f = \alpha^g = \alpha$. Moreover, the property of the H_i^j is the utility from public consumption goods equal X^j, defined by the sum of expenditures on both public consumption goods: $H^j(F^j, G^j) = X^j :- F^j + G^j$. Hence, marginal utility of public consumption goods is 1.

The government budget constraints for both periods are as follows:

$$
\begin{aligned}
I + G_1 + F_1 &\leq \tau\overline{Y}, \\
G_2 + F_2 &\leq \tau Y(I),
\end{aligned} \tag{8.3}
$$

where τ, Y, and $\overline{Y}$ represent the income tax rate, income of the first period, and income of the second period, respectively. From (8.3), two kinds of government expenditure are available: public consumption, G or F, and public investment, I. As assumed by Bohn (2007), the income of period 2, $Y(I)$, is a concave, increasing, and differentiable function of I.

We assume the budget constraints of private sector are independent in each period:

$$
\begin{aligned}
C_1 &\leq (1-\tau)\overline{Y}, \\
C_2 &\leq (1-\tau)Y(I),
\end{aligned} \tag{8.4}
$$

where the utility from public consumption goods has an implication for the optimal choice by two alternative governments, f and g. First, utility derived from type f's choice of incumbent government is equal to the public consumption goods utility derived from type g's choice: $H^f(F^f, G^f) = F^f + G^f = X^f = X = X^g = F^g + G^g = H^g(F^g, G^g)$. Second, government g's optimal choice for F and G is suboptimal for government f, that is, $X^f = H^f(F^f, G^f) > H^g(F^g, G^g) = ((1-\alpha)/\alpha)X^g$.

In period 1, the incumbent government chooses the quantity of public consumption goods in period 1; however, it can only choose in period 2 if it does not lose power. The utility function (8.1) becomes the following:

$$\begin{aligned} W &= V_1(C_1) + X_1 + Z^f(I) + \rho \\ &\quad \left[(1-P)(V_2(C_2) + X_2) + P\left(V_2(C_2) + \tfrac{1-\alpha}{\alpha} X_2\right) \right] \\ &= V_1(C_1) + X_1 + Z^f(I) + \rho\left[V_2(C_2) + \beta X_2\right], \end{aligned} \tag{8.5}$$

where $\beta = 1 - P + P\left(\frac{1-\alpha}{\alpha}\right) \in [0, 1]$.

Assume that private firms undertake public investments and that these private firms constitute special interest groups that can lobby the government. As these special interest groups can provide contributions, Z^f, to the government in return for influencing public investment, I, special interest groups offer a differentiable contribution schedule for public investment, $Z^f(I)$, to policy makers ($Z^{f'}(I) > 0$). Consequently, the payoff for the special interest group is as follows:

$$\Pi_f = \pi_f - Z^f(I), \tag{8.6}$$

where π_f represents gross profit of private firm.

Following Grossman and Helpman (1994), we focus on the truthful contribution schedule; $Z^f(I) = \max\{0, \pi_f - b\}$, where b represents constant correspondence to the reservation profit. Thus, the private firm's maximization condition must satisfy the following:

$$\frac{\partial \pi_f}{\partial I} = \frac{\partial Z^f}{\partial I}, \tag{8.7}$$

where this satisfies $Z^f > 0$.

Next, we derive the social optimal level of public investment by solving the social planning problem. In this case, because there is no political uncertainty, the problem can be written as follows:

$$\max V_1\left((1-\tau)\overline{Y}\right) + \tau\overline{Y} - I + \rho\left[V_2((1-\tau)Y(I)) + \tau Y(I)\right]. \tag{8.8}$$

Thus, the condition of social optimal public investment is as follows:

$$-1 + \rho\left[V_2'(1-\tau)Y'(I) + \tau Y'(I)\right] = 0. \tag{8.9}$$

Equation (8.9) shows that marginal utility must equal the marginal cost of public investment in the social optimal. The first term, -1, means marginal cost of public investment, the second term is the marginal utility of consumption in private sector,

$V_2'(1-\tau)Y'(I)$, and third term is the marginal utility of public consumption $\tau Y'(I)$ through public investment.

8.2.2 *Effect of Political Uncertainty and Lobbying on Level of Public Investment*

In this section, we show the effect of political uncertainty and lobbying activities from special interest groups organized by private firms on the public investment level. From Eq. (8.5), the incumbent government maximizes the following objective function in the truthful equilibrium:

$$W = V_1\left((1-\tau)\overline{Y}\right) + \tau\overline{Y} - I + \pi_f(I) + \rho\left[V_2\left((1-\tau)Y(I)\right) + \beta\tau Y(I)\right]. \tag{8.10}$$

The first-order condition is as follows:

$$-1 + \pi_f'(I) + \rho\left[V_2'(1-\tau)Y'(I) + \beta(P)\tau Y'(I)\right] = 0. \tag{8.11}$$

Comparing (8.8) and (8.11), we see that (1) if $\beta(P) < 1$, the government evaluates by discounting marginal utility of public consumption, $\beta(P)\tau Y'(I)$, through public investment, while (2) since $\pi_1'(I) > 0$, lobbying activity from private firm has the effect of increasing level of public investment.[1] Thus, the level of public investment is determined by the effect of underinvestment due to political uncertainty and overinvestment due to lobbying.

Bohn (2007) analyzed only the effect of political uncertainty but showed that an increase in the parameter of political uncertainty exacerbates underinvestment. Conversely, our model shows that if lobbying by a private firm exists, it may be mitigated. Considering that both effects coexist in most developed countries, which effects are stronger is an empirical question.

8.3 Empirical Analysis

In the previous section, the theoretical model clarified that political uncertainty and special interest group politics affected the composition of government spending. Based on this result, we empirically investigate whether ruling parties facing political uncertainty increase public consumption or public investment as a result of lobbying. In the next subsection, we describe the political situation in Japan during

[1] Effect of political uncertainty is in Appendix.

the period of political uncertainty (2007–2017) and examine it through a panel data analysis with dummy variables.

8.3.1 Japanese Politics Between 2007 and 2017

Before we present our data and analysis of political uncertainty and lobbying, in this section, we describe changes in the political environment from 2007 to 2017.

The House of Councilors election in 2007 was held amid the pension record problem and a series of scandals involving cabinet members. The Liberal Democratic Party suffered a historic defeat with 37 seats and surrendered the position of the first party of the House of Councilors for the first time since party formation. The Democratic Party won a record high of 60 seats and became the first party in the House of Councilors[2] (Nippon Hoso Kyokai Senkyo WEB).

As the cabinet approval rating remained low in 2009, the Liberal Democratic Party Prime Minister Aso's term of office expired effectively, resulting in the dissolution of his cabinet and a general election. Consequently, the Democratic Party won a major victory by winning 308 seats, which was the largest number of seats acquired by one political party after the war. The Liberal Democratic Party and Komeito Party were defeated, and the Democratic Party came to power (NHK Senkyo WEB).

However, the Democratic Party was defeated in the 2010 House of Councilors election and in the 2012 House of Representatives election. Hence, the Democratic Party was forced to change power again. Subsequently, the Democratic Party never regained its power. There was criticism of the policies and administration of the Liberal Democratic Party government at the beginning; the public had high expectations of the Democratic Party government. However, the Democratic Party was unable to meet the expectations of the people in fields such as response to the Great East Japan Earthquake, the relationship between the government and bureaucrats, and the relationship between the government and the ruling party (Murata 2020). This was the first postwar change of government by the Democratic Party, even though the Democratic Party's government ended up being in office for 3 years and 3 months, and it can be said that it was a time when political tensions were rising in Japan. It is assumed that both parties were making political decisions heavily relying on the political expectations of the next term because a change in power has been realized and the myth that the Liberal Democratic Party will continue to be in power no longer held true in this period.

Our dataset included the time period when voters' decisions were more sensitive than ever, and we will focus on how political parties react to government fund allocation during politically unstable times. Our hypothesis is that if the government is unstable, it will increase public consumption and execute attractive policies for

[2] NHK Senkyo WEB: https://www.nhk.or.jp/senkyo/database/history/.

voters (such as cash benefits). However, public investment, which is not directly related to the benefits of individual voters, is likely to decrease.

8.3.2 Definition of Variables

In this section, we define the three dependent variables examined in our analysis. The three dependent variables are share of public investment in aggregate government expenditure (GI/G), the ratio of public investment (GI/GDP), and public consumption to GDP (GC/GDP).

Independent variables are divided into political variables, which are our interests, and economic variables, which are the control variables. Political variables from our explanatory variables measure political power at the local government level, and this analysis considers the following two points: (1) the influence of the Liberal Democratic Party and the Democratic Party of Japan on national politics and (2) influence of the Liberal Democratic Party and the Democratic Party of Japan on local politics.

Regarding (1), we used the ratio of the number of diet members per capita to the national average. Based on previous studies (Kondoh 2008), both the House of Representatives and House of Councilors were included in this analysis. As the variable for (2), we used the relative value of the number of the Liberal Democratic Party and the Democratic Party members in each prefectural assembly to the national average.

As control variables, we used road investment, income level (real GDP per capita by prefecture), tax burden share (amount of national tax collected by each prefecture divided by the national value), jobs-to-applicants ratio, ratio of the young population, ratio of the elderly population, and fiscal capacity index. The ratio of construction workers is used as a variable to represent the political power of the construction industry that benefits from public work orders. Data sources are listed in the Appendix, and the summary statistics are shown in Table 8.1.

8.3.3 Methodology

Following Kondoh's (2008) empirical work, we analyze the impact of political instability and lobbying through standard panel analysis using prefecture-based data.

The estimation function is as follows:

$$y_{it} = a + \sum_k \beta_k \cdot \mathrm{Pol}_{k,it} + \sum_l \gamma_l \cdot X_{l,it} + \sum_m \delta_m \cdot \mathrm{RD}_{m,it} + c_i + d_t + u_{it}.$$

Table 8.1 Summary statistics

	Observations	Mean	Median	Maximum	Minimum	Std. Dev.
Liberal Democrats' Vote Share	517	0.474411	0.473819	0.728186	0.032009	0.095987
Liberal Democratic Party in the House of Representatives	517	1	0.734375	4.936073	0	0.847678
Liberal Democratic Party in the House of Councilors	517	0.989279	1	2.457143	0	0.65712
Liberal Democratic Party of Local Councilors	517	1.524095	1.387245	3.64503	0.126894	0.776953
Democratic Party Vote Share	517	0.290193	0.288164	0.608074	0	0.154381
Democratic Party in the House of Representatives	517	1	0.425339	11.05882	0	1.467227
Democratic Party in the House of Councilors	517	0.992447	0	4.7	0	1.295383
Democratic Party of Local Councilors	517	1.106252	0.891904	7.339117	0	0.872145
Ratio of Construction Workers	517	0.001648	0.001043	0.006842	0.000331	0.001454
GDP per capita by Prefectur	517	3.653937	3.572015	7.896392	2.432588	0.762533
Share of Tax Burden	517	0.021277	0.004756	0.787131	9.65E-05	0.078777
Effective Job Offer Rate	517	0.827917	0.771736	1.935483	0.212563	0.359475
Young Population Rate	517	0.130861	0.13	0.181	0.101	0.01054
Elderly Population Ratio	517	0.260727	0.261	0.356	0.169	0.034218
Financial Index	517	0.490344	0.44031	1.40598	0.22137	0.197982

Note: The Liberal Democratic Party (LDP), the Democratic Party (DP)

Pol_{it} is a set of political variables, X_{it} is a set of control variables, RD_{it} is a set of variables related to road investment, c_i is a fixed-effects dummy for each prefecture, and d_t is a fixed-effects dummy in the time direction. Data sample period is from 2007 to 2017 as follows.

8.3.4 Result

Table 8.2 shows the estimation results. In all results, the null hypothesis of the F-test was rejected, and the fixed-effects model was appropriate compared to the pooled model. The estimation method adds year dummies to the fixed-effects model to consider individual and time effects.

For the political variables, three important results appear in the stable estimation results. The first is political instability. The number of democratic seats in local legislature is negative and significant for public investment/GDP and public investment/government expenditures; however, it is positive and significant for public consumption/GDP. This result means that public consumption will increase in prefectures wherein the Democratic Party has a relatively large number of local legislators. Since the political situation was not stable, local Democratic Party members are assumed to gain popularity with policies involving public consumption. The second concerns the Democratic Party vote share. Increasing the number of the Democratic Party vote shares decreases public investment/GDP and public investment/government expenditure. The third is lobbying activity. The ratio of construction workers is positive and significant. This implies that lobbying by a constructor may indicate pressure to increase public consumption.

These results are consistent with our theoretical expectations. That is, as political uncertainty affects the decision-making of local politicians who determine each local expenditure, democratic local legislators reduce public investment and instead

Table 8.2 Estimation results

Dependent Variable	Public Investment/GDP		Public Consumption/GDP		Public Investment/Government Expenditure	
	(1)	(2)	(3)	(4)	(5)	(6)
Liberal Democrats' Vote Share	-0.013	-0.012	-0.003928	0.002	-0.029	-0.026
	(-1.461)	(-1.228)	(-0.538)	(0.187)	(-1.435)	(-1.241)
Liberal Democratic Party in the House of Representatives	0.000	0.002 **	0.001	0.000	0.000	0.004 **
	(0.336)	(2.011)	(0.833)	(0.459)	(0.229)	(2.056)
Liberal Democratic Party in the House of Councilors	-0.003 **	-0.004 **	-0.002 **	-0.002 **	-0.005 **	-0.007 **
	(-2.836)	(-4.141)	(-2.129)	(-2.285)	(-2.501)	(-3.607)
Liberal Democratic Party of Local Councilors	-0.001	0.000 **	-0.002 **	-0.003	-0.001	0.002
	(-0.397)	(0.192)	(-1.303)	(-1.324)	(-0.257)	(0.308)
Democratic Party Vote Share	-0.027 **	-0.032 **	0.000	-0.004	-0.051 **	-0.059 **
	(-3.755)	(-4.158)	(0.006)	(-0.601)	(-3.320)	(-3.562)
Democratic Party in the House of Representatives	0.001 **	0.001 **	0.000	0.000	0.003 **	0.002 **
	(2.842)	(2.155)	(1.421)	(0.715)	(2.744)	(2.131)
Democratic Party in the House of Councilors	-0.001 **	-0.001 **	-0.001 **	-0.001	-0.002	-0.002 **
	(-2.067)	(-2.497)	(-1.945)	(-1.292)	(-1.554)	(-2.033)
Democratic Party of Local Councilors	-0.003 **	-0.002 **	0.002 **	0.004 **	-0.006 **	-0.005 **
	(-2.959)	(-2.138)	(3.227)	(4.014)	(-2.897)	(-2.342)
Ratio of Construction Workers	35.87 **	52.05 **	20.62 **	18.47 **	71.45 **	110.27 **
	(5.1)	(7.3)	(3.7)	(3.0)	(4.7)	(7.2)
GDP per capita by Prefecture	0.008		-0.048 **		0.045 **	
	(1.501)		(-11.551)		(3.958)	
Share of Tax Burden	-0.055 **		-0.023		-0.123 **	
	(-2.769)		(-1.433)		(-2.878)	
Effective job Offer Rate	0.020 **		0.024 **		0.034 **	
	(4.568)		(6.988)		(3.618)	
Young Population Rate	-1.723 **		-1.469 **		-2.697 **	
	(-5.604)		(-6.044)		(-4.074)	
Elderly Population Ratio	-0.342		-0.121		-0.676 **	
	(-2.358)		(-1055)		(-2.163)	
Financial Index	0.0 **		0.0 **		0.1 **	
	(3.2)		(4.2)		(2.8)	
Constant	0.271 **	-0.004	0.550 **	0.197	0.429 **	0.063 **
	(3.883)	(-0.347)	(9.961)	(17.880)	(2.853)	(2.281)
Observations	517	517	517	517	517	517
Adjusted R-squared	0.891029	0.870168	0.980637	0.973259	0.838601	0.808369

Note: OLS regressions; Robust *t* statistics in parentheses (*significant at 10%; **significant at 5%)

increase public consumption to attempt to increase their parties' support. These results mean that political uncertainty increases public consumption. However, as expected, lobbying activities by special interest groups also increased public investment in 2007–2017.[3]

Under political uncertainty, more money is spent on government consumption and less on investment with the goal of gaining support from voters in the next election. Essentially, legislators in short-term administrations are assumed to work to prevent optimal investments in the social infrastructure needed in the long term. However, lobbying by the construction industry encourages road construction,

[3] Kondoh (2008) has clarified that local public investment policy has been strongly affected by the construction industry as a local interest group in Japan.

which is social infrastructure, and encourages investment in social infrastructure. These two variables can be interpreted as having exactly opposite effects on long-term infrastructure.

In addition to the main results above, there were two interesting results. The first is the sign of the number of Democratic parties in the House of Representatives on public investment, and public investment/government expenditures are positive. This suggests that, in contrast to local members, opposition parties may make decisions to maintain the level of public investment. The second is the sign of the Liberal Democratic Party in the House of Councilors on public investment/GDP and public consumption/GDP and public investment/government expenditure are negative. From the former two results, a larger number of the Liberal Democratic Party in the House of Councilors implies a lower level of government spending. The latter result indicates that members of the Liberal Democratic Party of the House of Councilors value government consumption. These two results are only revealed by the empirical analysis, which cannot be clarified by the model analysis described in the previous section and may be unique to Japan.

Returning to the main results, these findings suggest that policy decisions by short-sighted legislators in short-term administrations will negatively impact long-term social infrastructure. However, this effect may be offset by lobbying activities in the construction industry, and the level of investment in long-term infrastructure may not be affected. Essentially, lobbying may have the effect of directing social infrastructure investment in a more optimal direction for short-term administrations. In this analysis, the number of legislators and percentage of construction workers were used, and simply comparing the magnitude of the impact was not possible. Quantifying and comparing these two effects will be the subject of our next analysis.

8.4 Conclusion

This chapter investigates why desirable public investment does not occur under political uncertainty and lobbying. First, we theoretically show that the increase in public investment is because of the activities of special interest groups, while the decrease is because of political uncertainty. Second, we investigated whether the theoretical hypotheses were empirically justified using Japanese data from 2007 to 2017. The results show that (1) public consumption increases when the number of local legislators increases in this period and (2) public investment and consumption increase in regions where the number of construction workers, which we consider as a proxy variable for special interest groups, increases. This result could be interpreted as the coexistence of these two factors and may lead to political policy in the desired direction because the effect of political uncertainty and the effect of special interest groups have opposing directions for public investment.

Regarding the results of this study, some future issues need to be considered. First, political uncertainty must be included as an explanatory variable. To do this, the EPU index of the regional version in Japan is required, as created by Saxegaard et al. (2022). Second, the composition of government spending must be considered in more detail. As shown in Kondoh (2008), government expenditures include livelihood, industry, agricultural, forestry and fishery, and land conservation investments. Of these, agricultural, forestry, fishery, and land conservation investments are considered influenced by interest groups in the agriculture, forestry, and fishery industries.

Acknowledgements We wish to thank Professor Emeritus Shuetsu Takahashi, Akihiko Kaneko, and Kojun Hamada for their valuable comments and suggestions, supported in part by MEXT/JSPS Grant-in-Aid for Scientific Research (C) No. 19K01679. The usual disclaimer applies.

Appendix

Differentiating the first-order condition, we get the following:

$$\left\{V_2''((1-\tau)\,Y'(I))^2 + V_2'(1-\tau)\,Y''(I) + \beta(P)\tau Y''(I) + \pi_1''(I)\right\} \\ \mathrm{d}I = -\left\{\beta'(P)\tau Y'(I)\right\}\mathrm{d}P.$$

Thus, the increase in reelection probability increases the public investment as follows:

$$\frac{\mathrm{d}I}{\mathrm{d}P} = -\frac{1}{\delta}\left\{\beta'(P)\tau Y'(I)\right\} = -\frac{1}{\delta}\left\{\frac{\tau Y'(I)}{\alpha}\right\} > 0,$$

where $\delta = V_2''((1-\tau)\,Y'(I))^2 + V_2'(1-\tau)\,Y''(I) + \beta(P)\tau Y''(I) + \pi_1''(I)$ is negative from second-order condition in the maximization problem.

References

Baker SR, Bloom N, Davis SJ (2016) Measuring economic policy uncertainty. Q J Econ 131(4):1593–1636
Besley T, Coate S (1998) Sources of inefficiency in a representative democracy, a dynamic analysis. Am Econ Rev 88:139–156
Bohn F (2007) Polarisation, uncertainty and public investment failure. Eur J Polit Econ 23(4):1077–1087
Bohn F (2019) Political instability and seigniorage: an inseparable couple—or a threesome with debt? Rev Int Econ 27(1):347–366
Darby J, Li CW, Muscatelli VA (2004) Political uncertainty, public expenditure and growth. Eur J Polit Econ 20(1):153–179
Elder EM, Wagner GA (2015) Political effects on pension underfunding. Econ Polit 27(1):1–27
Grossman GM, Helpman E (1994) Protection for sale. Am Econ Rev 84(4):833–850
Kondoh H (2008) Political economy of public capital formation in Japan. Public Policy Rev 4(1):77–110

Murata T (2020) The ups and downs of the Democratic Party of Japan. Otemon Bus Manag Rev 26(1):89–100

Persson T (1998) Economic policy and special interest politics. Econ J 108(447):310–327

Persson T, Tabellini G (1999) Political economics and macroeconomic policy. In: Handbook of macroeconomics, vol. 1C. North-Holland, Amsterdam, pp 1397–1482

Saxegaard ECA, Davis SJ, Ito A, Miake N (2022) Policy uncertainty in Japan. J Jpn Int Econ 64:101192

Chapter 9
A Historical Perspective on the Role of Public Electric Utility in Modern City Formation in Japan

Sachiko Kumoshikari

Abstract In this section, we examine the urbanization process in Sendai, a representative standard local city in Japan, from the Taisho period to the early Showa period. We focus on regional public utility, which is vital to economic development. Notably, the Sendai Municipal Electricity Utility aimed for fiscal stabilization while providing electricity to the city. We find that the local government used revenue from this utility to compensate for fiscal shortages in general accounts. Moreover, we confirmed that this revenue was used to advance urban development projects (e.g., the construction of municipal roads, trains, and schools).

Keywords Local city of modern age in Japan · Sendai city · Municipal electricity utility

JEL Classification: N95, R58

9.1 Introduction

After the collapse of the Tokugawa Shogunate in 1868, Japan developed a new political and economic system. At that time, the new Japanese government developed various systems and organizations based on the political and economic systems of European countries (e.g., Britain, France, and Prussia) and the United States.

For example, in economic systems, the Tokyo Stock Exchange (in 1878, now designated Tokyo Stock Exchange Inc.) and Yokohama Specie Bank (in 1879) were established to promote trade. The Bank of Japan (BOJ, in 1882) was established as the central bank. Currently, the BOJ continues to issue legal tender and Bank of

S. Kumoshikari (✉)
Miyako Junior College, Iwate Prefectural University, Miyako, Iwate, Japan
e-mail: s_kumoshikari@iwate-pu.ac.jp

S. Takahashi et al. (eds.), *Modern Macroeconomics with Historical Perspectives*, New Frontiers in Regional Science: Asian Perspectives 67,
https://doi.org/10.1007/978-981-99-1067-0_9

Japan notes. Thus, it can be considered as the period when the foundation of Japan's monetary system was established.

Furthermore, in terms of the fiscal system, the land tax reform was implemented in 1873, and a system of tax payments in cash was thoroughly established in place of payments with crop yields, such as rice paid as land tax. In terms of the political system, the cabinet system was established in 1885, and the Constitution of the Empire of Japan (promulgated in 1889 and enforced in 1890) was enacted, establishing a constitutional monarchy. During the same period, the Japanese Imperial Diet (1890–1947) was established through bicameral legislation. During these periods (Meiji era)[1], moves to abolish the status system and adopt Western ideas were made, termed "Civilization and Enlightenment."

Through these policy developments, a centralized state system centered on the emperor was established in Japan, and capitalism was promoted. In addition to introducing British and French technology and machinery, the government aimed to develop the Japanese economy, centering on light industry (especially spinning and silk manufacturing) with the help of foreigners hired by foreign engineers.

Simultaneously, "the policy of fostering and promoting industry," or state-led industrial development, was also emphasized to facilitate "the wealthy nation and strong military" policy. In addition to introducing British and French technology and machinery, the government aimed to develop the Japanese economy, centering on light industry (especially spinning and silk manufacturing), with foreign specialists in government.

After the Sino–Japanese War (1894–1895) and the Russo-Japanese War (1904–1905), heavy chemical industrialization progressed in Japan. With the increase in special procurement during World War I (1914–1918), Japan's economy boomed, and heavy and chemical industrialization accelerated further. People's lives stabilized, political and ideological controls relaxed, and the "Taisho Democracy" era began, wherein democratic ideas were emphasized.

Japan's administrative and urban systems underwent major changes in the early Meiji period. In 1871, after the abolition of feudal domains followed by the establishment of prefectures established administrative districts throughout the country, the development of the local administrative system was greatly influenced in1878 by the three new local laws (the Act on the Formation of Counties, Wards, Towns, and Villages; the Rules of Prefectural Assemblies; and the Rules of Local Taxation), and the local administrative system was developed. Japan's administrative and urban systems underwent major changes in the early Meiji period.

These laws and systems were replaced by the city and town/village system (enforced in 1889) and the prefectural and county system (in 1890). This established local autonomy in institutional terms and made "self-government" possible in urban areas. The Municipal System Law was amended in 1911 to strengthen the authority

[1] In Japan, the Christian era is separated from the era name during the Emperor's reign. After the fall of the Tokugawa Shogunate, the eras are Meiji (1868–1912), Taisho (1912–1926), Showa (1926–1989), Heisei (1989–2019), and Reiwa (2019–).

over local autonomy. This amendment to the municipal system allowed cities to establish special accounts in their finances, making it possible to conduct urban development projects. This has led to further economic development in Japanese cities.

In this chapter, we examine the period from the beginning of the twentieth century to World War II (1941–1945). In particular, our analysis focuses on the Taisho and early Showa periods (the 1910s–the mid-1930s). This reflects the fact that the Japanese economy experienced economic panic after World War I (the 1920s), the Great Kanto Earthquake (occurred in 1923), the Great Depression of 1929, and the Showa Depression (1930–1931) reaching, which peaked in 1936 before the outbreak of World War II.[2]

The strong Japanese economy during the Taisho period produced a new urban development system wherein various projects were promoted at the expense of individual cities. This was encouraged by City Planning Law (established in 1919). This law stipulates that (1) development-ready areas called city planning zones could be established, (2) zoning could be established within city planning zones, and (3) special accounts could be established to secure financial resources for promoting city planning, with beneficiaries bearing the burden of the projects. Initially, the system was only applied to six major cities—Tokyo, Yokohama, Nagoya, Osaka, Kyoto, and Kobe—but the scope of its application gradually expanded to include other Japanese cities. At that time, cities were not allowed to levy inhabitant taxes (local taxes) as freely as they could today; hence, securing financial resources for city planning projects was key to achieving urban development.

According to the first national census (enforced in 1920), much of Japan's population is concentrated in the six largest cities. Therefore, various national projects are centered on these cities. Nagasaki, the seventh most populous city, was home to shipbuilding facilities (mainly Mitsubishi Heavy Industries) and was a prosperous international trading city; however, its population was less than half that of Nagoya and Yokohama. Hiroshima, ranked eighth in terms of population, was a city with military facilities, whereas Kure was positioned as a military port and naval arsenal city. Sendai, later identified by Oishi and Kanazawa (2003) as representing a "standard local city," was ranked 12th in terms of population, had a smaller population than these distinctive cities, and was less developed in terms of industrial production than other cities.

Sendai city is located approximately 350 km north of Tokyo. This distance was approximately the same as that between Tokyo and Nagoya. Sendai is located in the northeastern part of Honshu in the Tohoku region and is the largest city in the region. The large divisional headquarters of the Imperial Japanese army, the second division, and Tohoku Imperial University (1907–1949, now Tohoku University) were established in Sendai, second only to Tokyo. For this reason,

[2] For Japan, the Japanese–Chinese War broke out in 1937 and a wartime regime was established. Total war under the National Mobilization Law then unfolded, and we believe that the progress of the Japanese economy and development of cities must be analyzed from a different perspective.

citizens called this the "Military City" and "Academic City." Compared to the six major cities developed as production cities, Sendai was not an industrial cluster and was sometimes referred to as the "Forests City" in a derogatory reference to its rich natural surroundings.[3] Nevertheless, these three appellations describe Sendai as a consumer city. Owing to these characteristics, Sendai is a case study in this chapter.

Decentralization and securing financial resources are key factors in the urban development process in modern Japan (Kanazawa 2010). Decentralization increases the degree of freedom of local governments. Under the guidance of local councils, fiscal management contributes to residents' economic welfare (Davoodi and Zou 1998; Akai and Sakata 2002; Iimi 2005; Hanif et al. 2020).

While many studies have been conducted on modern Japanese urban history and urban finance (Iwanami 1979; Kojita 1991; Numajiri 2002; Ishita 2004; Mochida 1984, 1985, 1993), few studies have focused on the issues of urban decentralization and financial resources (Kanazawa 1979; Sekino 1982a, 1982b). Moreover, few studies in this field have examined local cities (Oishi and Kanazawa 2003; Kumoshikari 2011, 2013, 2017, 2021; Itoh 2018).

This chapter reviews the urban development process of Sendai, a typical Japanese regional city, from the Taisho period to the early Showa period from the perspective of decentralization and securing financial resources in a regional city. Urbanization of Sendai began with the five municipal utilities in Sendai or the "Five Major Projects" (i.e., water supply, electricity, revision of municipal districts, construction of streetcars, and development of parks), which appeared approximately 20 years after the Municipal System Law. These were selected as important social infrastructure projects in modern Japan to achieve the major goal of transforming Sendai City from a "consumer city" to a "production city." This also became the starting point for a systematic modern urban development project in Sendai. Essentially, the project aimed to transform the city from a "military city," "academic city," or "forests city" (i.e., a consumer city) to a city with a concentration of modern industries, such as the six major cities.

[3] The designation "Military City" (*Gun-to* in Japanese) had been in use since the Meiji era. It represented significant economic and social impact of the military establishment in Sendai city. The second Division and its fourth Infantry Regiment were established in Sendai city in the early Meiji period. Some stores in the city were contracted to provide cleaning services for the army, and procure and dispose off foodstuffs. Newspapers of the time reported that removing the army from Sendai would surely shrink the city's economy to less than one-third of its current size. It was reported that the name "Sendai City with the Army" was a natural (*Kahoku Shimpo*, July 11, 1906). The term "Academic City" (*Gakuto* in Japanese) represented the social impact of having various types of schools within the city. National and public schools, such as the Second High School (founded in 1887) and Tohoku Imperial University (founded in 1907), as well as various private schools, were established one after another in Sendai. The "Forest City"(*Mori-no-Miyako* in Japanese)represented the livability of Sendai City. It also indicated that the city was behind in modern industrialization. This name had been in use since the late Meiji period (late nineteenth century). It indicated that Sendai City had maintained its natural beauty since its days as a castle town in the Edo period (1603–1867) and made fun of the fact that the city had few factories and had not developed into a modern city. These three designations are names that clearly indicate the characteristics of Sendai as a "consumer city" with a weak foundation of modern industry, compared to the six large cities that are "production cities" and advanced industrialized cities.

In the late 1910s, these five municipal utilities were followed by the "Great Sendai Concept," a large-scale urban development project accompanied by the amalgamation of surrounding towns and villages that would become part of the urban planning area along with Sendai City.[4] However, the realization of these projects requires financial resources. Unable to establish its own financial resources, the city of Sendai was able to do so by utilizing profits from its publicly operated electric power utility, which were publicly operated. We then examine Sendai's financial data, including data from general and special accounts for electric power utility, to clarify the interrelationship between the two.[5]

Public demand is subdivided into government consumption, public investment, and changes in public investment. Public investment promotes the development of social infrastructure, increases private capital stock and employment, and increases productivity. In the long term, this is a source of strength for economic growth. This relationship holds true for the gross regional product (GRP).

This chapter examines the formation process of local cities based on fiscal data on modern Japanese cities, particularly general and special account data. General and special account data represent a cross section of government consumption and public investment in the GRP of the region in question and serve as a bridge to macroeconomic analysis.

This chapter is organized as follows: Sect. 9.2 provides an overview of Sendai Electric Utility; Sect. 9.3 describes the relationship between urban policy and Sendai City; Sect. 9.4 provides a perspective on local city finances; Sect. 9.5 provides a detailed analysis of Sendai Electric Utility; and Sect. 9.6 provides an overview of the performance of Sendai Electric Utility.

9.2 Overview of Sendai Municipal Electric Utility

Sendai Municipal Electricity Utility (SMEU) was a publicly owned project operated by the city of Sendai for approximately 30 years, from July 1911 to March 1942. This was established by acquiring and transferring two private companies that operated electric utilities in Sendai. The SMEU had five hydroelectric power plants and one thermal power plant (including the Sankyozawa Power Plant, which generated Japan's first hydroelectric power) and supplied electricity not only to the former Sendai City area but also to the neighboring areas. From the mid-Taisho period onward, revenues from the electric power utility gradually began being

[4] In 1923, Sendai City was approved as an applicable city under the City Planning Law.

[5] For this analysis, we used the Sendai City Council Administration Reports and the Sendai City Council Resolution Minutes and general and special account reports of the city of Sendai in the first half of the twentieth century. We also used articles from newspapers published in Sendai City then (e.g., *Kahoku Shimpo*) to correct the limitations of the primary source documents and confirm the factual process. Owing to the large number of these documents, they are omitted from the References section.

allocated to Sendai City's finances, and as a "The Fiscal Treasury," the revenues became a major source of funds for general and special accounts (e.g., municipal district revision projects, streetcar installation projects, urban planning projects). From the end of the Taisho era (1912–1926), the company was responsible for managing the streetcar business. However, when state control of electric power was strengthened in the late 1930s under the wartime regime, all electric supply businesses, except the streetcar business, were forcibly integrated into Tohoku Electric Power Distribution Co. Ltd.

The concept of SMEU appeared in 1907 as five municipal utilities in Sendai City called the "Five Major Projects." This was a plan for a comprehensive regional development project to secure the city's water supply, electric lighting, and electricity supply through water conservancy projects of waterworks and electricity and improve the infrastructure of Sendai as a modern city through the revision of city districts (road (street) expansion and park development) and construction of an urban electric railroad (tram line).

SMEU was established in 1911, and with the revision of the municipal organization in the same year, the project was placed under a special account. Initially, the entity was strongly characterized as a "public utility," which provided a stable and inexpensive electricity supply. However, from the mid-Taisho period onward, especially around the time the City Planning Law (enforced in 1919) was enacted, its role changed in response to "The Great Sendai" concept that emerged then. Proceeds and reserves from the project were diverted under the names of "transfer payments" and "operation fund" to the city of Sendai's general account and special accounts for other municipal projects and invested in urban development projects that would support citizens' daily lives. For these reasons, Tokuzaburo Shibuya, who later became the mayor of Sendai, described the municipal electric utility as "The Fiscal Treasury."

9.3 Urban Development Policy and Sendai City

Sendai's urban development policy was developed in response to national urban policy. From the mid-1900s, especially after the end of the Russo–Japanese War (1904–1905), there was a growing public opinion in Japan that cities, especially urban areas, should be developed in a manner befitting a "first-class" country. In response, cities across the country, especially the six major cities, have launched various urban development projects.

The same was true for Sendai City, which was required to promote modern urban infrastructure projects, particularly cityward revision projects, streetcar installation projects, park development, and water supply and sewage system development. Sendai transformed its urban structure from a modern castle town to a modern city as one of its policy goals, and both the city's administrators and citizens demanded that the city implement various policies to achieve this goal.

At this time, heavy industry began to develop in six major cities. In response, the development of industry was cited as an "urgent problem" in Sendai, and newspaper articles reported the need to promote industrial development by supplying low-cost electricity to factories that had been attracted to or established in the city ("Sendai City and Industry," *Kahoku Shimpo*, December 15, 1906).

In August 1907, during these developments, the Sendai City Assembly proposed Sendai's urban development policy called the "Five Major Projects." The five major projects consisted of five municipal utilities: waterworks, electricity, municipal district revisions, streetcar installations, and parks. These projects were infrastructure improvement policies selected to transform the city from a castle town in the early modern period to a modern city.

The Sendai City Assembly established a committee to investigate and study the five major projects in detail, but not all were initiated. For example, the project to revise the municipal districts, which was considered one of the pillars of the "Five Major Projects," made little progress because the city faced financial difficulties owing to the large amount of money required to acquire land and the tramline construction project. Hence, the project was not easily initiated and lasted for 10 years in an empty period. However, the idea of a municipal electric utility was initiated as the "first project." This project began with the establishment of two private electric companies in 1911.

It was not until the late 1910s that major changes occurred in the development of urban policies. The outbreak of World War I (1914–1918) created a boom (the Great War economy) in the late 1910s owing to a marked increase in foreign demand in Japan. Industrial urbanization in Japan has begun to progress, particularly in large cities. Heavy industry began to take over from the light industry centered on textile manufacturing, which had previously dominated the industrial structure. Therefore, the population of large cities has grown rapidly owing to an influx of people into the labor force, and urbanization has progressed rapidly.

In May 1918, the Japanese government established the City Planning Investigation Committee to analyze and deliberate policies related to city planning. Consequently, the City Planning Law and Urban Building Law were promulgated in April 1919. The city planning law differs from the Tokyo Municipal Revision Ordinance enacted in the Meiji period as follows: (1) urban development projects could be initiated as national projects, (2) zoning could be implemented in "city planning areas," and (3) it would be possible to secure its own financial resources for urban development projects implemented as "city planning" (e.g., by establishing rules on beneficiary responsibility and authorizing the imposition of special taxes).

Item (3) was very attractive to cities that did not have the authority to levy what is now called inhabitant tax (city tax) as their source of revenue. However, the City Planning Law applied to six major cities and other cities that required government approval as designated cities. Therefore, local cities had to undertake various applications and projects to apply for the "City Planning Law."

Sendai City was also prepared to apply the law. The law was enacted in response to the rapid population growth and urban problems that erupted during World War I and the unplanned expansion of urban areas. Sendai City, the central city of the

Tohoku region, was no exception to this population growth and intensification of urban problems.

The core of these measures was the "Great Sendai" concept. In 1918, the year before the City Planning Law was promulgated, *Kahoku Shimpo*, a local newspaper published in Sendai and its surrounding areas, reported that Sendai City should incorporate its neighboring towns into its city limits to create "Great Sendai." Around 1921, the city of Sendai established the Sendai City Planning Temporary Investigation Committee, which conducted various studies on city planning projects based on the City Planning Law. In April 1922, Sendai established the Sendai City Planning Preparatory Investigation Department to apply the City Planning Law. In May 1923, Sendai and 24 other cities were subjected to City Planning Law.

After becoming a city subject to the City Planning Law, Sendai began pursuing urban planning projects. According to the City Planning Law, various infrastructure projects (e.g., roads, squares, parks, harbors, electric tracks, sewers, markets, and housing) have been systematically outlined and constructed per "plans for important measures to permanently maintain public peace and promote public welfare in terms of transportation, sanitation, security, economy, etc." In Sendai City, various projects that had already been started or were yet to be started were positioned in this new city planning project.

In conjunction with these developments, Sendai began developing its infrastructure. The city of Sendai began implementing the city-area reform project proposed in the "Five Major Projects." At the Sendai City Assembly in February 1919, Keiichi Yamada, the Mayor of Sendai, proposed the "Regulations for the Establishment and Management of the City District Reform Project Fund," which was passed by the assembly, and "The Big Fire in Minamimachi" (Sendai Fire) that broke out in March of the following year, triggering the full-scale launch of the project. The project was undertaken by the city of Sendai as a "city planning project." A city planning law was applied to the cities.

The tramway construction project was discussed frequently at the Sendai City Assembly from 1918 onward and was launched in earnest in 1923, with streetcars beginning to operate in the late 1920s. Thereafter, with the development of city planning projects, various urban improvements have been implemented, including urban street planning in place of cityward revisions, park development, electric utility industry development, streetcar lines expansion, and water and sewage system development.

City planning projects have also taken over the concept of industrial concentration in Sendai. During the development of these projects, surrounding towns and villages that had seen a concentration of industries merged. For example, Nagamachi (town), Haranomachi (town), and Minami-Koizumi (part of Shichigo village) merged into one area in April 1928.

9.4 Overview of Local City Finances

9.4.1 Local City Finances in the Late Taisho Period

The Taisho period (1912–1926) was a period of significant change in the finances of modern Japanese local cities. With the outbreak of World War I (1914), Japan shifted from "austerity" to "proactive" fiscal policy. This has led to a significant expansion in national and local government financing.

In annual government expenditures during the Taisho period (1912–1926), both central and local governments presented an increasing trend; however, the growth in local government expenditures exceeded that of the central government (Fig. 9.1). Local governments had the costs of dealing with various urban and social problems that became prominent during rapid economic development, a "godsend." Local governments also had to manage the long-term recession that followed the "reactionary depression" (from around 1920) and the costs of recovery and reconstruction after the Great Kanto Earthquake (occurred in 1923). In summary, this situation of local government spending implies the function of local government finances as agents of the national government (Fujita 1949).

The Japanese tax system then allowed the national government to levy and collect national taxes and prefectural taxes for each prefecture but did not allow cities, towns, villages, and counties to levy and collect taxes that they could collect on their own (taxes that would be equivalent to the Japanese inhabitant tax today). Therefore, these municipalities had to raise tax revenue through "additional taxes" on national and prefectural taxes or rely heavily on subsidies and grants based on laws and systems enacted by the national government.

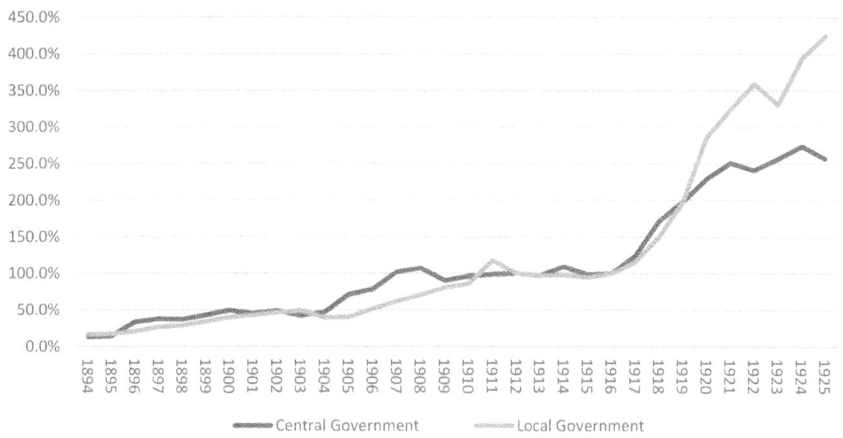

Fig. 9.1 Changes in central government and local government (total of prefectures and municipalities) expenditure (*1912 = 100) (Source: Ohkawa et al. (1969))

9.4.2 Finances of Sendai in the Late Taisho Period

Next, we examine the main trends in annual expenditures (*Saishutsu* in Japanese) and revenues (*Sainyu* in Japanese) of Sendai City. One of the major characteristics of expenditure items is that education and government office expenses (*Jigyo-hi* in Japanese), which have accounted for a large proportion of total expenditure since the Meiji period, continued to increase significantly during the Taisho period. As personnel costs in expenditure natures account for a high percentage of total expenditures, these expenses have increased, driven by soaring prices, and eventually played a role in driving fiscal expansion. Along with rapid industrialization and urbanization, a series of expenses have played an increasingly important role in civil engineering, urban planning, social services, public health, hospital construction, and industrial promotion. Although projects related to these expenses were initiated according to national laws and policies, the government's financial measures, such as low-interest loans and small subsidies, were poor.

The total revenue also increased significantly, corresponding to the total expenditure. The main feature is that municipal tax revenue, which has been the largest source of revenue, began to decline in the latter half of the Taisho period, whereas revenue from grants and subsidies from the national government increased. A typical example is national subsidies for compulsory education. Generally, an increase in subsidies is linked to the strengthening of the central control system.

The prefecture levies household taxes as local taxes. Municipalities such as cities, towns, and villages collect household taxes for prefectures and additional household taxes. In the tax revenue system of those days, additional household tax revenue was the largest source of municipal tax revenue. In the composition of municipal taxation in Sendai, additional tax revenue accounted for approximately 60% until 1917. Local governments faced an urgent need to replenish financial resources in the face of the dramatic expansion of expenses following World War I. The national government revised the local tax system to raise various local tax rates. Therefore, additional tax revenue resulted in a decline in taxation composition in the late Taisho period.

In principle, the General Account (GA) records all revenues and expenditures in government finance. However, the Special Account (SA) of Sendai increased noticeably during the 1910s. The main reason for this was the major revision of Municipal System Law in 1911. Municipal System Law has been revised accordingly. In particular, Article 138 of the Law allowed cities to establish special accounts for various projects (public projects) as an exception to the "principle of inseparability of budgets." Hence, cities across the country have established special accounts, mainly for large-scale municipal projects, such as waterworks and electricity.

9.5 SMEU as a "The Fiscal Treasury"

This section aims to clarify that SMEU played an extremely important role in the city's modern urban development process by analyzing data from the SMEU Special Account [Special Account Electricity Utility Ordinary Revenue and Expenditure (SAEU ORE)] and Special Account Electricity Utility Reserve Fund (SAEU Reserve Fund). This clarifies two specific aspects of SMEU: publicness and profit-making. Through this, we clarify why SMEU is called the "The Fiscal Treasury."

9.5.1 Establishment of SMEU and Increase in Electricity Demand

Here, we briefly describe the establishment of the SMEU. SMEU was one of the municipal project concepts included in the "Five Major Project Research Proposal" submitted to the Sendai Assembly in August 1907. The concept of a municipal electric power project was included in the "Proposal for Investigation of Five Major Projects" as "to develop water conservancy works under the management of the City of Sendai and to supply motive power to industrialists," which suggests that the city of Sendai intended to implement the project as part of its urban infrastructure development project for industrialization.

The SMEU was established in July 1911, and in December 1912, it began full-scale operations as a public utility that provided a stable and inexpensive electricity supply. In the meantime, "Establishment of a Special Account for the Sendai Municipal Water Consumption and Electricity Utility" was submitted and passed at the Sendai City Assembly in December 1910, and it was decided that SMEU would be operated under a special account. "The Budget for the Water and Electricity Utilization Project" (FY1910) and "The Budget for the Water and Electricity Utilization Project" (FY1911) were thus established. With the revision of the municipal organization in 1911, the municipal electric utility was placed under a special account, and SAEU ORE was established. The SAEU Reserve Fund was established in 1915.

Population growth and the spread of electric light in Sendai have caused a rapid increase in the demand for electric light. Electric lights are widely used in almost all households in Sendai. With the expansion of city areas, an increase in the number of births has led to a significant increase in the number of people living in cities.

As in the case of the demand for electric lights, the demand for electric power is increasing, particularly in urban areas. The SMEU also supplies electricity to the electric heaters. For example, according to the "Electricity Utility Report," until the early 1920s, electricity was supplied to Osaki Hydroelectric Company and Nippon Carbon Shokai Co., Ltd. for use in X-rays, electric furnaces, and other electric heating equipment. After 1926, with the spread of electric heaters, the SMEU also supplied electricity to various equipment such as X-ray machines, centrifuges, electric stoves, electric irons, and money registers. By this time, electricity had deeply penetrated people's daily lives and production in Sendai.

These changes in electricity demand are closely related to Sendai City's urban policy. Sendai City's urban facilities are located in neighboring regions. Sendai City has begun to formulate urban planning projects that include these regions. In particular, Nagamachi (town) and Haranomachi (town) were positioned as the future centers of modern industry in the city planning stage in the late Taisho period and were recognized as important areas for the city of Sendai, which was aimed at the concentration and development of the industry. Sendai City merged with Nagamachi (town), Haranomachi (town), and Minami-Koizumi (a part of Shichigou village) in 1928 and with other neighboring regions in 1931. Herewith, SMEU became an entity that supplied electricity only to the Sendai City area, thus establishing a "regional monopoly."

9.5.2 Aspects of the Electric Utility Special Account

9.5.2.1 Special Account Electric Utility

We examined trends in SAEU ORE, which is composed of revenue and expenditure. In the first half of the 1910s, revenue and expenditure were balanced. However, from the latter half of the 1910s, revenues exceeded expenditures for many fiscal years. This difference was particularly large from 1918 to the late 1920s. This indicates that the SMEU is a profitable sector. The surplus portion (the difference between revenues and expenditures) is carried over to the next year and used as "carry-over funds" in the revenue.

A breakdown of the Special Account Electric Utility Revenue (SAEU Revenue) shows that "royalties and fees" accounted for a large proportion of the total revenue, except for FY1911. This item accounts for approximately 40–50% of SAEU Revenue. After FY1929, this accounted for more than 60% of the total population. As "royalties and fees" are collected from consumers or users of electric light, electric power, and electric heating, this reflects the increase in demand for electricity and the increase in revenue owing to higher electricity rates in the middle of the Taisho era (1919–1926). The abovementioned "carry-over funds" also account for a large proportion of total revenue. "Public bonds" from FY1913 to FY1915 show a large portion as Sendai City financed the acquisition cost of Miyagi Spinning and Electric Light Co.

What are the trends in SAEU Expenditure? In SAEU Expenditures (current account) from FY1911 to FY1942, "business expenses" and "office expenses" are accounted for a large proportion. Most of these expenses are incurred by personnel and other office heads. "Train business expenses" were established in the streetcar business in FY1926.

We examine the extraordinary section of SAEU Expenditure. The largest portion of the Expenditure (extraordinary section) from FY1912 to FY1915 was for the "acquisition of existing companies," the cost of acquiring Miyagi Spinning and Electric Light Co. The SAEU Expenditure (extraordinary section) includes the cost of constructing the Goishikawa Power Station from FY1920 to FY1923 and the Tsuchitoi thermal power station from FY1923 to FY1926. Additionally, from FY1924 onward, expenses related to streetcar projects, such as "electric track-laying expenses," were also included. However, "bond expenses," "transfer funds" (*Hennyukin* in Japanese), and "reserve funds" (*Tsumitatekin* in Japanese) account for a large proportion of the total. As mentioned earlier, "bond expenses" are used to redeem bonds for the construction of power plants.

The "reserve fund" was paid to the SAEU Reserve Fund as a reserve fund for electric utility operations. Conversely, "transfer funds" were originally described as "transfer funds for municipal utility." They were not for the electric utility operations themselves but were recorded to be paid to other accounts.

9.5.2.2 Special Account Electric Utility Expenditures

A breakdown from SAEU Expenditure (extraordinary section) was first recorded as "transfers in" (*Hennyukin*) in FY1914 and transferred to the general account. In FY1919, the amount was JPY 16,600; in FY1921, it increased even more sharply to 239,629.40 yen. The amount of this "transfer money" has presented an increasing trend since then, although there have been some fluctuations. Approximately 20 years later, in FY1939, the amount increased approximately 21-fold. The "transfers" went to a wide range of accounts, including "transfers to the municipal revision project fund," "transfers to the general account," "transfers to the waterworks project fund," and "transfers to the city planning project fund."

The establishment of the City Revision Project Fund began in February 1919, when Sendai Mayor Kiichi Yamada submitted the "Regulations for Establishment and Management of the Sendai City Revision Project Fund" to the Sendai City Assembly. This was proposed with the aim of starting a municipal district revision project that had made little progress because of the lack of financial resources since the appearance of the "Five Major Projects" by the Sendai Assembly in 1907. However, the city planned to increase the electricity rates of SMEU as a source of funds for use in the municipal district revision project. Considerable discussion was held at the Sendai City Council Meeting regarding this plan. Hence, the "Municipal Revision Project Fund and Management Regulations" were enacted. Article 2 of the Regulations clearly stated that the municipal revision project fund would be financed by providing profits generated from the electric power utility. Based on this, in February 1919, a special account municipal revision project fund was established in the FY1919 budget, and transfers were made from the SMEU Special Account. This was the first transfer from the SMEU Special Account.

The largest percentage of the "transfers in" from SMEU Special Account Expenses is accounted for by "transfers in" to the general account of the Sendai City. Transfer from SAEU expenses was first appropriated in the FY1921 budget.

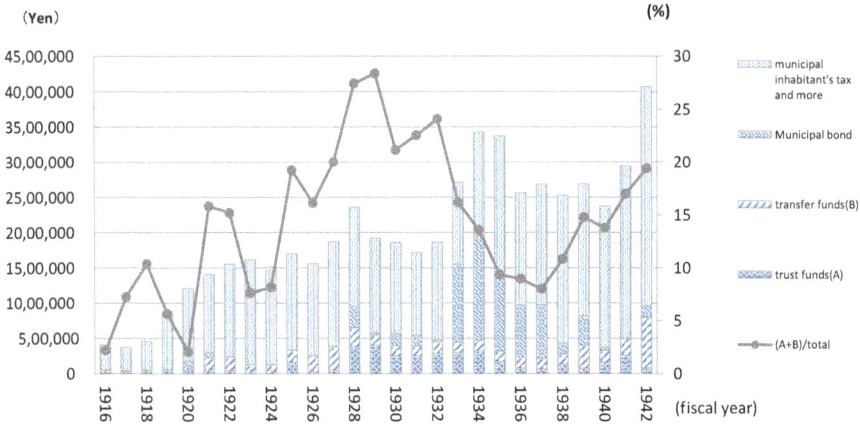

Fig. 9.2 "Transfers in" to the Sendai City General Account (Source: Statement of Revenue and Expenditure for General and Special Accounts in Sendai Ciy (FY 1916-1942))

Figure 9.2 presents the amount and breakdown of "transfers in" to the Sendai City General Account from FY1919 to FY1945. The largest portion of "transfers" in the Sendai City General Account is derived from SAEU ORE. In FY1921, when it was first recorded, it was 163,529.40 yen. In FY1931, it was 132,240 yen. Subsequently, the amount remained around 140,000 yen but increased again in the mid-1940s, reaching 239,983 yen in FY1941, just before the end of the municipal electric utility. These amounts accounted for a large proportion of the total "transfers," accounting for 80–90%.

9.5.2.3 Special Account Electric Utility Reserve Fund

Next, we examine the characteristics of the SAEU Reserve Fund, which is another utility account of the SMEU. The SAEU Reserve Fund was established based on the "Sendai City Electric Utility Reserve Fund Ordinance," enacted on July 28, 1915. The ordinance stipulates that a special account shall manage the electricity utility reserve fund and that its revenue and expenditure are segregated from the SAEU ORE (Article 1). The type of reserve fund shall be divided into the first, second, and third reserve funds according to use (Article 2), and the revenue from the reserve fund shall be appropriated from the "profits" of the electricity utility (Article 3). After establishing the reserve fund ordinance, 180,000 yen, relying on the second electric utility bond issue (480,000 yen) of SMEU, was allocated to the SAEU Reserve Fund and mainly funded as RF1 and RF2.

The type of reserve fund was divided into the first, second, and third reserve funds (RF1, RF2, and RF3) according to their use. RF1 was used to accumulate funds to amortize various facilities and equipment related to municipal electric utilities. The accumulated amount for the "electric utility" increased from 154,000 yen in

1919 to 298,000 yen in 1925, nearly doubling. Since RF2 was originally intended to cover the cost of Sendai City's waterworks projects, the cumulative amount was not as large as that of the first and third reserve funds. Nevertheless, in 1917, a portion of the RF2 was invested in SAEU Expenses. RF2 of 98,690.25 yen in 1917 was reduced to 45,129.76 yen the following year. The boundaries between the two became indefinite. RF3 accumulated only when there was a surplus in the SAEU ORE.

For what kinds of projects were the electric utility reserve funds used? As mentioned earlier, the SAEU Reserve Fund was established under the "Sendai City Electric Utility Reserve Fund Ordinance" every year to accumulate the operating expenses of the municipal electric utility itself. However, since the middle of the Taisho period, it has moved to other accounts. The reserve fund was managed based on the assumption that it would eventually be moved back to the SAEU Reserve Fund. Therefore, the "operation fund" amount accumulates yearly unless it is "repaid" from the utility account.

The electric utility reserve fund was used to pay out "operation funds" to various utility accounts, including the special account for electric utilities. However, its largest payout was the general account of Sendai.

At the breakdown of "operation funds (OF)," OF were divided into "electric utility operation funds" (EU-OF) and "general account operation funds (GA-OF)." Sendai City promoted a shift in funds from the revenue of the electric utility to the general account in 1919, bringing the cumulative total of the GA-OF to 63,000 yen in 1920. Thereafter, the amount in EU-OF decreased, and the amount in GA-OF increased.

For what kinds of projects were the electric utility reserve funds used? According to the "Sendai City Administration Report," the purpose of operating the electric utility reserve fund is as follows.

OF from RF1, "general account operation fund," includes donations for the founding of the National Institute of Technology of Sendai, expenses for renovation works of small public roads, civil engineering expenses, civil engineering expenses for education, school expansion, and renovation expenses, municipal office building expenses for facilities, expenses for the acquisition of the former site of Sendai Preparatory Military School, and general account appropriations (expenses). OF from RF2 comprises expenses for the Ceramics Research Institute and disinfection station site acquisition. The third reserve consists of general account appropriations and expenses for the relocation of the Sendai Technical School. OF from RF1 were removed from other special accounts via the general account of waterworks subject expansion expenses and gas project expenses. OF from RF3 were removed from municipal hospital renovation expenses, small industrial loan funds, and other special accounts.

The "history of the electric utility industry in the city of Sendai" (1941) describes this as follows:

> *The method of operating and reversing the reserve fund was often revised whenever necessary, and the city council passed resolutions to ensure the smooth operation, development, and enhancement of the electric utility.*

The city has contributed to the planning and execution of important projects in the city, such as the renovation of public roads, disinfection station civil engineering expenses, general accounting, city planning projects, waterworks projects, and municipal hospitals. Electric utility is the "The Fiscal Treasury," and it has been a source of brilliant achievements.

Thus, the utility accounts of the SMEU have stable financial management. "Electricity utility earnings" were appropriated to the general account and other special accounts and were used for "transfer funds" and "operation funds."

9.6 Concluding Remarks

In this chapter, we examine the process of formation and development in Sendai, a local city in Japan, from the Taisho period to the early Showa period using a basic framework to secure stable financial resources for fiscal decentralization. We would like to conclude by summarizing what we have discussed so far.

Since the middle of the Taisho period, revenues in SAEU have continued to exceed expenditures, and utility operations were so strong that the difference was carried over to the next fiscal year. There was a marked increase in electricity usage fees, owing to the strong demand for electricity. In the early part of the Showa period (1926–1945), revenue from municipal electricity utilities also increased. Revenue growth supports redemption. From FY1919 onward, "transfer funds" were established and used as a source of funds for other accounts. The "transfer funds" were used to finance important projects that were indispensable for Sendai to become a modern city, such as the municipal revision project fund and the waterworks project. Additionally, a breakdown of general account revenue "transfers" shows that they were almost entirely composed of "electric utility transfers."

The role of reserve funds in SAEU changed after the middle of the Taisho period. "Reserve funds" in the SMEU were actively invested in accounts other than the SMEU. Many reserves have been invested in general accounts and urban development projects, such as the construction of municipal hospitals. The portion allocated by the electric utility account accounted for nearly 30% of the general account revenue at its highest point. Although public bonds also accounted for a large proportion of general account revenues, they were positioned as the second-largest independent financial resource after tax revenue.

We have confirmed that SMEU was as critical as the "The Fiscal Treasury" of the City of Sendai. At present, we have experienced a structural transformation toward solar, wind, and biomass from hydroelectric and thermal sources in the generation of electricity. We believe the above basic framework can be applied to local cities with power shortages in developing countries.

Acknowledgements We would like to thank Professor Emeritus Shuetsu Takahashi, Shoichi Nishoji, Professor Kei Hosoya, Tsuyoshi Shinozaki, and Tatsuhiko Tani for their valuable comments and suggestions.

References

Akai N, Sakata M (2002) Fiscal decentralization contributes to economic growth: evidence from state-level cross-section data for the United States. J Urban Econ 52(1):93–108

Davoodi H, Zou HF (1998) Fiscal decentralization and economic growth: a cross-country study. J Urban Econ 43(2):244–257

Fujita T (1949) Capitalism and public finance in Japan. Jitsugyo no Nihonsha, Tokyo

Hanif I, Wallace S, Gago-de-Santos P (2020) Economic growth by means of fiscal decentralization: an empirical study for federal developing countries. Sage Open 10(4):2158244020968088

Iimi A (2005) Decentralization and economic growth revisited: an empirical note. J Urban Econ 57(3):449–461

Ishita Y (2004) The development of urban planning in modern and postmodern in Japan, 1868–2003. Municipalities Research, Tokyo

Itoh Y (2018) The birth of the "Great Tokyo Metropolis": the era of urban remodeling and publicness, 1895–1931. Minerva Shobo, Tokyo

Iwanami K (1979) Accumulation of municipal debt and fiscal contradiction under the Showa depression. Chuo University, Tokyo

Kanazawa F (1979) A study of urban finances in the 1910s: focusing on the establishment of the Tokyo municipal electric utility industry. J Econ Stud 22:77–89

Kanazawa F (2010) A study of the history of local public finance in modern Japan. Nihon Keizai Hyoron Inc, Tokyo

Kojita Y (1991) An introduction to the study of modern urban history in Japan. Kashiwa Shobo Inc, Tokyo

Kumoshikari S (2011) The problem of the raise of the electricity rate of Sendai-City in Taisho era. Econ Rev 177:165–193

Kumoshikari S (2013) Consideration by the statistics data of the municipal electric power business in Sendai City as "financial treasure": the analysis of the special accounts of the municipal electric power business. Bull Tohoku Inst Ind Econ 31:63–114

Kumoshikari S (2017) Historic meaning of "five municipal business" of Sendai in the end of Meiji era: the process of establishing of the municipal electricity business in Sendai City. Bull Inst Cult Res Northeast Jpn 49:1–27

Kumoshikari S (2021) Consideration on the development of "Great Sendai" project in modern era: with the focus of on community activities. Econ Rev 194:137–180

Mochida N (1984) The emergence of modern municipal government finances in Prewar Japan (I). J Soc Sci 36(3):95–142

Mochida N (1985) The emergence of modern municipal government finances in Prewar Japan (II). J Soc Sci 36(6):49–197

Mochida N (1993) A study of urban finance. University of Tokyo Press, Tokyo

Numajiri A (2002) Factory location and urban planning: characteristics of Japanese urban formation, 1905–1954. University of Tokyo Press, Tokyo

Ohkawa K, Shinohara M, Umemura M (1969) Estimates of long-term economic statistics of Japan since 1868, GOvernment Expenditure. Toyo Keizai Shinpo Inc, Tokyo

Oishi K, Kanazawa F (eds) (2003) A study on the history of Japanese cities in the modern era: reconstruction from local cities. Nihon Keizai Hyoron Inc, Tokyo

Sekino M (1982a) Hajime SEKI's theory of urban finance. Econ Rev 129(12):94–113

Sekino M (1982b) Hajime SEKI's Osaka municipal utility. Econ Rev 129(13):77–96

Sendai City Hall (1917-1943) Statement of Revenue and Expenditure for General and Special Accounts in Sendai City (FY 1916-1942)

Chapter 10
Concentration and Agglomeration in Spatial Monopoly, Spatial Duopoly, and Spatial Competition

Tohru Wako and Shuetsu Takahashi

Abstract This chapter examines the structure of the urban economy and urban growth under spatial monopoly, spatial duopoly, and spatial competition. We find: First, for any external utility level, the wage rate is the largest under spatial duopoly, followed by spatial monopoly and dispersed spatial competition. Second, the rent profiles depend on the maximum commuting distance under each competition scenario. For example, if the maximum commuting distance under spatial monopoly is more than twice of that under dispersed spatial competition, the order of the three scenario's rent profiles is the same as that of the wage rate. Third, there exists a sustained point of dispersed spatial competition and a break point of concentration in the city. The conditions for both points depend on the external utility level and labor productivity in the urban space. Spatial duopoly, rather than spatial monopoly, in a centralized city leads to agglomeration.

Keywords OAK model · Spatial monopoly · Löschian dispersed competition · Spatial duopoly à la Cournot

JEL Classification: R11, R12, R13, R23

10.1 Introduction

In the late 1980s and early 1990s, the per capita income of Japanese urban workers exceeded that of their US counterparts following several years of appreciation of the yen. Still, Japanese workers were afflicted by a feeling of poverty. Bronfenbrenner and Ohta (1990) explained this using a simple model involving the firm, household,

---

T. Wako · S. Takahashi (✉)
Faculty of Economics, Tohoku Gakuin University, Sendai, Miyagi, Japan
e-mail: wako@mail.tohoku-gakuin.ac.jp; shu@mail.tohoku-gakuin.ac.jp

S. Takahashi et al. (eds.), *Modern Macroeconomics with Historical Perspectives*, New Frontiers in Regional Science: Asian Perspectives 67,
https://doi.org/10.1007/978-981-99-1067-0_10

and landowner. The authors showed how rapid urban economic growth with skyrocketing land prices, such as those in Tokyo, can possibly be related to or even supported by the poor workers confined in their "rabbit hutches."

Spatially, increasing returns to scale imply positive agglomeration effects; that is, concentrating production in one economic area allows for higher productivity. The implications of these effects on the spatial distribution of activities have been analyzed in the new economic geography literature (e.g., Krugman 1991a, b; Ottaviano and Puga 1997; Fujita et al. 1999; Fujita and Thisse 2002). The new economic geography literature emphasizes the spatial consequences of agglomeration forces that are necessary to understand endogenous growth.

Meanwhile, in the spatial competition literature, Ohta et al. (1990) (abbreviated to OAK) presented a general equilibrium model of three related markets in economic space; the authors analyzed the behavior of wages, rents, and profits in a linear space with spatially differentiated labor, land, and product markets under spatial monopoly and spatial competition. Others, such as Kohlhase and Ohta (1990) and Nakagome (1986), analyzed spatial competition in product and labor markets. Finally, Gronberg and Meyer (1982) integrated land rents into a model of spatial monopoly, while Fujita and Thisse (1986) extended the Hotelling model to account for land rents.[1]

Undoubtedly, OAK's contribution to urban spatial economics is remarkable; however, several problems remain unresolved. First, the authors did not derive rent profiles under spatial monopoly or Löschian dispersed spatial competition (where an entrant enters some distance away from the incumbent firm; Lösch 1954). Here, we express the rent profiles under differing conditions of spatial monopoly and alternative spatial competition.

Second, when an entrant enters the spatial monopolist's site, the authors only deduced that the rent would increase by assuming that the resulting wage rate is higher than that in the monopoly case due to wage competition; they did not construct any duopoly models of concentrated competition. Here, we reexamine OAK's findings based on their ad hoc hypothesis and probe deeper into the labor market under centralized employment using a spatial labor market model à la Cournot (1897) (where an entrant enters the spatial monopolist's site).

Third, the authors did not consider concentration and agglomeration. We focused on city size as the urban fringe distance, that is, the maximum commuting distance from the central business district (CBD) in the OAK model. City size is different from the types of spatial monopoly, spatial duopoly, and dispersed spatial competition, depending on the external utility level and labor productivity. We then find the sustained point of dispersed spatial competition and the break point of

[1] See Hotelling (1929). For overviews of spatial economics, see, for example, Alonso (1964), von Thunen (1966), Christaller (1966), Muth (1969), Kanemoto (1980), Henderson (1985), Mills (1987), and Fujita (1989) on urban land use; Fujita et al. (1999) and Fujita and Thisse (2002) on new economic geography; DiPasquale and Wheaton (1996) on real estate markets; and Beckmann and Thisse (1987), Greenhut et al. (1987), and Ohta (1988) on spatial competition.

concentration in the city. In a centralized city, a spatial duopoly rather than a spatial monopoly leads to agglomeration.

Wako (1992) has also attempted to numerically clarify the first and second problems of OAK which were left. This chapter generalizes Löschian dispersed spatial competition and the spatial labor market à la Cournot to solve these two problems. Furthermore, we present a new third problem to examine the alternatives between prosperity and decline in the city.

The remainder of this chapter is organized as follows. Section 10.2 outlines our basic assumptions to revisit the three-sector model of OAK in an economic space with three agents: consumers, landowners, and firms. Each subsection in Sect. 10.3 then describes firm behavior in a spatial monopoly, Löschian (dispersed) spatial competition, and spatial duopoly à la Cournot to derive the wage rate, rent profile, and commuting distance. Section 10.4 examines the unsolved problems from OAK. We prove the validity of OAK's ad hoc hypothesis and the structure of rent profiles. Section 10.5 notes the concentration and agglomeration through city size calculated numerically. Finally, Sect. 10.6 presents the conclusions of this study.

10.2 The Model

10.2.1 Framework

We set the following basic assumptions about the spatial character in urban areas[2]

1. The city is monocentric in both spatial monopoly and spatial duopoly. Firm(s) and all job opportunities are located in the CBD.
2. Firms in the Löschian dispersed spatial competition are separated by a constant interval from their boundaries. Job opportunities are located in each CBD.
3. Each household is uniformly and continuously distributed along a one-dimensional linear market.
4. The household earns wages per unit time, spends on a composite consumer good, and enjoys leisure.
5. The only travel is that of workers commuting between residences and workplace.
6. The urban market here is *open* and *closed*.[3]
7. Absentee landowners own all the land for residential use, while the land needed for factory sites is owned by the firm(s).

---

[2] This section and Sect. 10.3.1 are mainly based on OAK (1990).

[3] Our linear market is not only open in the sense that households are free to migrate to and from outside the market but also closed in the sense that the population size is exogenous after considering the migration to and from that market. Definitions of open and closed as well as small cities were introduced by Wheaton (1974).

The households depend on landowners for their housing and on nearby firm(s) for their wages. Landowners and firms depend on each other via workers (households) as the ultimate source of their rewards in the form of rent and profit.

10.2.2 Households

Each household has identical tastes and maximizes its utility, subject to their budget constraints. We specify their utility functions as $U(q, h, s)$,where q, h, and s represent the amount of a composite good consumed (the numeraire), the amount of leisure, and the lot size of the house, respectively.

Each household is endowed with total time, H, which is spent on working, commuting, and leisure. Commuting time is assumed to be directly proportional to distance.

We consider the cases of spatial monopoly, Löschian dispersed spatial competition, and spatial duopoly à la Cournot. First, we explain cases of spatial monopoly and spatial duopoly. If a household is located at distance of x from the CBD, which implies commuting time x from the CBD, their budget constraint is given by $w(H - x) - R(x)s = q + wh$, where w and $R(x)$ are the wage rate and land rent, respectively. $R(x)$ depends on the commuting time x from the CBD. In the case of Löschian dispersed spatial competition, the above distance (time) should be read as the distance (time) from each firm site.

The pioneering work of Fujita (1989) assumes that h is not a choice variable, while OAK (1990) assume s as a constant, especially, $s = 1$, for simplicity. We now follow OAK' (1990) assumption for the analysis of the centralized and decentralized city. Then, the household optimization problem may be formally stated as follows:

$$\max_{q,h} U(q.h) \quad \text{subject to} \quad w(H - x) - R(x) = q + wh. \tag{10.1}$$

Furthermore, OAK (1990) specify the utility function $U(q, h)$ for simplicity, as $U(q, h) = qh$. OAK (1990) and Wako (1992) derive the demand functions of q and h to obtain the bid rent function at commuting time x from the CBD.

However, the easiest method to solve the optimization problem is to apply Fujita's (1989) bid rent function approach based on duality theory. Let U_* be the (expected) utility level or some minimum standard of living that households can obtain in the outside economy. The above duality problem reduces to maximize the bid rent function (rent profile), that is:

$$\max_{h} R(x) = w(H - x) - q - wh \quad \text{subject to} \quad U^* = qh. \tag{10.2}$$

Thus, we have the compensated demands as:

$$h^*(x) = \sqrt{\frac{U^*}{w}}, \tag{10.3}$$

$$q^*(x) = \sqrt{wU^*}. \tag{10.4}$$

The consumer optimum $[h^*(x), q^*(x)]$ at any location depends on U^* and w alone, and is completely independent of location x. Furthermore, we obtain the bid rent function (rent profile):

$$R^*(x) = w\,(H - x) - 2\sqrt{wU^*}. \tag{10.5}$$

Letting $R^*(x) = 0$, we obtain the maximum commuting time, X^*, defined as:

$$X^* = H - 2\sqrt{\frac{U^*}{w}}. \tag{10.6}$$

10.2.3 Firms

Under spatial monopoly, only one firm exists in the CBD. It acts as a monopolist in both the product and labor markets. Under Löschian spatial competition, there are two city centers, and each firm is located in each CBD at a certain distance. Finally, under spatial duopoly, two firms are located in the CBD and face wage competition in the labor market.

A one-factor production technology, the sole input of which is labor, is assumed. Let α and L be labor productivity and labor input, respectively; we then denote output as αL, where α is exogenously given.

The mill price of output, the numeraire, is unity; hence, the profit function for the firm is given by the following:

$$\pi = (\alpha - w)\,L. \tag{10.7}$$

The firm under spatial monopoly and two firms under Löschian dispersed spatial competition try to maximize their profit, π, by setting their strategic variable, w, the wage level. Differentiating (10.7) with respect to w and setting $d\pi/dw = 0$, we obtain:

$$L = (\alpha - w)\,\frac{dL}{dw}. \tag{10.8}$$

Meanwhile, the firm under spatial duopoly à la Cournot tries to maximize its profit with respect to its labor input, conjecturing that the employment levels of its rival firm remain unchanged. We describe this in detail in Sect. 10.3.3.

10.3 The Centralized and Decentralized Cities

10.3.1 The Centralized City: Spatial Monopoly

The labor supply of each household is $H - x - h^*(x)$ from the discussion in Sect. 10.2.2. The amount of leisure $h^*(x)$ is represented by (10.3), which implies the complete independence of location x. The maximum commuting distance X^* is given by (10.6). Here, the superscript m stands for "Monopoly." X^{m^*} represents the maximum commuting distance under spatial monopoly.

The aggregate labor supply under spatial monopoly, L^m, is given by the following:

$$L^m = 2\int_0^{X^{m*}} \left(H - x - h^*(x)\right) \mathrm{d}x = H\left(H - 2\sqrt{\frac{U*}{w^m}}\right), \tag{10.9}$$

The aggregate labor demand under spatial monopoly is given by (10.8). Thus, we have the optimal wage rate w^{m^*} for the monopolist given in an implicit form as follows:

$$Hw^{m^*}\sqrt{w^{m^*}} = \sqrt{U^*}\left(\alpha + w^{m^*}\right). \tag{10.10}$$

Further, the rent profile $R^{m^*}(x)$ via (10.5) can be expressed as follows:

$$R^{m^*}(x) = w^{m^*}\,(H - x) - 2\sqrt{w^{m^*}U^*}. \tag{10.11}$$

The maximum commuting time is rewritten as follows:

$$X^{m^*} = H - 2\sqrt{\frac{U^*}{w^{m^*}}}. \tag{10.12}$$

10.3.2 The Decentralized City: Löschian Dispersed Entry

Here, we change our viewpoint from a concentrated city to a decentralized one and from a spatial monopoly site to plural spatial competition sites. OAK (1990) consider a case of interest in which the entry of firms results in a dispersed location pattern.

OAK (1990) and Wako (1992) assume a Löschian landscape, whereby firms are separated by a constant interval over the entire market area. This implies that any firm's market area touches that of neighboring firms and is fixed.

We assume that firms are located at a distance of $\delta/2$ from their boundary and, therefore, are separated by δ. We denote 0 as the coordinates of the point of the boundary and x as the distance (time) from the boundary. Therefore, the commuting distance (time) from the firm site is $\delta/2 - x$ for $0 \leq \delta/2 - \theta \leq x \leq \delta/2$ and $-\delta/2$ for $\delta/2 \leq x \leq \delta/2 + \theta$, where θ is the maximum commuting distance from the firm site.

We then derive the aggregate labor supply L^l for a firm located on the right-hand side of the boundary as follows:

$$L^l = \int_{\frac{\delta}{2}-\theta}^{\frac{\delta}{2}} \left(H - \left(\frac{\delta}{2} - x \right) - h^*(x) \right) \mathrm{d}x + \int_{\frac{\delta}{2}}^{\frac{\delta}{2}+\theta} \left(H - \left(x - \frac{\delta}{2} \right) - h^*(x) \right) \mathrm{d}x = \theta \left(2H - 2\sqrt{\frac{U*}{w^l}} - \theta \right), \tag{10.13}$$

where the superscript l stands for the Löschian.

A one-factor production technology and constant labor productivity are again assumed. Profit maximization for each firm under Löschian competition is given by (10.8). However, each firm is unable to take the effect of wage rate w^l on θ into its competitiveness. If the firm's wage rate is lower than that of another firm, households move their residence and working site to the higher wage location. Thus, we have the optimal wage rate w^{l^*} for the Löschian firm with a distance of $\delta/2$ from the boundary, given in an implicit form as

$$(2H - \theta)\, w^{l^*} \sqrt{w^{l^*}} = \sqrt{U*} \left(w^{l^*} + \alpha \right). \tag{10.14}$$

Further, the rent profile $R^{l^*}(x)$ can be expressed by the following:

$$\begin{aligned} R^{l^*}(x) &= w^{l^*} \left(H - \left(\tfrac{\delta}{2} - x \right) \right) - 2\sqrt{w^{l^*} U*} \quad \text{for } \tfrac{\delta}{2} - \theta \leq x \leq \tfrac{\delta}{2}, \\ R^{l^*}(x) &= w^{l^*} \left(H - \left(x - \tfrac{\delta}{2} \right) \right) - 2\sqrt{w^{l^*} U*} \quad \text{for } \tfrac{\delta}{2} \leq x \leq \tfrac{\delta}{2} + \theta. \end{aligned} \tag{10.15}$$

For each household, $R^{l^*}(x) = 0$ in (10.15) represents their maximum commuting distance $x*$ from firm site $\delta/2$. Taking the difference of $\delta/2$ into consideration, we have the maximum commuting distance θ from the firm site in absolute value as follows:

$$\theta = H - 2\sqrt{\frac{U*}{w^{l^*}}}. \tag{10.16}$$

An equilibrium is a point at which w^{l^*} for the Löschian firm with the anticipated commuting distance corresponds to the maximum commuting distance θ for the household, which depends on w^{l^*}. Thus, we obtain the wage rate $w^{l^{E*}}$ in equilibrium from (10.14) and (10.16) as follows:

$$Hw^{l^{E*}}\sqrt{w^{l^{E*}}} = \sqrt{U^*}\left(\alpha - w^{l^{E*}}\right). \tag{10.17}$$

If $\delta/2 > \theta$, each residential area and each firm's market area are at least separated by $\delta - 2\theta$ (Case A). If $\delta/2 = \theta$, each residential area is adjacent at $x = 0$ (Case B). As $w^{l^{E*}}$ in (10.17) is completely independent of the Löschian distance of $\delta/2$, it does not substantially affect θ and the rent profile $R^{l^*}(x)$.

If $\delta/2 < \theta$, each residential area overlaps (Case C). Assuming that two households are unable to live in one lot, we need to remove the labor supply from the overlapped residential area to reconsider the aggregate labor supply in (10.13). The aggregate labor supply L^l for each firm should be then changed to:

$$\begin{aligned} L^l &= \int_0^{\frac{\delta}{2}}\left(H - \left(\frac{\delta}{2} - x\right) - h^*(x)\right)\mathrm{d}x + \int_{\frac{\delta}{2}}^{\frac{\delta}{2}+\theta}\left(H - \left(x - \frac{\delta}{2}\right) - h^*(x)\right)\mathrm{d}x \\ &= \left(H - \sqrt{\frac{U^*}{w^l}}\right)\left(\theta + \frac{\delta}{2}\right) - \frac{1}{2}\left(\theta^2 + \left(\frac{\delta}{2}\right)^2\right). \end{aligned} \tag{10.18}$$

We obtain the optimal wage rate w^{l^*} for each firm under Löschian competition from profit maximization (10.8) as:

$$\left[H\left(\theta + \frac{\delta}{2}\right) - \frac{1}{2}\left(\theta^2 + \left(\frac{\delta}{2}\right)^2\right)\right]w^{l^*}\sqrt{w^{l^*}} = \frac{1}{2}\left(\theta + \frac{\delta}{2}\right)\sqrt{U^*}\left(w^{l^*} + \alpha\right). \tag{10.19}$$

Further, the rent profile $R^{l^*}(x)$ can be expressed by the following:

$$\begin{aligned} R^{l^*}(x) &= w^{l^*}\left(H - \left(\tfrac{\delta}{2} - x\right)\right) - 2\sqrt{w^{l^*}U^*} \quad \text{for } 0 \le x \le \tfrac{\delta}{2} \\ R^{l^*}(x) &= w^{l^*}\left(H - \left(x - \tfrac{\delta}{2}\right)\right) - 2\sqrt{w^{l^*}U^*} \quad \text{for } \tfrac{\delta}{2} \le x \le \tfrac{\delta}{2} + \theta. \end{aligned} \tag{10.20}$$

From $R^{l^*}(x) = 0$ in (10.20), we again get (10.16). Thus, we have the wage rate $w^{l^{E*}}$ in equilibrium, given in an implicit form as:

$$\begin{aligned} \left[H(H+\delta) - \left(\frac{\delta}{2}\right)^2\right]w^{l^{E*}}\sqrt{w^{l^{E*}}} &= \left(H + \frac{\delta}{2}\right)\sqrt{U^*}\left(\alpha + w^{l^{E*}}\right) \\ &\quad - \frac{2U^*}{\sqrt{w^{l^{E*}}}}\left(\alpha - w^{l^{E*}}\right). \end{aligned} \tag{10.21}$$

$w^{l^{E*}}$ in (10.21) depends on the distance $\delta/2$. This implies that the distance affects the maximum commuting distance θ and the rent profile $R^{l^*}(x)$ through $w^{l^{E*}}$. In the specific case of $\delta/2 = 0$, the aggregate labor supply L^l in (10.18) is half of that in both Cases A and B, as shown by (10.13); meanwhile, the wage rates are the same as in both cases because (10.21) returns to (10.17) as:

$$\left[Hw^{l^{E*}}\sqrt{w^{l^{E*}}} - \sqrt{U^*}\left(\alpha - w^{l^{E*}}\right)\right]\left[H\sqrt{w^{l^{E*}}} - 2\sqrt{U^*}\right] = 0. \qquad (10.22)$$

The Löschian firm can define the distance δ from its neighboring firm with flexibility. Hereafter, we focus on the case of $\delta = 2\,\theta$ (i.e., Case B) for simplicity.

10.3.3 The Centralized City: Entry at Market Center à la Cournot

In the case in which an entrant enters the spatial monopolist's site, OAK deduced that the rent would increase, assuming that the resulting wage rate is higher than that in the monopoly case due to wage competition. Even if this is the case, we must reexamine OAK's findings since they are based on the ad hoc hypothesis set up without constructing any appropriate models; consequently, we probe deeper into the labor market under centralized employment.

Here, we use a spatial labor market model à la Cournot to compute the profit-maximizing employment levels and optimal wage rates. Applying the Cournot duopoly model for a homogeneous product to our analysis of the spatial labor market, we obtain the following behavioral hypothesis for firms: Each firm sets its employment levels simultaneously to maximize its profits, conjecturing that the employment levels of its rival firm remain unchanged. Letting the employment of firms 1 and 2 be L_1^c and L_2^c, respectively, we have:

$$\frac{\partial L^c}{\partial L_1^c} = \frac{\partial L^c}{\partial L_2^c} = 1, \qquad (10.23)$$

where aggregate employment in the entire market is defined as $L^c = L_1^c + L_2^c$ and superscript c stands for "Cournot."

The aggregate labor supply in the spatial labor market model à la Cournot, L^c, is given by the original aggregate labor supply schedule in (10.9) as:

$$L^c = H\left(H - 2\sqrt{\frac{U^*}{w^c}}\right). \qquad (10.24)$$

Again, a one-factor production technology and constant labor productivity for each firm are assumed. The profit function for each firm is given by the proximate of (10.7). By differentiating this proximate with respect to L_i^c $(i = 1, 2)$ and setting $\mathrm{d}\pi_i/\mathrm{d}L_i^c = 0$, we have the labor demand for each firm à la Cournot in an implicit form as:

$$L_i^c \frac{\partial w^c}{\partial L_i^c} = \alpha - w^c \qquad (i = 1, 2). \tag{10.25}$$

Hence, the aggregate labor demand in spatial labor à la Cournot is:

$$\sum L_i^c \frac{\partial w^c}{\partial L_i^c} = 2\left(\alpha - w^c\right) \quad (i = 1, 2). \tag{10.26}$$

The effect of the labor demand increase on wages in labor market equilibrium is derived from (10.24) as:

$$\frac{\partial w^c}{\partial L_1^c} = \frac{\partial w^c}{\partial L_2^c} = \frac{w^c}{H}\sqrt{\frac{w^c}{U*}}. \tag{10.27}$$

Therefore, we obtain the optimal wage rate w^{c^*} from (10.26), (10.27), and (10.24) as:

$$Hw^c\sqrt{w^c} = 2\alpha\sqrt{U*}. \tag{10.28}$$

We obtain the rent profile $R^{c^*}(x)$ and the maximum commuting time X^* as follows:

$$R^{c^*}(x) = w^{c^*}(H - x) - 2\sqrt{w^{c^*}U*}, \tag{10.29}$$

$$X^{c^*} = H - 2\sqrt{\frac{U*}{w^{c^*}}}. \tag{10.30}$$

10.4 Comparative Statistics

10.4.1 Comparative Static Properties

We examine comparative static properties in spatial monopoly, Löschian spatial competition, and spatial duopoly à la Cournot.

OAK (1990) find the following comparative static properties in spatial monopoly and posit it as their Proposition 1: if $w^{m^*} \in [0, \alpha]$, then:

$$\frac{\partial w^{m^*}}{\partial \alpha} > 0, \quad \frac{\partial X^{m^*}}{\partial \alpha} > 0, \quad \frac{\partial w^{m^*}}{\partial U*} > 0 \text{ and } \frac{\partial X^{m^*}}{\partial U*} < 0. \tag{10.31}$$

We also reconfirm the above inequalities from (10.10) and (10.12).

We derive similar properties in Löschian competition from (10.16) and (10.17), and in spatial duopoly à la Cournot from (10.28) and (10.30) as follows:

$$\frac{\partial w^{l^{E*}}}{\partial \alpha} > 0, \; \frac{\partial \theta}{\partial \alpha} > 0, \; \frac{\partial w^{l^{E*}}}{\partial U*} > 0 \text{ and } \frac{\partial \theta}{\partial U*} < 0, \tag{10.32}$$

$$\frac{\partial w^{c^*}}{\partial \alpha} > 0, \; \frac{\partial X^{c^*}}{\partial \alpha} > 0, \; \frac{\partial w^{c^*}}{\partial U*} > 0 \text{ and } \frac{\partial X^{c^*}}{\partial U*} < 0. \tag{10.33}$$

These results indicate that a rise in the productivity α and external utility level $U*$ increases the wage rate. Furthermore, the former (latter) increases (decreases) the maximum commuting distance.

Before proceeding further, we reconfirm that $U*$ is sufficiently low. w^{m^*} in (10.10) is a monotonically increasing function of $U*$, as proven by OAK (1990). We obtain $U*= \frac{\alpha H^2}{4}$ when $w^{m^*} = \alpha$. For $w^{m^*} \leq \alpha$, $U*$must satisfy the relationship, $U^* \leq \frac{\alpha H^2}{4}$.

10.4.2 Structure of the Urban Economy

OAK assume that the wage rate in spatial duopoly is higher than that in spatial monopoly because of wage competition. Based on our model's framework, we derive OAK's findings founded on their ad hoc hypothesis. In addition, the structure of rent profiles remains an unsolved problem in OAK. We clarify this structure related to wage rates.

The wage rates in spatial monopoly, Löschian competition, and spatial duopoly à la Cournot are represented by (10.10), (10.17), and (10.28), respectively. We have $w^{m^*} = w^{l^{E*}} = w^{C*} = 0$ when $U* = 0$, and $w^{m*} = w^{C*} = \alpha$ when $U^* = \frac{\alpha H^2}{4}$. As w^{m^*}, $w^{l^{E*}}$, and w^{C*} are monotonically increasing functions of $U*$, their respective inverse functions also exist. Denoting U^{m^*}, $U^{l^{E*}}$, and U^{C^*}as $U*$ in each case, we obtain the following relations for any $w \in (0, \alpha)$:

$$\sqrt{U^{m*}} - \sqrt{U^{l^{E*}}} = \frac{Hw\sqrt{w}}{\alpha + w} - \frac{Hw\sqrt{w}}{\alpha - w} = \frac{-2Hw^2\sqrt{w}}{(\alpha + w)(\alpha - w)} < 0, \tag{10.34}$$

$$\sqrt{U^{C*}} - \sqrt{U^{m*}} = \frac{Hw\sqrt{w}}{2\alpha} - \frac{Hw\sqrt{w}}{\alpha + w} = \frac{-(\alpha - w)\,Hw\sqrt{w}}{2\alpha\,(\alpha + w)} < 0. \tag{10.35}$$

This implies $U^{C^*} < U^{m^*} < U^{l^{E*}}$for any $w \in (0, \alpha)$. In turn, this means that $w^{c*} > w^{m*} > w^{l^{E*}}$ for any $U*$ ($0 < U^* \leq \frac{\alpha H^2}{4}$).

We immediately have leisure $h_*(x)$ and consumption $q_*(x)$ as $h^{c*} < h^{m*} < h^{l^{E*}}$ and $q^{c*} > q^{m*} > q^{l^{E*}}$ at any location for any U_* ($0 < U^* \le \frac{\alpha H^2}{4}$) from (10.3) and (10.4), and the above relations of $w^{c*} > w^{m*} > w^{l^{E*}}$.

Here, we consider the city size (the length of city) as the urban fringe distance, which relates to the maximum commuting distance, that is, X^{m_*} or X^{c^*} from the CBD and θ from the point of the boundary in Case B of Löschian competition. The city size is a double of $X^{m_*}$and X^{c^*}, and a quadruple of θ. For simplicity, we compare $X^{m_*}$and $X^{c^*}$with 2θ. For $w^{c*} > w^{m*} > w^{l^{E*}}$, we have $X^{c_*} > X^{m_*}$ for any given $U^* \left(0 < U^* \le \frac{\alpha H^2}{4}\right)$ from (10.12) and (10.30). However, the size relations for 2θ are ambiguous. Table 10.1 in the next section shows that $X^{c_*} > X^{m_*} \ge 2\theta$ for a relatively high U_* and $2\theta > X^{c_*} > X^{m_*}$ for a relatively low U_*.

In summary, we have the following proposition.

Proposition 10.1 *For any external utility level U_* ($0 < U^* \le \frac{\alpha H^2}{4}$), the wage rate in spatial duopoly à la Cournot is higher than that in spatial monopoly due to wage competition. Moreover, the latter is higher than the wage rate in Löschian spatial competition. In each case, the consumption quantity (leisure), in descending order for the three scenarios, is the same (opposite) as the wage rate in descending order.*

OAK (1990) find the following properties of rent profiles in spatial monopoly and posit it as their Proposition 10.3: if $w^{m^*} \in [0, \alpha]$, then:

$$\frac{\partial R^{m^*}(x)}{\partial \alpha} > 0, \qquad \frac{\partial R^{m^*}(x)}{\partial U^*} \gtrless 0 \quad \text{as} \quad \gtrless \frac{\left(\alpha^2 - 2\alpha w^{m^*} - w^{m^{*2}}\right) H}{\left(\alpha + w^{m^*}\right)^2}. \tag{10.36}$$

We also reconfirm the above inequalities from (10.10) and (10.11).

Here, we examine the rent profiles represented by (10.11), (10.15), and (10.29). The bid rents of $R^{m^*}(0)$ and $R^{c^*}(0)$ at the CBD and the bit rent of $R^{l^*}\left(\frac{\delta}{2}\right)$ at $\frac{\delta}{2}$ from the boundary point in Löschian competition are $wH - 2\sqrt{wU^*}$, depending on the wage rate in each type and the external utility level U_*. Therefore, we have $\frac{\partial}{\partial w}\left(wH - 2\sqrt{wU^*}\right) = H - h > 0$,which implies $\frac{\partial R^{m^*}(0)}{\partial w^{m*}} > 0$, $\frac{\partial R^{c^*}(0)}{\partial w^{c*}} > 0$, and $\frac{\partial R^{l^*}\left(\frac{\delta}{2}\right)}{\partial w^{l^{E*}}} > 0$. Further, considering $w^{c*} > w^{m*} > w^{l^{E*}}$, we have $R^{c^*}(0) > R^{m^*}(0) > R^{l^*}\left(\frac{\delta}{2}\right)$ for any $U^* \left(0 < U^* \le \frac{\alpha H^2}{4}\right)$.

Next, comparing the bid rents of $R^{m^*}(x)$and $R^{c^*}(x)$, we have $R^{c^*}(x) - R^{m^*}(x) = (w^{c*} - w^{m*})(H - x) - 2\sqrt{U^*}\left(\sqrt{w^{c*}} - \sqrt{w^{m*}}\right)$. For the same reason as described above, we have $R^{c^*}(x) > R^{m^*}(x)$.

We consider $R^{m^*}(x)$ and $R^{l^*}(x)$. Case B in the Löschian competition reduces $\frac{\delta}{2}+\theta$ to 2θ. Because $R^{m^*}(2\theta) = w^{m^*}(H - 2\theta) - 2\sqrt{w^{m^*}U^*} = w^{m^*}\left(X^{m^*} - 2\theta\right)$, we have $R^{m^*}(2\theta) \ge R^{l^*}(2\theta) = 0$ for $X^{m^*} \ge 2\theta$. Hence, $R^{m^*}(x) \ge R^{l^*}(x)$ holds for $X^{m^*} \ge 2\theta$ from the linearity of $R^{m^*}(x)$ and $R^{l^*}(x)$ and the properties mentioned above, that is, $w^{m*} > w^{l^{E*}}$, $R^{m^*}(0) > R^{l^*}\left(\frac{\delta}{2}\right)$ and $R^{m^*}(2\theta) \geq R^{l^*}(2\theta) = 0$. Thus, we obtain $R^{c^*}(x) > R^{m^*}(x) > R^{l^*}(x)$ for $X^{m^*} \geq 2\theta$.

Similarly, we obtain $R^{m^*}(2\theta) = 0 \leq R^{l^*}(2\theta) \leq R^{c^*}(2\theta)$ for $X^{m^*} \leq 2\theta \leq X^{c^*}$ and $R^{m^*}(2\theta) = 0 \leq R^{c^*}(2\theta) \leq R^{l^*}(2\theta)$ for $X^{m^*} \leq X^{c^*} \leq 2\theta$. Denoting x^{ml} as x satisfying $R^{m^*}(x) = R^{l^*}(x)$, we have $R^{c^*}(x) > R^{m^*}(x) > R^{l^*}(x)$ for $0 \leq x \leq x^{ml}$ and $R^{c^*}(x) > R^{l^*}(x) > R^{m^*}(x)$ for $x^{ml} \leq x$ in $X^{m^*} \leq 2\theta \leq X^{c^*}$. Denoting x^{lc} as x satisfying $R^{l^*}(x) = R^{c^*}(x)$, we obtain $R^{c^*}(x) > R^{m^*}(x) > R^{l^*}(x)$ for $0 \leq x \leq x^{ml}$, $R^{c^*}(x) > R^{l^*}(x) > R^{m^*}(x)$ for $x^{ml} \leq x \leq x^{lc}$, and $R^{l^*}(x) > R^{c^*}(x) > R^{m^*}(x)$ for $x^{lc} \leq x$ in $X^{m^*} \leq X^{c^*} \leq 2\theta$.

In summary, we have the following propositions.

Proposition 10.2 *For any external utility level* $U*$ ($0 < U^* \leq \frac{\alpha H^2}{4}$), $R^{c^*}(0) > R^{m^*}(0) > R^{l^*}\left(\frac{\delta}{2}\right)$ *holds for the bid rents in spatial duopoly, spatial monopoly, and Löschian competition.*

Proposition 10.3 *For any external utility level* $U*$ ($0 < U^* \leq \frac{\alpha H^2}{4}$), *the following relations hold between rent profiles in spatial duopoly, spatial monopoly, and Löschian competition*:

If $X^{m^*} \geq 2\theta$, $R^{c^*}(x) > R^{m^*}(x) > R^{l^*}(x)$,
if $X^{m^*} \leq 2\theta \leq X^{c^*}$, $R^{c^*}(x) > R^{m^*}(x) > R^{l^*}(x)$ *for* $0 \leq x \leq x^{ml}$,
$R^{c^*}(x) > R^{l^*}(x) > R^{m^*}(x)$ *for* $x^{ml} \leq x$,
if $X^{m^*} \leq X^{c^*} \leq 2\theta$, $R^{c^*}(x) > R^{m^*}(x) > R^{l^*}(x)$ *for* $0 \leq x \leq x^{ml}$,
$R^{c^*}(x) > R^{l^*}(x) > R^{m^*}(x)$ *for* $x^{ml} \leq x \leq x^{lc}$,
$R^{l^*}(x) > R^{c^*}(x) > R^{m^*}(x)$ *for* $x^{lc} \leq x$.

The next section reveals the effects of spatial monopoly and spatial duopoly on concentration and agglomeration.

10.5 Concentration and Agglomeration

Various external levels of utility $U*$ and labor productivity α have significant effects on X^{m*}, 2θ, and X^{c^*}. For simplicity, we numerically evaluate these effects by assuming $H = \alpha = 1$. The minimum standard of living $U*$ must be less than or equal to 1/4 subject to $U^* \leq \frac{\alpha H^2}{4}$. Here, we specify $U*$ as 1/48, 0.04918, 1/16, and 1/12 to examine the urban structure.

First, we solve Eqs. (10.10), (10.17), (10.28), etc., to summarize Table 10.1 numerically, which provides a comparison of the effects of spatial monopoly and alternative imperfect competition. We confirm the framework of the model in Table 10.1 as follows.

The city size (the length of city) is twice the maximum commuting distance from CBD X^{m*} and X^{c^*}, or a quadruple of the maximum commuting distance from the point of the boundary, θ. The aggregate working hours of all households are equal

Table 10.1 City size and utility level

U^*	Maximum commuting distance	City size	Working hours of all households	Wage rate	Leisure hours	Rent income	Wage income	Profit income	Total income 1	Total income 2	Population density
	0.50000	1.00000	0.50000	0.33333	0.25000	0.08333	0.16666	0.33333	0.58332	0.58332	1.00000
1/48	0.39932	1.59728	0.79864	0.23096	0.30034	0.07364	0.18445	0.61419	0.87228	0.87228	0.62606
	0.56320	1.12640	0.56320	0.43679	0.21840	0.13855	0.24600	0.31720	0.70175	0.70175	0.88778
	0.35623	0.71246	0.35623	0.47467	0.32185	0.06023	0.16909	0.18714	0.41646	0.58453	1.40358
0.04918	0.17813	0.71252	0.35627	0.29124	0.41089	0.01848	0.10376	0.25251	0.37475	0.52595	1.40346
	0.41841	0.83682	0.41841	0.58158	0.29077	0.10182	0.24334	0.17507	0.52023	0.62167	1.19500
	0.31033	0.62066	0.31033	0.52560	0.34484	0.05061	0.16310	0.14721	0.36092	0.58151	1.61119
1/16	0.10183	0.40732	0.20367	0.30990	0.44909	0.00642	0.06312	0.14055	0.21009	0.51578	2.45507
	0.37003	0.74006	0.37003	0.62996	0.31498	0.08625	0.23311	0.13692	0.45628	0.61654	1.35124
	0.25258	0.50516	0.25258	0.59669	0.28706	0.03806	0.15071	0.10187	0.29064	0.57534	1.97957
1/12	0.00000	0.00000	0.00000	0.33333	0.38407	0.00000	0.00000	0.00000	0.00000	0.00000	–
	0.30663	0.61326	0.30663	0.69336	0.26630	0.07570	0.21261	0.09402	0.38233	0.62343	1.63062

Note: The first column, the second column, and the third column corresponding to each U^* show calculation values in spatial monopoly, Löschian competition (case B), and spatial duopoly, respectively to the maximum commuting time (distance). The aggregate working hours are equal to the sum of wage and profit incomes.

In each U^*, the city size, aggregate working hours, wage rate, wage income, and rent income in spatial duopoly à la Cournot (the third row in each U^*in Table 10.1) are higher than those in spatial monopoly (in the first row in each U^*), while relations in profit income become the opposite due to competition. When U^* increases, city size decreases, regardless of monopoly or duopoly, while the wage rate increases.

With $U^* = 1/48$, the city size in spatial monopoly is unity, which is smaller than that in Löschian competition (the second row in $U^* = 1/48$). In addition, wage and rent incomes in the former are lower than those in the latter. When $U^* = 0.04918$, the city size in the former is almost equal to that in the latter; thus, $U^* = 0.04918$ is the break point of city formation. Until U^*reaches 0.04918, the city in Löschian competition is better in terms of city size and various economic variables than the city in spatial monopoly. By contrast, above this critical value, the city in spatial monopoly gains predominance. Concentration to the city center occurs under spatial monopoly and spatial duopoly, while the city under Löschian competition shrinks sharply.

Note that calculating the break point numerically is difficult. Therefore, we theoretically show the existence of breakpoints. We obtain X^{m*}, 2θ, and X^{c^*} from (10.10) and (10.12), and their counterparts, respectively, as follows:

$$X^{m^*} = \frac{H\left(\alpha - w^{m^*}\right)}{\alpha + w^{m^*}},\quad 2\theta = \frac{2H\left(\alpha - 3w^{l^{E*}}\right)}{\alpha - w^{l^{E*}}},\quad X^{c^*} = \frac{H\left(\alpha - w^{c*}\right)}{\alpha}, \tag{10.37}$$

where w^{m^*}, $w^{l^{E*}}$, and w^{c*} satisfies (10.10), (10.17), and (10.28), respectively. X^{m*}, 2θ, and X^{c^*} are decreasing functions of U^*. In particular, for $U^* = 0$, we have $X^{m*} = H$, $2\theta = 2H$, and $X^{c^*} = H$. For $U^* = \alpha H^2/12$, we have $2\theta = 0$, $X^{m*} > 0$, and $X^{c^*} > 0$. For $U^* = \alpha H^2/4$, we have $X^{m*} = 0$ and $X^{c^*} = 0$. This means that U^* values satisfying both $X^{m*} = 2\theta$ and $X^{c*} = 2\theta$ exist, implying the existence of breakpoints. Denoting the former as $U^{*^{ml}}$ and the latter as $U^{*^{lc}}$, we obtain $X^{m*} \leq 2\theta$ for $U^* \leq U^{*^{ml}}$ and $X^{c*} \leq 2\theta$ for $U^* \leq U^{*^{lc}}$. Thus, the dispersed city in Löschian competition dominates. If $U^* > U^{*^{ml}}$ (or $U^* > U^{*^{lc}}$), the concentration to the city center occurs.

We obtain $U^* = \alpha H^2/1\ 2 = 1/12$ from (10.16) with $\theta = 0$ and (10.17). "$\theta = 0$" means the double-headed city in Löschian competition is no longer sustainable. An increase in the external utility level increases the wage rate; this, in turn, reduces the maximum commuting distance and city size. Shrinking the maximum commuting distance decreases the labor supply and employment, which reduces firms' profits. With $U^*=1/12$ and $w = 1/3$, the maximum commuting distance declines to zero and nobody works and firms stop operations. Then, the spatial structure of the city becomes monocentric. Thus, $U^* = 1/12$ is the sustain point of Löschian competition.

In each U_* between 0.04918 and 1/12, the city size, wage income, and others in spatial monopoly and spatial duopoly at the CBD are higher than those in Löschian dispersed spatial competition. Furthermore, these values in spatial duopoly facing a competitor in the CBD are higher than those in a spatial monopoly without competition. Firm location and competition lead to agglomeration.

Thus, we make the following propositions.

Proposition 10.4 *For a relatively low external utility level* U_* ($0 < U^* < U^{*^{lc}}$), *the dispersed city in Löschian competition gains predominance over the concentrated city in spatial monopoly and spatial duopoly.*

Proposition 10.5 *For a relatively high external utility level* U_* ($U^{*^{ml}} < U^* < \alpha H^2/12$), *the concentration to the city center occurs. Spatial duopoly in the concentrated city brings higher wage income, city size, and others than a spatial monopoly without competition.*

Proposition 10.6 *Löschian dispersed spatial competition is no longer sustainable at* $U_* = \alpha H^2/12$.

The population size and density may affect this explanation. The modifications in (10.7) and (10.8) are required. Here, we tighten the assumption of *open* and *close*d city to *a close*d city; that is, we assume a constant population size in each case and house residence inside the urban fringe distance. Assuming a weak effect of these factors on employment, we neglect the effect on the wage rate and others. Total income 2 of the 11th column in Table 10.1 shows the correcting values of total income 1 in the tenth column. Here, we calculate the values considering only population density as the reciprocal of the length of the city. However, we do not need to calculate the values for population density which are less than unity because all house residence in the case can be located inside the urban fringe without the use of multistory buildings. The column for total income 2 shows that the above discussion still holds true.

From a historical perspective, urban concentration is often accompanied by urban extensions (see Chap. 9 in this book). Table 10.2 summarizes the effects of labor productivity α on city size and various economic variables when $U_* = 1/12$. Here, the sum of wage and profit incomes is the aggregate working hours of all households multiplied by α.

$\alpha = 1$ is the sustain point of Löschian competition. The double-headed city disappears. Under high labor productivity as $\alpha = 1.5$ or 2, Löschian competition extends the city size. Especially at $\alpha = 2$, Löschian competition restores the city size to include spatial monopoly and spatial duopoly.

A more abundant life increases the external utility level. Then, a high external utility level accelerates spatial concentration and leads to agglomeration. The enhancement of labor productivity causes the city size to extend and concentration to decelerate. Both the external utility level and labor productivity are key drivers of converting a double-headed city to a monocentric one. The interrelation between

Table 10.2 City size and labor productivity

α	Maximum commuting distance	City size	Working hours of all households	Wage rate	Leisure hours	Rent income	Wage income	Profit income	Total income 1	Total income 2	Population density
	0.25258	0.50516	0.25258	0.59669	0.28706	0.03806	0.15071	0.10187	0.29064	0.57534	1.97957
1	0.00000	0.00000	0.00000	0.33333	0.38407	0.00000	0.00000	0.00000	0.00000	0.00000	–
	0.30663	0.61326	0.30663	0.69336	0.26630	0.07570	0.21261	0.09402	0.38233	0.60630	1.63062
	0.33333	0.66666	0.33333	0.74999	0.25605	0.08333	0.24999	0.25000	0.58332	0.87498	1.50001
1.5	0.14024	0.56096	0.28049	0.45095	0.33021	0.01774	0.12649	0.29425	0.43848	0.78166	1.78265
	0.39429	0.78858	0.39429	0.90856	0.23263	0.10182	0.35824	0.23320	0.69326	0.92912	1.2681
	0.38636	0.77272	0.38636	0.88523	0.26571	0.13214	0.34202	0.43071	0.90487	1.17101	1.29412
2	0.22682	0.90728	0.45364	0.55760	0.33479	0.05738	0.25294	0.65434	0.96466	1.06324	1.10219
	0.44968	0.89936	0.44968	1.10064	0.23830	0.08625	0.49494	0.40442	0.98561	1.24746	1.1119

Note: Values in $U^* = 1/12$

the utility level and labor productivity determines the degree of spatial concentration and extension in the city. A link between both is needed for our future study.

10.6 Concluding Remarks

Although OAK's simple model provides several important insights into the structure of the urban economy, several unresolved problems remain. We approach these problems from a different aspect by constructing a model of dispersed spatial competition à la Löschian, which is slightly different from OAK, and a model of concentrated spatial competition (spatial duopoly) à la Cournot. We show that the wage rate, in descending order, comes from concentrated spatial competition à la Cournot, spatial monopoly, and dispersed spatial competition à la Löschian for any external utility level. In addition, rent profiles are in the same order of the wage rate if the maximum commuting distance under spatial monopoly is more than twice that under dispersed spatial competition.

The most important factor seems to be the concentration and agglomeration in the city. The different structures of competitiveness in the spatial economy bring prosperity and decline. Beyond the sustain point of Löschian dispersed spatial competition, the double-headed city is no longer sustainable. The city's spatial structure becomes monocentric. The city size, wage income, and others in concentrated spatial competition à la Cournot are higher than those under spatial monopoly without competition. Importantly, concentration and competition lead to agglomeration.

However, there is another aspect to concentration. We conjure the image of households inside the urban fringe distance in a metropolitan area. Households may live in multistory buildings in highly restricted areas. An acute housing shortage then breaks the assumption of the same lot size for houses. This causes the skyrocketing of land and house prices, as well as land and house rents. Poor workers are forced to live in small and narrow houses, or "rabbit hutches." The deteriorating residential environment reduces the external utility level; this, in turn, may lead to the break point of the transformation from a monocentric city to a double-headed city.

Beyond OAK, many unknowns remain. The role of urban concentration and agglomeration is an important theme that needs to be further investigated in detail, including population size and density, bid-max lot size, and the linkage between utility level and labor productivity.

Acknowledgements The authors are grateful to Professors Mitsuyoshi Yanagihara, Kei Hosoya, and Tsuyoshi Shinozaki for comments on and critiques of earlier versions of this chapter.

References

Alonso W (1964) Location and land use. Harvard University Press, Cambridge

Beckmann MJ, Thisse J-F (1987) The location of production activities. In: Nijkamp P (ed) Handbook of regional and urban economics: regional economics, vol 1. North-Holland, Amsterdam

Bronfenbrenner M, Ohta H (1990) Japanese economic growth and the Takuboku lament. Taiwan Econ Rev 17:435–457

Christaller W (1966) The central places in southern Germany. Prentice-Hall, Englewood Cliffs

Cournot A (1897) Researches into the mathematical principles of the theory of wealth (translated by N. T. Bacon). Macmillan, New York

DiPasquale D, Wheaton WC (1996) Urban economics and real estate markets. Prentice-Hall, Englewood Cliffs

Fujita M (1989) Urban economic theory: land use and city size. Cambridge University Press, Cambridge

Fujita M, Thisse J-F (1986) Spatial competition with a land market: Hotelling and von Thunen unified. Rev Econ Stud 53(5):819–841

Fujita M, Thisse J-F (2002) Economics of agglomeration: cities, industrial location, and regional growth. Cambridge University Press, Cambridge

Fujita M, Krugman P, Venables AJ (1999) The spatial economy: cities, regions, and international trade. MIT Press, Cambridge

Greenhut ML, Norman G, Hung CS (1987) The economics of imperfect competition. Cambridge University Press, Cambridge

Gronberg TJ, Meyer J (1982) Spatial pricing, spatial rents and spatial welfare. Q J Econ 97(4):633–644

Henderson UJ (1985) Economic theory and the cities, 2nd edn. Academic Press, New York

Hotelling H (1929) Stability in competition. Econ J 39:41–57

Kanemoto Y (1980) Theories of urban externalities. North-Holland, Amsterdam

Kohlhase JE, Ohta H (1990) Löschian spatial competition and the related labor market. Environ Plan A 17(2):1223–1238

Krugman PR (1991a) Geography and trade. MIT Press, Cambridge

Krugman PR (1991b) Increasing returns and economic geography. J Polit Econ 99(3):483–499

Lösch A (1954) The economics of location (translated by W.H. Woglom and W.F. Stolper). Yale University Press, New Haven

Mills ES (ed) (1987) Handbook of regional and urban economics, vol 2. North-Holland, Amsterdam

Muth RF (1969) Cities and housing. University of Chicago Press, Chicago

Nakagome M (1986) The spatial labor market and spatial competition. Reg Stud 20(4):307–312

Ohta H (1988) Spatial Price theory of imperfect competition. Texas A&M University Press, College Station

Ohta H, Asami Y, Kohlhase J (1990) Land, labour and product markets under spatial monopoly and spatial competition. In: Chatterji M, Kuenne R (eds) New frontiers in regional science essays in honor of Walter Isard, vol 1. Macmillan, London

Ottaviano GIP, Puga D (1997) Agglomeration in the global economy: a survey of the “new economic geography”. World Econ 21(6):707–731

von Thunen JH (1966) Von Thunen’s isolated state (translated by C. M. Wartenberg and edited by P. Hall). Pergamon Press, New York

Wheaton W (1974) A comparative static analysis of urban spatial structure. J Econ Theory 9:223–237

Wako T (1992) Effects of alternative types of competitive location on rent profiles and aggregate rent. Stud Reg Sci 22(1):243–259

The manufacturer's authorised representative in the EU is Springer Nature Customer Service Centre GmbH, Europaplatz 3, 69115 Heidelberg, Germany. If you have any concerns regarding our products, please contact ProductSafety@springernature.com

Printed and bound by CPI Group (UK) Ltd, Croydon, CR0 4YY
30/09/2026
02225314-0003